LETTERS OF WARWICK GREENE
1915–1928

WARWICK GREENE
As a Young Man

LETTERS OF
WARWICK GREENE
1915–1928

EDITED BY
RICHARD W. HALE

With Illustrations

Boston and New York
HOUGHTON MIFFLIN COMPANY
The Riverside Press Cambridge
1931

The Riverside Press

CAMBRIDGE · MASSACHUSETTS

PRINTED IN THE U.S.A.

I dedicate this book to
my grandson
Warwick's nephew

FRANCIS VINTON LINDLEY

BELLE CHEVALLIÉ GREENE

PREFACE

WARWICK GREENE was given by Fate a seat in the front row at the great war drama of 1914. He did not bury his talent. Fortune had fitted him for this opportunity. His career in the Philippines put him where he could see the wood and not the trees. His transfer to the Rockefeller War Relief Directorship gave him a private view of Armageddon and took him behind the scenes in Entente, Central Power, and neutral countries.

Then we came in and he transferred to our Aviation Service. After the war he served the Peace Conference as Wilson's Commissioner to the Baltic States. Then he remained in Europe upon a private errand.

In the pages which follow the reader may judge for himself of the talent or ten talents which made him discerning, critical, judicial, and prophetical. Those who were fortunate enough to know the man will tell you more.

RICHARD W. HALE

CONTENTS

ILLUSTRATIONS

INTRODUCTION

THE object of this book is to give the reader for his enjoyment Warwick Greene's war letters as they come hot from the Front. They are linked together with the irreducible minimum of connecting and explanatory matter. They must be preceded by an account of the man sufficient to show who wrote.

The obituary in the 'Harvard Alumni Bulletin' tells the story in skeleton form:

'01 — WARWICK GREENE, LL.B. '05. Died at Boston, Mass., November 18, 1929. His death followed a surgical operation. He was born in Washington, D.C., December 18, 1879, the son of the late Major-General Francis V. Greene, and Belle Eugénie (Chevallié) Greene, the latter now residing in New York City. From 1910 to 1915, Greene was Director of the Bureau of Public Works at Manila, Philippine Islands. He was also Director of the War Relief Commission of the Rockefeller Foundation in 1916. Greene's war work was largely confined to Red Cross activities and aviation. He served with the American Red Cross Commission in France and Belgium from June through August, 1917. He was commissioned a major of the Aviation Section, Signal Corps, in September of that year, assigned to the office of the Assistant Chief of the Air Service, appointed Executive Assistant, and transferred to the office of the Chief of the Supply Section, Air Service, in December. He was promoted to lieutenant-colonel in March, 1919, and later was attached to the American Commission to Negotiate Peace, in Paris. Subsequently he was appointed chief of the mission to the Baltic, Russia. He was discharged from the service, in France, in October, 1919. After the war he became associated with the New England Oil Refining Company, of which he became president. Later he was vice-president of the Petroleum Heat and Power Company of Boston. At the time of his death, he was associated with some of the business enterprises in which W. Cameron Forbes, '92, is interested. Greene was unmarried, and lived in Boston.

Three weeks after his death 'Peter' Bowditch [1] wrote this account of him:

December 10, 1929

Brigadier General Francis LeJ Parker, U.S.A. [2]
Wardman Park Hotel
Washington, D.C.

DEAR FRANK:

Yours of December 8th has just been received and I hasten to answer it. I am sorry to have missed you in New York and am sorry that I will not see you at the Philippine Club dinner, as I must be out of town on Saturday....

You ask me for certain details regarding dear old Warwick.

[1] Major Edward Bowditch, Harvard 1903, aide-de-camp to General Pershing during the Great War.

[2] President of the Philippine Club. This letter was written for use at its annual gathering.

xiv

MARTHA BARRETT
DANA GREENE

GENERAL GEORGE
SEARS GREENE

BELLE EUGENIE
CHEVALLIÉ GREENE

GENERAL FRANCIS
VINTON GREENE

WARWICK GREENE
LIEUT.-COL., WORLD WAR

WARWICK GREENE
LANDSMAN, SPANISH WAR

INTRODUCTION

Warwick was born in December, 1879, and died on Monday, the 18th of November, just about one month short of fifty years of age. As you know, he was the son of General Francis Vinton Greene and Belle Chevallié Greene, and was the oldest of a family of six children.

He went to Cutler School in New York and entered Harvard University in the class of 1901. His father and his grandfather were distinguished generals in the service of the United States. Due to this fact I think his father wished him to go to West Point; but his predilection was for the sea and even as a youth he became a daring and accomplished yachtsman. It was natural, therefore, that when the Spanish War broke out, he should take to the sea. He enlisted in the New York Naval Reserve as a landsman and saw service with Bronson on the converted yacht Yankee in Cuban waters. This boat was in action in several engagements along the Cuban coast. Warwick rose in the service and was discharged as an able seaman. He has often told me yarns about his experiences.

When he returned from the Spanish War, he resumed his college activities and received the degree of A.B. in the spring of 1901. Due to a very severe appendicitis operation in his youth, he was unable to take part in athletics while in college. He was notable, however, for his literary ability and was one of the favorites of George Santayana and of the other intellectual giants at Cambridge. He was prominent socially and was a member of the Alpha Delta Phi and of the other social and literary undergraduate clubs.

INTRODUCTION

From the beginning, Warwick's mechanical abilities interested him in the then novel automobile, and he achieved a great reputation among us undergraduates with his over-powered Stanley runabout. He fitted this with two boilers and used to attain the unbelievable speed of over fifty miles an hour. This interest in mechanics, which at times amounted to inventive genius, was always a factor in his life-work. He was about the best and safest driver of motor cars that I have ever known.

Following graduation, he studied at the Harvard Law School and graduated with the degree of LL.B. in 1904. Almost immediately he went to the Philippine Islands as law clerk for the Honorable W. Cameron Forbes, who was then Philippine Commissioner and Secretary of Commerce and Police. Thus started the deep and lasting friendship which was broken only by Warwick's death.

Shortly after Mr. Forbes arrived in the Islands, he decided to make a drive for the construction of Baguio. In order to encourage others, it was his wont to take the lead in all such matters and he decided to build a permanent house for himself in the mountain capital of the Islands. The work of building 'Top Side' was given to a contractor, and speed in construction was of importance, as he desired his house ready for a family party which was expected at the end of the rainy season. As I remember it, construction did not begin until sometime in June. The work dragged and all sane and conservative engineers said the house could not be completed in time. It certainly looked so and it certainly would not have been completed on time had not Mr. Forbes sent Warwick to push the work. He went to Baguio in the height of the rainy season and took charge with a foreman, who had the usual failings of drink, but who knew his work and when sober was a hustler. The material difficulties were unbelievable. The site chosen for the house was on top of one little peak and the stone had to be quarried on another peak, and was being carried by Igorrotes from the quarry to the site of construction. Warwick, as always, saw the essential factors of the situation and, with his mechanical genius, solved the difficulties by doing something which all the Bureau of Public Works engineers said was impossible. As one tells it, it seems simple. Perhaps all real solutions are simple. He bought a length of cable in Manila, had it carried up from San Fernando, and ran the single length of cable from the quarry to 'Top Side.' The engineers said it could not be done and would not work. It did work, and with Warwick's punch and energy and with the foreman's loyal support — for he never got drunk while Warwick was on the job — the house was finished on time so that when Mr. Forbes's mother and party arrived, at the end of the rainy season, 'Top Side' was there awaiting their arrival.

I have gone into this detail, as it is significant of all of his later achievements. He was destined for one difficult job after another, to wring success from failure, and the abilities that he showed here were to be displayed again and again throughout his life.

You may remember that in those days the road

INTRODUCTION

situation in the Islands was bad, that the Commission had appropriated large sums of money for public improvements, but the roads that had been put in were badly constructed or were washed away and the Bureau of Public Works was not well organized for big work. Mr. Forbes saw this and decided to appoint Warwick, who was not an engineer, as Director of Public Works. This, of course, was a radical thing to do, as the position had been considered only possible for an experienced engineer. Mr. Forbes induced Major Case, who had successfully constructed the City of Manila water-works, to accept the directorship of the Bureau for a few months and appointed Warwick as his assistant. The plan worked well. Major Case started the reorganization of the Bureau and Warwick succeeded him a few months later, amidst the jeers and head-shakings of the engineers and of many of the Manila fraternity. This, I think, occurred sometime in 1908. Warwick's career as Director of Public Works was a great success. Under his direction, roads were constructed all over the Islands and were maintained. Permanent bridges and buildings were constructed. Artesian wells were dug. Irrigation systems were started. Before the end of his term of office, the Bureau had assumed all of the road and construction work throughout the Islands, reaching even into the sacred precincts of the special provinces under the zealous domination of Commissioner Worcester, and in the Moro Province, which was at that time changed into the Department of Mindanao and Sulu under Frank W. Carpenter, the ablest Governor the Moros ever had.

INTRODUCTION

From an organization which was almost hostile to him at the beginning of his administration, Warwick had built up and welded together a machine which was efficient and loyal to the last man.

I think it was in 1916 that he returned to America for a leave of absence. In any event, he resigned from the Philippine service about this time and accepted the directorship of the Rockefeller War Relief Organization. It was international in scope, and therefore Warwick had an extraordinary opportunity of visiting and seeing all the nations at war, with the exception, I think, of Russia. As usual, he showed great intelligence and drive in this work, and had among his assistants such men as Colonel John R. White, Dwight Davis, and 'Wild Bill' Donovan, all of whom were his loyal friends. I remember that one of his plans was the organization of an international committee for war prisoner relief, which he discussed with the Crown Princess of Sweden. I think he hoped to have the Pope head the committee. In any event, his plans, as always, were on a grand scale.

Our entry into the war put an end to the international phase of the Rockefeller war relief. At that time, Warwick was in Paris and had an office organization there, when General Pershing and his staff arrived in the spring of 1917. Warwick offered his services and turned over his organization to our Aviation. He joined the forces as a major and started to work with his usual enthusiasm to help build the American Aviation organization in France. I will not go into detail, except to say that his activities were centered on the procurement and construction of 'matériel' and that he served loyally a succession of chiefs, some of whom were most difficult to work under.

During the war, Warwick came very close to ending his career. With some British officers he was inspecting the bombing groups of the British Independent Air Force which were stationed in our sector near Neufchâteau. The incident occurred while he was returning to one of the fields. The British squadron was preparing to start on a raid up the Moselle. The Germans had the jump on them and sent over a squadron of Gothas who successfully bombed the airdrome and the squadron which was about to take the air. One of the Germans saw the car approaching the field and, singling it out, he dropped three bombs. The first one fell in the field close by, the second fell in the road in front of the motor car, killing the driver, and, I think, one of the officers and wounding the others. The only hurt that Warwick had was that he was deaf for a few weeks and he received a slight scratch on his arm from a shell fragment.

After the Armistice, he was chosen to head the mission which was sent by the American Peace Commissioners to the Baltic Provinces to find out conditions there and report back to Paris. This brought him further interesting experiences, for he saw the retaking of Riga from the Bolsheviks by the German Iron Division under Von der Goltz. The mission examined conditions and returned to France to report. As always Warwick's recommendations were constructive. I do not think, however, they were followed: for that was the fate of most of the recommendations of the various missions which were sent out at that time. He made another trip for the Peace Commission to this area and inspected thoroughly this Eastern Front, where the Germans and the 'Whites' were battling against the invading Bolsheviks. As usual, his stay was marked by many deeds of kindness and consideration to the people of the country. I remember that Prince and Princess Lieven were beneficiaries of his generosity and became his devoted admirers, and there were many others. Warwick returned to Paris and resigned from the Army as a Lieutenant-Colonel of Aviation and this ended his long and faithful service for the United States Government, which covered, with certain exceptions, a period from 1898 to 1919.

He was now given by private New York parties a very interesting secret service mission which involved the getting in touch with a Russian who was supposed to be in Moscow. This was at the height of the Bolshevist reign of terror. He returned to the Baltic Provinces and was lost to his friends for perhaps a period of a year, although we heard from him from time to time. During this time he was travelling in the troubled border states of Russia and Poland. I think he entered Russia, although of this I am not certain. In any event, he succeeded in this mission and returned to New York and reported success. As I recall, this was about 1921.

His return to New York coincided with the final illness of his father, and his energy was for a time taken up in looking after his father's estate and arranging for his mother. He took a summer course

INTRODUCTION

at the Business School at Columbia and learned thoroughly the theory and principles of corporation finance. It was about this time that Governor Forbes offered him the position of vice-president and general manager of the Petroleum Heat and Power Company, which was then a struggling infant. He then moved to Boston, which became his headquarters and home until the day of his death. Here again his mechanical ingenuity and genius stood him in good stead and his powers of coördination and organization were used to the utmost. He was so successful that, at the insistence of Mr. Bradley Palmer, he was allowed also to take over the management of the New England Oil and Refining Company, a large organization which had already passed through one receivership and was in a bad way. He resigned after a while from the Petroleum Heat and Power Company and battled for some years to save the other corporation. He finally decided to leave this company, whose history has been one of litigation and trouble into all of which he was dragged, although he was not responsible for any of it. He now took up a development project in which some of his friends were interested, where his creative and mechanical genius had full scope. Warwick was happy in his work, and was, I believe, on the threshold of great financial success when he died.

Probably you can use little of this in your address. There are one or two more things, however, that I want to tell you, and perhaps you may be able to use them, as they are indicative of his great quality. As a schoolboy, he first showed one of the traits that marked him throughout life, and that is great courage,

xxii

INTRODUCTION

and the ability to act quickly in a dangerous situation. As a lad of ten or twelve, he was in a train wreck. The engine was overturned and the steam was gushing out of the broken boiler tubes. Warwick went through the cloud of steam under the engine to get out the fireman.

Warwick was a man of tremendous physical force and vitality. His mind was one that was suited to the conditions of modern life. He was always looking forward and dreaming of the possibilities of what our civilization could bring to mankind. To outward appearances he may have seemed only brusque and strong, but there was another Warwick whom I perhaps knew better than any one else, a man who was gentle as a woman, kind and thoughtful. He was always doing generous things, helping those who needed help and upholding the underdog. His devotion to his widowed mother and sisters was all that the most loving mother could ask for, and after his father's death his efforts were largely centered in enabling her to live in comparative comfort and enjoy many of the pleasures to which a lady of her position had been accustomed. Warwick loved children and they clung to him. He loved animals and had a very special way with dogs and cats. Although not a natural horseman, he was a keen polo player, and finally, by hard work and intelligence, he became a very good horseman, indeed. Coupled with his tremendous physical and mental vitality, he was one of the most sensitive men I ever knew. He was an enthusiastic oarsman and one of the delights of living in Boston was his association with the men of the Union Boat

INTRODUCTION

Club and his long rows of a Sunday in Boston Harbor. Rowing and polo were his chief relaxations. When he could do neither, he would take long runs at night before turning in. As I have said, he was probably the best motorist that I have ever seen.

Warwick's life was one of achievement. I did not expect him to die and had looked forward to his success and to his being in a position to do one thing that he had always wished to do. Perhaps few people know that he had an extraordinary literary gift. His dream was that sometime, when he had achieved a financial competence, he could then begin what he had always dreamed of doing, and that was to write. He knew the use of words and could describe things so that they lived before you.

It was fitting that such a soldier (for, in spite of himself, he was the last of a great line of soldiers) should die fighting. About the last words he uttered was his remark to Frank Carpenter when he and I saw him for the last time on the morning of his death and after the doctors had given up all hope. He was lying there in his hospital bed in great suffering. He turned to Carpenter and said: 'Well, C. P., I nearly kicked the bucket this time.' His mother was with him when he passed beyond. On that morning there was a northeasterly gale howling in from the Atlantic Ocean, and at about the hour of his death an earthquake shook Boston and the towns of New England in the vicinity. It was the last salute to a dying soldier. After his death, the wind and storm died down.

I hope that this may give you something which will

WARWICK GREENE
Captain of Manila Polo Club Team 1913–14

INTRODUCTION

help you to pay a tribute to Warwick at the dinner. I am sorry that I cannot be there.

Sincerely yours

PETER

Warwick was a loyal friend and he and I were friends.

LETTERS OF WARWICK GREENE
1915–1928

LETTERS OF WARWICK GREENE

1915–1928

I

WAR RELIEF WORK

To W. Cameron Forbes

MANILA, *May 12*, 1915

MY DEAR GOVERNOR,

I am off for the United States in a short time. My leaving is unexpected and due to personal matters at home. I had not planned to leave before August or September.

The authorities here are kind enough to express regret and to hope that I will return as soon as possible. Many of the leading Filipinos, including Quezon, tell me I must come back and that they all hope to see a still greater expansion in public works. How genuine these flattering statements are I don't know. Carpenter tells me that they are sincere.

I am rather planning to return, especially if the public works outlook is encouraging and if the Administration will sanction a fresh start on irrigation with the idea of carrying it through to big results, as we have done with the roads.

Physically I am perfectly fit and don't believe that

I

I have a sign of deterioration from the results of over nine years' service in the tropics. I attribute that largely to polo. Mentally and nervously, however, I feel very stale and petered out. My capacity for sustained, accurate, or concentrated work has fallen off forty or fifty per cent. I have been in Manila right through this hot season, and that on top of five strenuous years of work (including the past two very trying years) has been too much for me. I hope that a vacation and cooler climate will fix that up, though I am rather curious to see how long it takes one to 'come back' after tropical nervous debilitation.

I hope to have an opportunity to see you not very long after you get this letter and to talk over with you many of the Philippine happenings of the past year and a half. In particular I want to discuss with you the future of the Polo Club and the property in Pasay.

Sincerely yours.

WARWICK GREENE

From Greene's portfolio of drafts and miscellaneous writings, undated [1]

As we look back on history, we see that never has a coming event cast before itself a more portentous shadow than the Great War. In the sky and on earth it was there plain to read, ever growing blacker and more menacing. So inevitable did it seem that by very reason of its inevitableness, almost, men had be-

---

[1] Among Mr. Greene's manuscripts was found a loose-leaf portfolio of typed passages. Apparently he had put into it every experiment which he had tried in expressing his feelings or in recording the interesting events which passed under his eye.

gun to doubt. So often, in the forty years that bridged the nineteenth and twentieth centuries, had Europe been to the edge of the precipice without going over that people began to say she never would go over. They lived like mountaineers on the cliff's brink, who, by reason of never having fallen over, have persuaded themselves that gravitation does not really exist.

Oh! this passionate experience of life which has been mine — can I do nothing to render it again to the world?

Have I taken everything in and given nothing out? Must I go to the grave with this locked within me, must the colors fade and the dream perish with my dust?

Vast and haunting Asia, bright Europe, the gleam of the tropics, booming America — how deeply they are pictured on my heart!

The streets, the cities, the seas, the shining railroads, sports, great navies, the beauty of the human body, the vast drama of night and day, God in his Heaven, man on his radiant earth — how I have thrilled to them!

Childhood, home, school, college, travel (blessed of the Lord!), love, dear friendship, war — how they have crowded in and dressed naked life with dear colors!

Has the kaleidoscope perished when I die? Can I re-create nothing of it?

LETTERS OF WARWICK GREENE

From Rockefeller Foundation Minutes

February 29, 1916

RESOLVED that Mr. Warwick Greene be, and he hereby is, appointed Director of the War Relief Commission to serve from January 24, 1916.

March 14, 1916

The Secretary reported that arrangements had been made whereby Mr. Warwick Greene, Director of the War Relief Commission, accompanied by Messrs. W. J. Donovan, R. C. Foster and H. D. Topping, would sail for Europe on the 18th instant.

To William Phillips, Under-Secretary of State

61 BROADWAY, NEW YORK
March 17, 1916

Personal and confidential

DEAR BILL:

The passports have arrived and everything is in good shape for us to sail Saturday on the St. Paul.

I am strongly impressed with the necessity for maintaining the spirit of neutrality on the part of the men to whom the State Department has granted these general passports. I feel that our usefulness will depend on the maintenance of an impartial attitude that would carry conviction to all with whom we came in contact, so I shall see to it that they feel in honor bound to conduct themselves in such manner that no Government will ever regret having given

4

permission to any member of our party to cross their boundaries.

Very sincerely yours.

WARWICK GREENE

Memorandum by Mr. Greene

NEW YORK, *October* 24, 1916

Little that is worth while can now be accomplished in war relief by impulsive or spasmodic efforts; it must be done by slow, hard, sustained work, as in other undertakings of magnitude. The countries of Europe have settled down in the grimmest earnest to the business of war, and a condition that I call 'war normal' has been reached in all warring countries. This means that human life is as precarious and of as little value as in the Middle Ages; that widespread horror and misery are accepted as inevitable and living conditions adjusted to meet them; that individual rights have almost ceased to exist; that the energies of the entire community are concentrated on self-preservation.

The United States has come into rather ill repute in both warring and neutral Europe. In the Entente Powers we are regarded as a greedy, commercial race, lending money to them at the highest rates, and feathering our own nest a bit too ostentatiously, while the best manhood of Europe is dying; in the Central Powers our extraordinary war prosperity is considered to rest on German blood and German dead; in the neutral States, all of them small and all of them surrounded by peril, yet most of them straining every nerve to mitigate the suffering in their warring

5

neighbors, we are thought of as a fat and heedless State which has failed to assume the humanitarian and relief leadership in this war to which our position as the greatest of the neutrals and the richest nation in the world entitles, or rather obligates, us.

The above feelings are not communicated to one in the course of the polite insincerities with which one is greeted on one's first interview at foreign offices, nor are they fully grasped during a galloping trip through Europe. But if one lives successively in these warring and neutral European States, and gets close to the people, one discovers that the position of our country in the European imagination is susceptible of improvement.

It is true that under Mr. Hoover's leadership, the Commission for Relief in Belgium has been a great achievement, but it must not be forgotten that the greater part of the enterprise of feeding Belgium and Northern France is financed by the Allies and not by American philanthropy.

It is also true that our generosity in gifts to France has earned us some regard and some gratitude in that country, but our gifts would be doubly welcome and our prestige much enhanced if our relief efforts for France, looking at them as a whole, were directed with more centralized control, with more efficiency, and with more discipline. Some individual American relief undertakings in France are so directed, but not the majority.

At the risk of repetition I wish to say that in European opinion we, of the United States, have crowded our energies into making the greatest com-

6

mercial use of the war; we have coined our billions
out of Europe's appalling misfortune; we have given
perhaps thirty, perhaps forty million dollars (probably the first figure), to relief work; and we have
not assumed the relief leadership as we should have
done.

From Rockefeller Foundation Minutes

October 25, 1916

RESOLVED that the hearty thanks of the Trustees
be given to Mr. Warwick Greene for his satisfactory
presentation of war relief matters, and for the admirable and efficient manner in which he has directed
the work of the War Relief Commission.

Cablegram to the Rockefeller Foundation, September 22, 1917

Rockefeller Foundation, N.Y.

Your sixty eight my personal Major Murphy says,
'I am entirely willing for you to go with army. Your
connection with aviation corps is made with my
entire approval and good wishes.' August twenty
second he said, 'You have my cordial approval and
all my best wishes for your entrance army air service
it is a fine thing for you to do and Foundation ought
to be proud and undoubtedly will be proud of it.' My
relations with Red Cross always most cordial and I
would have been glad to have continued to work for
Murphy and Perkins if I had not felt my duty lay
here. I have worked on trial but my commission as

major is now approved and soon will become effective.

WARWICK GREENE

To General Francis Vinton Greene

PARIS, *September* 15, 1917

DEAR PAPA:

During July and August I had some unusual opportunities to visit the British and Belgian zones of operations and also a bit of the French. Altogether I spent nearly three weeks in the neighborhood of the Front, during the course of which I visited — among other places — the following towns: Compiègne, Noyon, Ham, Péronne, Bapaume, Arras, Bethune, Aire, St. Omer, Hazebrouck, Cassel, Poperinghe, Ypres, Kemmel, Wytschaete, Elverdinghem, Reninghe, Loo, Nieucappelle, Oudecappelle, Caeskerke, Furnes, La Panne, Adinkerke, Dunkerque, Calais, Boulogne, Abbeville, Amiens, Havre, and Rouen. If you take a good map of the Western Front you will realize what an extraordinary chance I had to see things. The trips were all made in automobiles and I was in Flanders long enough to go over every road in the unoccupied part.

In all I had three separate trips, during the first and second of which I actually lived for a short while in Flanders. The last trip I arranged for Major Murphy and accompanied him during it. We motored from Paris to Compiègne, then to Péronne and Bapaume, across the devastated regions and the site of the long battle of the Somme last year, through ruined Arras, then by the famous Vimy Ridge, past

8

Lens (which was being shelled by the British), and so on up to the seacoast at La Panne, where we spent the night.

Next day we saw the Queen of the Belgians in the morning, Major Murphy had an audience with the King (I had one the previous visit), and then we went to lunch at Belgian G.H.Q., which was given to us by the Commanding General, General Rucquoy, and his staff. We were all photographed after lunch and the General afterwards sent me one, which will make an interesting souvenir after the War.

After lunch we were taken out to the front-line trenches, where we could look at the German trenches (about thirty or forty yards away) through a periscope and got four German bullets on the outside of the parapet while we were doing it.

We spent the balance of the afternoon in the trenches or with the batteries, returning to La Panne that night.

Next day we motored to Vinckem, Wulveringham, and Poperinghe, and after lunch on to Hazebrouck, and finally, about midnight, Le Havre.

The fourth day we saw the Belgian Ministers of Finance and of the Interior in the morning and then motored to Rouen for lunch and to Paris that night.

Sounds like a pretty interesting four days' trip, doesn't it? But my two previous trips, where I lived for days at a time in Flanders, were the ones where I got the deepest impression of life at the Front. For example, I lived for two or three nights in a bombarded town — and nothing hardens you up at first faster than that!

I also had a chance to visit Ypres itself — one of the most fascinating and dangerous places in the world today. This was just before the recent British advance, when the Ypres salient was seething with activity.

The British Army is marvellous. It looks like an army of the picked manhood of the world and its equipment is superb. The best of everything produced in the British Empire is concentrated in that little area in Flanders and Northern France — the best men, the best horses, the best motor trucks and automobiles, the best doctors and hospitals, and such a wealth of stores, guns, ammunition, motor tractors, tanks, and equipment as were never dreamt of before this War. 'Ils font la guerre riche,' as they truly say of the British. And such a healthy, good-tempered, and determined army! I admire it enormously.

The small section of the French Army that I saw in Flanders was also splendid. I was with them the afternoon before the advance whereby they took Steenstraate and Bixschoote and they certainly were a tanned, jolly, and competent-looking lot.

I was very glad to have had these little outings with the British and Belgian armies, as I am now working until after midnight every day here in Paris and it is likely to be a long while before I get out again. But I am busy with very interesting work.

Your affectionate son
WARWICK GREENE

10

WAR RELIEF WORK

From Greene's portfolio of miscellaneous writings
— undated

And the British Army! One of the greatest
bromides of the war is that modern war has lost all its
beauty and romance. In reality it is saturated with
both. Nature would never have inflicted such unimaginable horrors on us, in order that we might fulfill
our destiny, without giving us compensations, without mixing the colors of tragedy with splendid and
vivid hues. She runs all her world of wild animals this
way; life for them bristles with peril and runs quickly
to disaster, so it is keen, colorful, healthy, and magnificent while it lasts. Temporarily we have gone
back to this life; at least our vigorous great armies
have. Life flows fast and strong to the edge of the
precipice and goes quickly over. In those marvellous
armies, sunburned and vigorous, clear-eyed, in handsome uniform, accompanied by the most lavish and
fascinating equipment of guns and great guns, tanks,
horses, gauzy airplanes, and a million other things,
one would never recognize the dull millions that
crowded the dreary streets of modern cities. It all
flows up to end in unspeakable filth and mud and
bitter pain; but it flows there in a marvellous pageant.
All that the world has of best she has crowded to that
short belt that runs from the Channel to the Adriatic,
with one pause to go round the mountains of Switzerland — the best men, the best horses, the best of
every human production, is picked and culled from
the entire globe and poured into that long charnel
trench.

11

The famous places of the war were there — not merely as names on the newspaper page, but as vivid realities, lit up by the warm July and August sun — or poured on by the August rains that were so fatal to the British offensive of 1917 — Bapaume, Péronne, Arras, the Vimy Ridge, Lens, Poperinghe, Ypres, Dixmude and Nieuport. The offensive began while I was there, on the thirty-first of July, and with what high hopes! Those hopes were to die in the mud of Passchendaele.

What a joy and pride the British Army was at that moment — a perfect marvel!

Into that long charnel ditch that runs from the Channel to the Adriatic — with one break for the mountains of Switzerland — pours the élite of the whole earth. And in that outdoor life, which, after all, is our natural life, the élite take on a heightened bloom, especially when they are accompanied by the very cream of everything the globe produces. The activity of every country in the world now terminates in that sacred belt of land that comprises Flanders, Picardy, Champagne, the Wœvre, and the Vosges and the Piave. Of course it is splendid and moving beyond description.

I saw the British Army at the height of its power and prestige. The victories of the Somme, of Vimy Ridge and of the Messines Ridge were just behind it. I passed close to Vimy, actually stood on the Messines Ridge, so shell and mine cratered that it was like a visit to the moon, and roamed about the ruins of Ypres. Into that whole Ypres salient was pouring the British Empire. Miles and miles and miles of heavy cannon tractoring up the main roads, miles and miles and miles of men up every side road. It seemed as though nothing this side of the Rhine could stop the shock of that effort. One who saw it starting can never bear to think how it ended. From Armentières to the sea the guns bayed unceasingly day and night, and after dark the northern sky was a palisade of flickering heat lightning. Occasionally a burning ammunition dump lit a great orange glow in the darkness.

I have never been so moved or impressed. I returned to Paris in a sort of daze.

In Paris our aviation was beginning to organize. Colonel Bolling had recently come from America and had just been put at the head of the supply, industrial and training part of aviation. I joined and had four or five of the most strenuous, most worth-while months I have ever known. Bolling was a real leader, whose friends swore by him and whose enemies swore at him. But there was no stopping him — by fair means. We worked morning, afternoon and evening, Sundays and holidays, with every imaginable obstacle against us, but always achieving.

II

IN THE AVIATION SERVICE

To General Francis Vinton Greene

FRANCE, *September* 25, 1917

DEAR PAPA:

A cable from Washington dated September fifteenth stated that I had been commissioned in the Officers' Reserve Corps as a Major in the Aviation Section of the Signal Corps. I have since taken the oath, but have not yet been officially assigned to duty through the usual delay in papers.

If I had stayed with the Red Cross it was Major Murphy's intention to have me go to Italy and Salonica for him.

But the call of the Army has naturally been strong on me since we entered the war, and when I was asked by the proper Army authorities if I would come into the administrative and business end of the Air Service, I accepted and jumped into active work as Executive Assistant to Colonel R. C. Bolling and have been exceedingly busy ever since. I began work about August eleventh and have been at it without a break since that date except a few days' intermission for a trip to the Front with Major Murphy. I appeared before the Examining Board about August twenty-third, was notified of my commission as Major on September fifteenth, and have just (since starting this letter) received official notification that I was assigned to active duty September twenty-fifth.

14

My transfer to the Army had Major Murphy's cordial approval. I will later send you copies of some of his letters to me.

It has been a long gap since the last mail from home. I feel as though it must have gone astray somewhere. It really seems several months since I last had word. I am keen to know how everything is going.

Your affectionate son

WARWICK GREENE

P.S. My address is now:

Major Warwick Greene
Air Service
American Expeditionary Forces
(via New York)   France

To General Francis Vinton Greene

HEADQUARTERS AIR SERVICE, L. OF C.
AMERICAN EXPEDITIONARY FORCES
November 12, 1917

DEAR PAPA:

Your letter postmarked October 25 has just arrived. Quite a rapid mail compared to others we have had.

L. of C. of course is Line of Communications. You will remember that when an expeditionary force is sent overseas there are three Zones — the Zone of the Interior, the Zone of the Line of Communications and the Zone of the Advance. I am on duty at the Headquarters of the Line of Communications of the Air Service, where I am Executive Assistant to the Colonel in command. In addition I am temporarily Chief of the Department of Production and Supply, though my trials and tribulations — as well as the glory — in this job will be brief, as I shall be superseded as soon as a certain colonel arrives from the United States. Meanwhile I am having a lively time and am working every day, Sundays included, from nine in the morning until after midnight — I haven't been to bed before one or two o'clock for over two months.

I expect to find a number of acquaintances and friends among the large crowd now on their way over for the Air Service. Indeed, I shall come into close contact with them, as I am the temporary head of the Department they are coming to organize.

It is great that Russell [1] is coming and I shall probably see a great deal of him.

Louis Neilson I see several times a day. He is in one of the Divisions of my Department, where he is doing good work. He is one of the few men we have who really knows the airplane business, in which he has been for the past three years.

I saw Peter Bowditch the other day. He just walked in the office, a Major in the Infantry. One has pleasant surprises like that every day. All the world seems to be assembling in France for the finale of this war. Undoubtedly we shall see Mackensen and great events on the Western Front next year.

I enclose a pictorial map of the British Front taken from the 'Graphic,' with my wanderings in the British Zone of Operations indicated in red. Remember that when I visited Ypres the original British line shown on this map was still the line of the trenches

---

[1] Russell W. Bryant married a sister, Emma Gertrude Greene.

and that the Germans were very, very close to Ypres. Since that time the British have advanced considerably. I remember looking at the heights of Passchendaele, then wholly in the possession of the Germans. They looked down on Ypres, and one wondered how the British had clung to their lines through three long years with the German positions commanding them as they did.

You are right in saying that one must visit fronts and battlefields to realize them. No description can ever bring the reality before one. And, of course, there have never been zones of operations that were as vast as these. They are incomprehensible, they are so enormous. But people are wrong when they say that there is no more color or romance to war. The British Army in Flanders is the most marvellous spectacle that has ever been seen. The side roads are crammed with kilted Scottish regiments marching to the Front with bagpipes playing as they go through the Flemish towns — not to mention English, Canadians, New Zealanders and Indian troops — and the main roads jammed with motor lorries, automobiles and huge traction engines dragging the big guns to the Front. The fields are crowded with camps, horses and camouflaged batteries. And the sky, of course, is full of life and excitement these days — observation balloons, airplanes, air fights and bursting archie shells.

But all this took place for me *before* I entered the Army. Since I entered I have been held down to the hardest, most gruelling and worrying administrative work I have ever been associated with. No more

Front for me for the present. Instead, long indoor office hours and continual trips to airplane and motor factories, to supply dépôts and airdromes, and to Bureaus and offices around Paris. But it is interesting and worth-while work, though not as healthy as the other, which, I hope, may come later for me.

Your affectionate son

WARWICK GREENE

To Conrad P. Hatheway [1]

HEADQUARTERS AIR SERVICE, L. OF C.
AMERICAN EXPEDITIONARY FORCES
FRANCE, *November* 17, 1917

DEAR CONRAD:

It seems a thousand years since I have heard from any of you.

Peter turned up the other day, however, and gave me the first news of any of you that I have had for a long while. He looked well. I hope to see him again before very long, as he was only here for a day or so and that during a tremendous rush when there seemed hardly a moment to sit down and talk things over.

Heiser was also here a little while ago and I presume that you have seen him since he got home. He can tell you a lot about things that it would take a long while to write about.

I have been commissioned as a Major and am having about the hardest work of my life — every day, Sundays included, all morning, all afternoon, and all

[1] Conrad P. Hatheway was secretary and right-hand man to Governor W. Cameron Forbes, Commissioner and Governor-General of the Philippines and now Ambassador to Japan.

evening until twelve or one o'clock. Even the worst days in the Philippines were not quite as bad. Consequently I am feeling a bit frazzled. But the work is immensely interesting. And anything to beat the Germans.

Give my best to Mabel and to little Mabel, and write. I am very keen to have all the news. I have practically been cut off from home news for the better part of a year. I certainly should like to take a run home and see things there again, including a trip to your place in Lincoln. But there is little chance of it until the end of the war. As for when the end of the war will be — well, I have my own opinions, but I enclose the best prediction I have seen.

Always

WARWICK GREENE

Absolute knowledge I have none,
But my aunt's washerwoman's son
Heard a policeman on his beat
Say to a laborer on the street
That he had a letter just last week,
Written in the finest Greek
From a Chinese coolie in Timbuctoo,
Who said the niggers in Cuba knew
Of a colored man in a Texas town
Who got it straight from a circus clown
That a man in Klondike heard the news
From a gang of South American Jews,
About somebody in Bamboo
Who heard a man who claimed he knew
Of a swell society female rake

Whose mother-in-law will undertake
To prove that her husband's sister's niece
Has stated in a printed piece
That she has a son who has a friend
Who knows when the war is going to end.

To Mrs. Conrad P. Hatheway

AIR SERVICE. A.E.F. FRANCE
March 14, 1918

DEAR MABEL:

Your nice, long Christmas letter has just reached me, having apparently chased me all about the pleasant land of France where I have been off on a long inspection tour. It has been only two or three months en route — long enough for a round of correspondence between Manila and New York in the old days. But — 'c'est la guerre'!

Those good old Philippines! In these cold and coal-less times I often think of the good heat that was wasted on us in the P. I., and how we groused about it. Often and often in some freezing little French country inn during my long trip did I think of the sunny Luneta. And oh! for a day or two right this minute back in my Pasay house. Good old house! I never expect to have another as attractive or that I shall love as much, or half as much.

But indeed the Philippines are well represented in these American Expeditionary Forces, from the Commander-in-Chief and the Chief of Staff right down. Why, on this last trip of mine I found an old Filipino (not a Goo-Goo, however) in every nook and cranny of our Army. You begin right with our Air

Service with Lindsey and Hirzel on the job just as in old days in Manila. Then the principal Major in our Supply Work — an ex-officer of the Scouts. And our well-organized Balloon Squadron — the first U.S. one in France — and who is the Commanding Officer but a very old-timer from the Philippines with sixteen years' service in those tricky Islands. I staid a day and a half at his camp, talking over old times and going out with him to see the artillery practice.

Another large aviation camp, and the first person I walk into is the Adjutant, who had barely had time to change his Constabulary uniform before sailing for France.

And a few days later I very formally salute the American Adjutant of a famous artillery school and present my credentials almost before I have time to recognize one of the old Polo Crowd. And so of course everything at the school is mine for the day or so that I stay there.

And when I went up to the British Front some months ago I collided with one or two of the Manila British colony almost before I had landed. As I have said, the Philippines are very much in evidence over here, from our C.-in-C. down.

Since I joined our Army I have seen nothing of the Front, though I have been pretty nearly everywhere else in France on behalf of the Air Service. Fat and middle-aged like myself are principally used — and useful — for the Line of Communication work, or, as they call it now, Service of the Rear. We are merely civilians camouflaged as Army officers and for all our shoulder straps, Sam Browne belts and jingling spurs we are here just to hold down the desks and speed up the typewriters. Don't waste any heroics or tears on us, except for the miles and miles of Government Red Tape in which we are wound up. Direct and swift action is something you may dream about, but you never see. I often wonder if the Kaiser's agents didn't draft the regulations creating War Department paperwork. Anyhow, whoever did deserves a ton of iron crosses. Because it is strangling us.

Last July and August, however, I had the opportunity of spending some weeks at the British, French and Belgian fronts. And they were wonderful weeks. The Front is like the pictures you have seen and the articles you have read, and yet again very different — all the articles and all the pictures, if you read and saw every one of them, don't give you the real, live actual *front* as you see it, and hear it and smell it for the first time. The earth teeming with the great armies, the splendid health and looks of the soldiers marching to the trenches — for miles and miles. I watched the British, and the Welsh, and the Scots, and the Canadians, and the Australians, and the New Zealanders marching up for the great 'push' in the Ypres salient last summer; the hideous bloody human rubbish that comes back on the stretchers; the grumbling and muttering of the great guns that goes up and down the horizon all day long; the skies that are full of sparkling adventure where the observation balloons hang high and the airplanes chase each other and fight and fall spinning down; the stinking trenches with shell bursts spouting dust and smoke and dirt all about the place and the enemy in his trenches just across the way — well! It is all very vivid and very startling and quite indescribable the first time you see it.

And yet it has become the most common sight and experience of these times. Millions and millions of men live their daily life — though it be a short one — in these surroundings. It is just a coarse, monotonous, grim business. And now it is our turn. And everybody, friend and foe, is watching to see how we are going to stand the gaff of real war, not just talking big about war. Will our soldiers stick to their trenches, with death, cold misery and vermin always snuggling close for month after month and the survivors for year after year? Will our civilians face those great endless, bloody casualty lists day after day, week after week and even year after year? Do we comprehend how hard and how long and how efficiently we must work and how many hundreds of thousands of Americans may have to die before Germany will lie down, licked, and acknowledge that an American is a better man than a German?

As far as our soldiers go, they are likely to turn out the toughest and most resourceful of the war. But will the supporting organization be behind them, stretching across five hundred miles of France, three thousand miles of ocean full of steel sharks, and running back to every state and city and farm in the whole United States, creating and shipping and hurrying to the Front the absolutely incredible amount of munitions, equipment and supplies which will be necessary? It is appalling when one thinks of the efficiency and discipline the whole hundred million people of the United States must develop to back up its Army on the Western Front and enable it to stand up and paste Hindenburg in the eye. Are we going to rout old General Red Tape and Colonel Fogey to start with? Are we going to put the skids under that easy-going, wasteful way of doing things that we had as long as all the real brains of the country were in business and all the duds and dodos in Washington Government bureaus?

Well, I suppose it is hard to say. But if the good people at home had been in Germany as much as I have and had seen how busy — and how effectively busy, too — those seventy or eighty million Germans are, they would certainly get an everlasting move on. Ships, guns, shells, airplanes, food, uniforms — we have simply got to pour them into France. But let's do it this year and next and not dawdle along until nineteen nineteen and nineteen twenty, when it may be too late.

As I wrote you, I have just completed a long, long inspection trip, which took me pretty much all over France. And I got back to Paris in time to take in the raid of two or three days ago. They are quite stirring, these raids. You hear the engines of the Gothas very distinctly as they push along over Paris, and you certainly do hear their 'eggs' when they let them drop into the buildings of the city. But you can't see them at all against the night sky. You hear the French machines, too, swarming along after them, aërial machine guns every now and then chattering very loudly overhead, though quite invisible.

I am quite tired of wanderings and of wars and rumors of wars. The supply and desk old guard over here, like myself, have a long, long job before us. Not dangerous, like the trenches — unless a Gotha should have the luck to shy a bomb on us some night. I am off to Italy.

Always

WARWICK GREENE

To Mrs. Francis Vinton Greene

AIR SERVICE, A.E.F.
March 29, 1918

DEAR MAMMA:

I am just back from Italy. I was only gone about ten days, but I had four of them in Rome. I am writing Papa about it and am sending you a little diary I kept.

This trip followed the long jaunt through France I have already told you about. And they were great trips — lots of interesting and worth-while things to see. And I hope that through them I will be more useful to the Air Service.

I find your fine, long letter of March 7 — rather quick for home mail. But letters have a hard time following me about in my flea-like existence — always hopping from one spot to the next.

If I write you gaily it is simply because things are so very bad that one had better take them lightly. Every chance I have for a bit of fresh air or a bit of amusement I take. It is part of the job of keeping fit for the tremendous strain which is before us all. I went through a terrific bit of strain from August to November, and if the powers that be don't care to work me hard now, why, I shall certainly get all the

25

rest and lay up all the health and reserve for the future that I get my hands on. For the period of stress will surely come again.

Yes! they certainly laid Colonel Bolling on the shelf. I have written you nothing about the matter because it doesn't seem to me very soldierly to fight out our internal difficulties in letters home. I didn't get to West Point, but something has come down to me from Papa's and Grandpapa's having been there. We must submit to individual injustice and to the unsoldierly use of soldiers' discipline for the good of that greater discipline which we must have to cement together our American Expeditionary Forces in France. Under no other circumstances would we have submitted to what has happened. All I can say is we worked like nailers during the Bolling régime, with an enormous responsibility laid on him and no personnel and no tools furnished with which to carry it out. We dumped into the organization every man we could lay our hands on. We ransacked the Rockefeller Foundation, the Red Cross, the banks, the business houses in England and France to build up, hastily and under the pressure of an enormous daily business, an organization for the Air Service, A.E.F. We worked morning, noon and night, every day, Sundays and holidays. Often we were going until two in the morning. We operated under terrific pressure and in great haste, and we were full of imperfections and we knew it and worried about them. We had to make bricks without straw and often of very poor clay. But we kept the furnace hot and we baked the bricks as fast as we could. There were but few experts about and our organization was largely made up of amateurs. But they knew they were amateurs and they were out to learn and to progress every hour of the twenty-four. They sat at the feet of the few professionals we could find very humbly and learned as fast as they could pack the information into their brains. There was always the feeling that we were only holding down the situation until the great, competent organization of trained men and of experts arrived from the other side. Then everything was to go wonderfully. In the meantime, however, our Air Service, L. of C. under Colonel Bolling and Lieutenant-Colonel Gorrell, was full of drive, esprit and enthusiasm.

That was our history from the beginning of August until the middle or end of November. Since that time there is nothing that I feel at liberty to write about. Much has happened, all of it trying and disheartening, much of it creating bitterness and resentment in all quarters. I shall, of course, work as hard as I know how for any and every Chief to whom I am assigned for duty. I would slave for Beelzebub if I thought it would help stay the conquering Germans or if he were my military Chief. But it is a bit difficult to be cheery about our situation.

And I like my present Chief, Lieutenant-Colonel Dodd, very much. He has treated me very well and I should like to see him make a success of his undertaking. But it remains to be seen whether or not my close identification with the Bolling régime really ends my usefulness in the Air Service. In that case I should ask for a transfer. But I don't like to give up the line I started in. I shall do my level best for the new régime. Whatever usefulness and energy I possess is at their disposal against the Germans. But I can't pretend that I don't think Bolling got a very 'raw deal.'

You know what a critical time this is. We don't know what the next day or week may bring forth. I have great faith in the doggedness of the English and in the military ability of the French Staff. I hope that the whole military direction of the war for the Allies has been placed under the French General Staff.[1] It is the only solution. There must be one supreme Allied military command. And the French General Officers are the only ones who have ever had great experience wielding large armies in manœuvres. I feel that there is a good chance that the French Staff may yet pull off some very brilliant coup — attack the Germans on the flank after they have let them overreach themselves, or something of the sort. But I don't underestimate German ability — I am only too sadly wise as to how very efficient they are.

And, oh! the priceless years that our country allowed to roll by and made no preparation! How those years accuse us now! At this moment our whole world is at stake, and all we can do is to stand by and wring our hands and offer sympathy to those who are making the fight! We are a hundred million people, the richest and most boastful on earth, and in this critical hour we can't strike one blow that the Germans can feel — not one!

And as I write this you can hear, at intervals of

[1] Done on March 26th, announced April 16th.

twenty minutes — very methodical are these particular German gunners — a loud thump! from some quarter of Paris, followed by a sort of muffled crash.

It is a shell from the mysterious German gun, the gun which is firing at us from some fantastic distance according to all artillery standards. But the shells are very real, and the one that fell an hour ago, I have just heard, killed five or six people. A little later it will stop. But tomorrow or the day after it will begin again. It is a very, very mild bombardment as compared to bombardments which even I have experienced in towns in the zone of operations.

But it is a very eerie sort of bombardment. In the middle of the day, in busy Paris, to hear that thump ... crash register itself, now near at hand, now far away. And the fighting front fifty or sixty miles away from Paris. Of course it is uncanny. A suggestion of being bombarded from another world. One can indulge in creepy speculations as to how many guns of this preposterous range are being prepared by the Huns. And what other devilish surprises along this line!

The Parisians take it very well. Business goes on as usual — that regular twenty-minute bump doesn't stop anything. They are well hardened. Gothas and guns are all a part of the natural course of events to this metropolis.

I am only here for a few days. And then on to Air Service Headquarters, which are not in Paris.

Did you know that Donovan has won the Croix de Guerre? And with very, very complimentary remarks from the French. He should make a wonderful officer, that fellow, and I hear good things about him from everybody. He ought to go far if he doesn't get killed first. There should be a marvellous opportunity for men with a natural gift for military command in our Army. And I should say that Donovan had very great gifts for handling and leading men. I am delighted to hear that he has won distinction so soon.

And in this connection I think our War Relief Commission has done well — I am going to write Mr. Rockefeller, Jr., and tell him about them. Donovan is a Major and has made the best military record of the bunch. White is also a Major, still in Washington. Steever is a Captain in the Air Service. Reggie Foster is a Second Lieutenant of Artillery — I ran across him at a well-known artillery school on my last trip. Paulding is a First Lieutenant in the Air Service, but has recently been transferred to Intelligence. He has done so well that there has been quite a quarrel between the two services as to which should have him. Intelligence exerted its prerogative and landed him. Hirzel — our Rockefeller accountant and formerly my Chief Accountant in the Philippines — has been one of the mainstays in the Disbursing Division of the Air Service. He refused to be considered for a commission unless he took military training. He is invaluable to his country as an accountant and we hope to keep him there. Leonard Jones is in the Red Cross.

Not such a bad record. Practically our whole establishment has continued over here in some military or semi-military job. Donovan, however, is way in the lead of all of us, as he is actually fighting on our American Front.

Well — rather a long letter, don't you think. But I feel as though I had still a great deal more to tell you about or to talk over with you. But there isn't time today. I am writing this in the midst of dark days here. Let's hope that things are much better before you receive this. I have a very deep faith in the innate genius of the French Staff. And, of course, the greatest faith in the sticking qualities of both Tommies and Poilus. Not so much faith, unfortunately, in the genius of the British Staff. You cannot extemporize great military leaders for modern warfare. They are only made by years and years of such military service as the great continental armies furnish. Neither the British nor ourselves have ever given our Army officers the practice in handling large armies grouped for manœuvres year after year. Neither of us have been fair to our little regular armies or their officers. And now we are paying for it — and we Americans are paying dearly for lots of our other shortcomings.

With dear, dear love

Your loving son

WARWICK

To Conrad P. Hatheway

AIR SERVICE, A.E.F.
March 30, 1918

DEAR CONRAD:

I have just come back from a trip to Italy, during which I had three days at Turin, four days at Rome and about an hour at Genoa. I went down on business for the Air Service and so had a chance to see the great plant of the Fiat Company at Turin, as this company is executing a large order from our Air Service for automobiles — and, by the way, I was able to borrow Grant Forbes to draft the contract many months ago.

The Fiat Company is also building airplanes and engines for us.

It is a splendid concern, with over thirty thousand employees and over a million square metres of factory area. And it seems to be run in the most vigorous, intelligent and progressive sort of way. I was very favorably impressed.

I drove cars and rode in cars and trucks on a number of tests made on the mountains near Turin, particularly on a mountain known as Soperga with a steep, narrow, and winding road where the grades reach eighteen and twenty per cent — a sort of little Italian Benguet Road, only much shorter. We put four thousand kilos on a three-and-a-half-ton truck of the type we are buying and it walked up to the top of the little mountain without a whimper and without boiling the water. •

I also had the luck to be taken up in one of the very fast airplanes. We climbed up as fast as the machine would go until we had made over four thousand metres of altitude and my ears were behaving very strangely. Just before or just after we started, the 'alerte' alarm was given, and from above we could see the defence squadrons flying below us in formation. The two machine guns in my place were loaded and with additional cartridges in readiness — but the Lord knows what I would have done if the Boches had actually hove in sight, as a machine gun is a mystery to me. But no hostile machines appeared. Indeed, Turin is pretty far to the west for enemy air attack.

It was a glorious day and the flight was wonderful. We were finally flying on a level with the crest of the Alps and indeed ultimately as high as their topmost peaks. They form a wonderful mountain wall all along the north of Italy, sweeping around in a long circle by Genoa and the sea. We could see the whole plain of Piedmont spread out below us, and, as we flew east, the great plain of Lombardy. Far below us the land was warm and brilliant in the spring sunshine, but up where we were the air was icy from the great snow-fields of the Alps. I should like to have flown over them to France, but no such luck. I would even like to have gone over and taken a peep at Switzerland that I know so well from old Rockefeller Foundation days. It all seems so easy when you are up in a good, buoyant machine, with a three-hundred horse-power engine yanking you along a hundred and twenty miles an hour. At least it is all very easy from the passenger's point of view. The pilot has to do all the worrying.

Both Rome and Turin seemed prosperous and gay, the war notwithstanding. The Rome hotels were doing a good business and the streets were full of people. I was there over a Saturday afternoon and Sunday and so had a chance to see Saint Peter's, the Vatican, the Roman Forum, the Coliseum, the ruins on the Palatine Hill, and a great deal more. All of which made a very good day and half's holiday.

Here in France we are at most critical times. By the time this reaches you things will either be very much brighter or very much darker. But I have great faith in the French General Staff. Their Generals have had the priceless experience of having handled troops in enormous numbers during their annual manœuvres. Owing to the neglect of our people and our Government's, neither the British or American Generals have ever had that opportunity. The present British Army has grown up in trench warfare. It is a marvellous army, splendidly equipped and with a great fighting spirit. But neither officers nor men have ever been trained for a warfare of movement. And ability of that kind cannot be extemporized. A great general must not only be born a great general, but he must also be made by a lifetime of experience and training in handling armies in warfare or in manœuvre. It is natural ability plus the technique acquired by a lifetime of special training. The French and Germans have it. And so today the hope of the Allies lies in the French General Staff, which saved France at the Marne and at Verdun and is capable of saving the whole Western Front and thereby the war if they are given the supreme military direction of the war for the Allies. Then we shall have that unity of military command which has been such a priceless asset to the Germans. The French Generals are capable of great strategic conceptions and they have the technique to put them into practical execution.

IN THE AVIATION SERVICE

Paris has her own taste of warfare these days. From time to time the Gothas appear and drop their eggs on the city. Then the few dim lights that are left go out as soon as the noisy alarm has been sounded over the city and the place becomes inky black. Cellars become very popular and streets are pretty soon deserted. There is a short interval and you hear the anti-aircraft guns about the city barking very angrily. They become noisier and noisier, and if you watch the show from a high roof the sky becomes brilliant with bursting barrages. But on come the German vultures and pretty soon you see the flash and hear the crash of the first bomb. And then they come thick and fast, falling on different sections of the absolutely black city. Presently a few glares appear where fires have started.

This goes on for several hours and then the racket gradually dies away, the 'all out' sounds, people emerge from the cellars, there is a bit of chattering, and then everybody goes to bed. I am reminded of it because the alarm sounded about ten minutes ago, and I am sitting in this upstairs room, with the window tightly wrapped up in blankets so that not a crack of light escapes, writing and waiting for the first guns of the barrage.

Then we had the great munitions explosion at Courneuve a short while ago — one of the most spectacular things I have ever seen. You can't picture the rumpus it made or the way in which it blew dozens and dozens of factories and houses flat and left only heaps of brick to mark their site.

And now it is the mystery cannon. Yesterday and

today it has been at work regularly. It goes on duty for several hours at a time and then quits. While doing business it fires regularly every fifteen or twenty minutes. And the shells come travelling some sixty or seventy miles and plump down in the city of Paris. It is uncanny. Nobody dreamed such a thing possible. But here it is. And it makes itself known in a very grisly fashion every now and again. Yesterday — Good Friday — it winged a church full of people and brought down the stone roof. Rather a ten-strike. Seventy-five people were killed and a great many wounded. I was walking a street not very far away and heard the thud and crash very clearly. Indeed you hear every shell. But this made a specially loud racket.

The Parisians take all this very well. Indeed it is extraordinary how quietly most people continue about their business while you hear those steady, twenty-minute interval crashes about the city. The French will to fight on will never be broken by Gothas or fantastic, long-range guns.

I find here your letter of February 28. Many thanks, especially for the trouble you have taken for me about the India House dues and other matters.

I am interested to hear about the boom in the Benguet gold mines. As far as I can gather, the Philippines are simply fat with prosperity these days. The war has done marvels for them. But after the war! If I were a Filipino I should be thinking pretty hard these days.

Sincerely yours
WARWICK GREENE

IN THE AVIATION SERVICE

To General Francis Vinton Greene

AIR SERVICE, A.E.F.
April 4, 1918

DEAR PAPA:

On my return here from my trip to Italy I found your note suggesting that if I should meet General Crozier, I should introduce myself as your son — as you had known him for years.

Well, I met him at lunch at the Frederick Allens' last Sunday, Easter. He was most cordial when I told him who I was and said that he had just received a letter from Mrs. Crozier stating that you had dined there.

The lunch was a pleasant one. Mr. Allen (now a Lieutenant in the Navy, one of his daughters, General Crozier, a French officer from General Foch's staff, an Italian officer, Phil Lydig (now a Major Q.M.), and one or two others. The Allens have a charming house out on the Rue Reynouard, where I think you have dined.

As we walked home with General Crozier we heard and saw two of the shells from the long-distance 'mystery gun' fall into Paris. And, by chance, later that afternoon I had tea with some people within half a block of the landing place of one of these shells. It tore off part of a mansard roof and killed one and wounded one.

Good Friday, as you know, the shell struck a supporting pier or arch in a church, thereby bringing down the stone vaulting on the congregation assembled below, killing seventy-five and wounding over eighty.

Today there have been only two or three shells.

But a few days ago they would fall quite steadily through the day, at fifteen- or twenty-minute intervals. It is very uncanny, of course, to be bombarded in this way from a range of over sixty miles, but business goes on much as usual and the Parisians take it very well. It is a very curious experience to walk about the streets of a busy capital and hear shells landing from time to time with a thump and crash. I have never heard any preliminary whistle or scream — as I used to when up in the Ypres salient. Simply a thump and crash, coming out of a clear sky. One wonders whether this is merely a freak gun of which there are only two or three, and which are not really practical except for their effect on the morale of the civilian population, or whether it is only the beginning of stupendous and successful long-range bombardment which will be developed by both sides.

Colonel Bolling is with the British, having gone there just before the beginning of the great German push. So he is very much in the thick of things. He is preparing, I understand, for a field command in our Aviation. He couldn't have selected a better time, as he will see the British air work at close range during one of the most critical periods of the war.

I am just back from Italy, where I had three days in Turin and four in Rome. At Turin I saw the great plants of the Fiat Company, employing over thirty thousand operatives and occupying more than one million square metres of factory area. They manufacture touring cars, light trucks, heavy trucks, tractors, airplanes, airplane engines and machine guns — the whole output now, of course, for war purposes. For our Air Service they are executing a large order for automobiles, trucks, airplanes and engines. I am particularly interested in this order, as I carried on a good part of the negotiations some months ago, and commandeered Grant Forbes to draft the contract which Bolling finally signed. It was one of the far-sighted acts of his administration, as we have been largely dependent on Fiat deliveries for automobile transportation for our Air Service.

. While at Turin I had a chance to go up in a S.I.A. airplane — the S.I.A. Company being a subsidiary company of Fiat. This machine is fast and a wonderful climber. We went up to an elevation of four thousand metres so fast that my ears rang for twenty-four hours afterwards. That put us on a level with the topmost Alpine peaks and gave me a good view of the greater part of northern Italy.

The best news of these critical times, it seems to me, is the appointment of Foch as the Supreme Allied Commander on the Western Front. It should have been done some time ago. The French Generals have had the experience of years and years of the great annual manœuvres. England never had the armies to have these great manœuvres and so her Generals never had the practical experience of handling great masses of men in the field. And her present Army, magnificent as it is, has grown up in the trenches and its leaders know little of a war of movement.

And, of course, our Army has had infinitely less chance than even the British.

Indeed, it seems to me that the only salvation for the present situation lies in the French General Staff. They only, on our side, have had the previous training which fits them to cope with the Germans in grand strategy.

Your affectionate son

WARWICK GREENE

To Mrs. Francis Vinton Greene

AIR SERVICE, S.O.S.
A.E.F. FRANCE
April 5, 1918

DEAREST MAMMA:

I have just come up from the medium-sized French town which is the Headquarters for our Air Service and also Headquarters for various other services. It is a charming French town, but full of American Generals and Colonels — too much rank for me!

Paris has been most peaceful for these times. No air raids for several days and not a shot from the Boche 'Long Tom' gun which fires at us from a distance of over sixty miles.

This afternoon Bill Hoffman and I walked down to look at the church that was struck by a shell on Good Friday and seventy-five people killed and over eighty wounded. The church had a high nave with heavy stone vaulting. The shell struck one of the piers just at the springing point of the arch, and the collapse of the vaulting sent tons and tons of massive masonry crashing down on the congregation below. It was very much as though a shell should strike Grace Church, New York, during Good Friday service and leave the interior a shambles. We saw the wrecked interior and could easily imagine what a ghastly scene it must have been.

Saw Perry Osborne tonight and his sister Virginia Sanger — Perry is a Lieutenant-Colonel — going some! He has recently arrived from the other side and was full of news.

I am here to learn to fly, but don't know whether permission will be given me. Am considered too old and stout. But I have not given up all hope.

We are worried about Colonel Bolling. He has been at the British Front and hasn't been heard from in twelve days. Under present circumstances this is very serious. We can only hope for the best.

With dear love
Your loving son
WARWICK

To Conrad P. Hatheway

Private

AIR SERVICE, S.O.S.
AMERICAN EXPEDITIONARY FORCES
May 3, 1918

DEAR CONRAD:

My Chief, Colonel R. C. Bolling, was killed by the Germans recently while on a trip to the British Front. He was not only a good personal friend of mine, but he was also my immediate Chief during one of the most strenuous periods of my life. I went into the Air Service last August as his Executive Assistant. From that time until the middle of November were some of the liveliest months of my

41

career — like the rush days long ago in Manila. We were at it morning, afternoon and evening, every day, Sundays and holidays included. Then a new crowd came over from the States. They poured in on us from the beginning of November. There was rank galore. And all sorts and kinds of officers, regular and reserve. And all kinds and conditions of character, ability and talent. Things turmoiled about a bit and then Colonel Bolling was deprived of most of his duties. In March he went up to the British Front to study field aviation at first hand. He got there just before the beginning of the great offensive. A few days after it started, he left Amiens driving his little car — a Fiat 15–20. He was never seen again. Some weeks afterwards we learned through the regular sources in Switzerland that he was shot and killed in the car. Ran into the Germans and that was the end.

He was a splendid fellow, full of brains, energy and initiative. He was aggressive and made enemies, but he was a marked personality in any work he undertook. I have very strong feelings about the way he was treated. But it is contrary to military requirements for me to express them. One can't help thinking, however, that a man of such marked ability in certain directions should have been kept at important work. We need initiative and pep in this air game, and he had both.

I had been very disappointed at not being able to accompany Colonel Bolling to the British. But about that time my orders to go to Italy came through. I rode down with him in his car the day he left town and felt very much out of luck that I couldn't go on with him. If I had, you would never have had this letter, or it would have come from a German hospital or prison camp. I am not so disappointed now as I was.

I see Gerrit Forbes from time to time. Had planned to take him to Italy if I had been ordered there for station. And this I had hoped for. Indeed I had the orders at one time. But they were temporarily suspended by other orders and have never been revived. I went to Italy, but only on a flying trip. I had wanted to go there for four or five months or even longer.

Here in Paris we have the long-range gun — 'la grosse Bertha,' as the Parisians call it — and the Gothas for excitement. The night raids are really quite theatrical. First the rushing about of fire-engines, blowing horns and small sirens. Then the wailing of the big sirens on the taller buildings. Then the scampering of the people to the shelters and cellars. Presently the guns, the very noisy anti-aircraft guns which encircle the city. And the most beautiful barrage of shrapnel bursting in the night skies. And then the noise of the German motors, though you can't make out the machines in the dark. But you hear the thrump of the bombs as they land and the great 'he' crashes as they burst. And presently the glare of burning buildings adds to the spectacle. By and by the noise dies down and finally things become entirely quiet again. Then the fire-engines rush about the streets once more, blowing the 'all out' on their bugles. And the church bells start to ring, people come out of the cellars and go back to bed. It is all over except for the poor devils under the wrecked buildings.

But the people stand it very well. And they also take the shells from the big gun quite cheerfully. It is uncanny the way they suddenly fall out of a clear sky in the middle of the day and into a busy city. They don't seem real, even when you see them kick the roof off a house in a cloud of splinters and dust.

Sincerely

W. G.

To Conrad P. Hatheway

AIR SERVICE, S.O.S.
AMERICAN EXPEDITIONARY FORCES
May 17, 1918

DEAR CONRAD:

I have just come back from quite a long cross-country flight with a French transfer pilot, that is, one of the pilots who fly the machines from the acceptance parks to the parks where they are delivered to the Army to be made up into squadrons, to be sent to the Front or to be sent directly to the Front to replace damaged machines in organized squadrons.

The trip itself took only a short time, but the return journey by automobile and rail required over an hour and a half — like the Chinaman's description of tobogganing.

It was a lovely, warm day — in fact, a blazing hot day, the first we have had this year — and the French countryside, in its spring green, was delightful. As we were in a great hurry, having started late owing to a balky motor, we flew low and as fast as

44

possible. We were so close to the hot ground that the air was full of holes and pockets and we plunged and wiggled and rolled like a boat in a tide chop when the wind is against the tide. And this in a Bréguet, which is a magnificent machine and very steady. It was the longest cross-country trip I have yet made, though I have been up for longer periods and, of course, much higher.

I am keen to learn to fly. I have been up as passenger a good deal, so that I am quite accustomed to the air, but I have not yet been able to get permission to learn the flying game. Considered too old. But men of my age are later on going to be useful in bombing work, where steadiness, reliability and judgment are more necessary than dash and agility.

But at present the American Air Service has more pilots than machines. Our personnel is superb — I have never seen a finer lot of men than our fliers and cadets. Let us hope that we will have material and an organization back of them which will be worthy of them. Like polo, one must be well mounted, and the best aviator is tremendously handicapped if his adversary has a better machine — if it is faster, climbs better and is more easily handled.

... There goes the 'alerte' or alarm. It is a warm night, with a clear sky and a young moon. We had expected the Kaiser's birds and now the sirens that are howling all over Paris tell us they are coming. First the sirens on the tall buildings begin to wail and shriek and then fire-engines rush through the streets with more sirens. It is quite theatrical. You hear the patter of feet in the street as people hurry to the nearest 'abri' or shelter — every strongly constructed building has a sign on the outside stating how many people the cellar will hold during a raid.

And from this window on the eighth story you can see the balloons starting up and the northern sky sprinkled with flashes of light where the anti-aircraft guns are lifting their barrages of exploding shrapnel shell to stop the passage of the Gothas. The muttering of these guns is incessant and grows ever sharper and louder as the guns nearer Paris come into action.

But all lights must be extinguished, including this office, and one must go to the cellar, if one is conservative, or to the roof, if one is curious and wants to see the show. It is usually not long after the alarm that one begins to hear the distant explosion of dropping bombs and then the noise of the hostile motors as they cross the city, invisible in the night sky, but quite audible. But this letter must wait until tomorrow.

May 18, 1918

Well, last night's raid was a tame one. No Gotha flew over the city. One heard a few dull and distant explosions of bombs which were dropped in the suburbs, but the city itself was untouched. Very different from some raids which I have watched from this roof, when the bombs fell thick and fast and the flash and crash of the explosions, as well as the glare from occasional fires, were quite startling. One would say that the aërial defence of the city had greatly improved. On the other hand, the Boche is a tricky and resourceful devil and is likely to spring some new surprise in night bombing. But Paris has quite adjusted itself to these night raids and accepts them with much the same psychology that one takes fires and railroad accidents at home — they excite people, but they go on living and doing their daily jobs just the same.

You probably know that Peter has been made A.D.C. to General Pershing. It is fine. He will make a splendid Aide. He is a good soldier, and, as he has lots of friends both among the regular and the reserve officers, he makes a good point of contact between the two groups.

Sincerely yours

W. G.

To Conrad P. Hatheway

AIR SERVICE, S.O.S.
AMERICAN EXPEDITIONARY FORCES
FRANCE, June 13, 1918

DEAR CONRAD:

There is little to say about the situation over here. The Front creeps on towards Paris and nobody knows what the events of the next two months will lead to. We can only trust old man Foch to find the best way possible out of the present situation. Our troops are going into the thick of things and are fighting splendidly. The attitude of the British and French has changed greatly since this has begun. Paris is repeatedly peppered by day with shots from 'grosse Bertha' and by night is constantly raided by the Gothas and other night-flying birds of the Kaiser. But the old city is game and holds tight.

Sincerely

W. G.

LETTERS OF WARWICK GREENE

To Conrad P. Hatheway

AIR SERVICE, S.O.S.
AMERICAN EXPEDITIONARY FORCES
June 21, 1918

DEAR CONRAD:

The Front has crept pretty close to Paris. Only thirty-nine miles away — fancy Boston with the Huns six miles this side of Worcester. And with air raids almost every night and Big Bertha chucking shells into the city every now and again. To realize the situation you must imagine yourself sitting in the Sears Building with a shell or two falling in the Common, another on the lower end of State Street, one on the Old South Church and six or seven down in the tenement house district. When you go out to lunch, one falls a few houses away, with a frightful racket, as happened to me a short while ago.

I only hope the Bostonians would stand it as well as these Parisians do. They are admirable.

Love to both Mabels.

Sincerely yours
WARWICK GREENE

To Mrs. Charles Fairchild

AIR SERVICE, S.O.S.
AMERICAN EXPEDITIONARY FORCES
FRANCE, *July* 5, 1918

DEAR MRS. FAIRCHILD:

Of course Neil lives for me yet. He was one of the dearest friends of my youth and his memory will never die with me. I remember his warm and strong young nature as though it were but yesterday. I can feel him taking his part in these passionate times if he

48

had been spared for them. But my recent trip to Italy brought back the past especially vividly. Not a color has ever faded from my recollection of that journey across France — the length of Italy in the glowing August heat — Brindisi — the gaunt mountains of Albania — Greece — the Dardanelles and Constantinople. It was my first experience of Europe and I was simply aquiver at each new sight. And no better companion than Neil with his ardent nature to share the delight with. I was simply intoxicated at each day's new experience. England, France, Italy, Greece and the East were one rich picture after the other. Neil was far more sophisticated about Europe than I, and often whimsical where I was merely dazzled, but his underlying enthusiasm was as great as mine.

And this April the sight of Turin, where we stayed seventeen years ago, brought the past back with a rush. If he had lived, how ardently he would have entered into the beauty and tragedy of this European convulsion!

Yesterday was a really joyful Paris. The city rippled with the pink of our good old American flag from one end to the other. When we were here seventeen years ago, who would ever have dreamed that a flood of American soldiers in steel helmets, some fresh from European battlefields, would ever pour down the Champs-Elysées? And that the Fourth of July would be celebrated as a French fête day. What trim, compact, tough fighters our men are beginning to look! We have still some way to go before our new Army has become a great, coördinated, efficient, scientific military machine; but our men fight like young wolves in khaki. Particularly in this open fighting are they cool, tough, aggressive, resourceful and savage.

And how Neil would have enjoyed that river of blue that followed the river of khaki down the Champs-Elysées — a river of blue that carried a sparkling forest of steel bayonets above it. And how the eyes of the Parisian crowd shone with affection at the sight of their own, their very own poilus! For the friendly American invaders the cries of 'Vive l'Amérique!' showed their appreciation, but oh! the burst of honest love and devotion when their own trench-stained blue soldiers appeared. And overhead silvery airplanes rushed about, cavorted, turned somersaults, darted down at the crowd, frolicked about just above the tree-tops and chimney-pots, and drew long ripples of applause from the crowd.

I had just returned from an inspection trip of several weeks — partly down through the heart of France and partly to the portion of the Front that runs from the St. Mihiel salient eastward towards Switzerland.

And I had one real adventure. Late one night we were hurrying out to an airdrome to see the machines get off on a bombing trip over Germany. Our party consisted of two British Lieutenant-Colonels, one American Lieutenant-Colonel, two American Majors, and a small dog. We were bowling along in a nice new Cadillac car when out of the dark night a Boche plane began to pepper us with his machine guns. He was invisible, but how arrogantly his great engines droned overhead and how viciously his tracer bullets spat down at us out of the darkness! We hastily extinguished our lights and fled along the road. Presently one of our brakes heated up and we had to stop. While it was being fixed, we were grouped around the rear of the car, but watching a whole flock of the Kaiser's night buzzards unloading their bombs on an objective *very* close at hand. Lord! what a show it was with the angry spurts of light into the night and the incessant splintering crashes! Presently one of the searchlights caught one of the great mechanical birds in its beam, but only held him for a few seconds.

But while we were watching it, like a lot of gawks, the fellow who had chased us down the road, and overrun us while we were stopped, wheeled back, and as he passed over us, dropped from two to four bombs, the evidence differs. The first landed in the field beside the road. The entire field seemed to rise in a black tornado against the low moon. The second hit the hard surface of the road about a metre and a half from the front of our automobile. As far as we were concerned, the world was instantly overwhelmed by a cataclysm of horrible noise, fire and fury. If two others fell near us, as was claimed, we were too mercifully blinded, deafened and stunned by the second bomb to register any more agony.

The rest was like an atrocious nightmare. We regained our sight, but not our hearing for some time. We found our poor Corporal chauffeur desperately wounded. When we finally got him to the hospital, they immediately took out one shattered eye and proceeded to measures to try and save the other. His head and back were also badly messed, as was the head of one of the officers. Another had splinters in his leg and another a slight wound in the same place.

I got off extraordinarily lightly. A tiny splinter went into my shoulder, but so small as to do no damage. I had a splitting headache for twenty-four hours, and I still have a slightly damaged right ear, though the left one seems entirely all right. Yet my trench coat which I was wearing is drenched with blood from the others and has several jagged holes through the skirt. But not one of the bullets or fragments which made the holes touched me. Except for the poor chauffeur we got off very lightly. Why we were not all blown into hash is unexplained. Fragments went right through the car from side to side. And the bark on the trees in the neighborhood was blasted off in great strips. Fragments tore holes in the trunks of the trees eight and nine inches deep. But by some freak of explosions the soft human bodies grouped near the rear wheel of the car survived, though one was seriously and another dangerously wounded.

But how an experience like this sharpens one up for the war! I am used to being in towns where you were being impersonally bombed; but in this case the Hun was very personally and directly chasing *us*. Like a hawk after a fat chicken on the road. Lord! how I should like to go on a bombing raid to that hawk's lair in German land — we think we know where it is....

WARWICK GREENE

52

IN THE AVIATION SERVICE

To Richard W. Hale[1]

AIR SERVICE, S.O.S.
AMERICAN EXPEDITIONARY FORCES
FRANCE, *July* 5, 1918

DEAR RICHARD:

I am just back from a series of inspection trips and find your good letters with the proposed will, power of attorney, etc. Many thanks.

You came near being prophetic about my will and a Gotha. For we had a lively run in with one of them on the Front. It happened this way:

We made a date to go out one evening with a British Lieutenant-Colonel and see his bombing fleet start off for Germany. I have been bombed enough in Paris and at various small towns to have a lively personal interest in reprisals. So I wanted to see this fleet flap off with juicy bombs for Mannheim, Cologne, Stuttgart, etc. I couldn't wish them too much success.

I finished an honest day's work checking up property accountability (my métier just now!) with our units, then sped over in a fast car and joined our British friend for dinner at a small town near the Front. The dinner was excellent — the place is famous the length of that Front — and very high-priced. Since the Americans came to France an excess profits tax on restaurants would pay off

---

[1] Richard W. Hale — a Boston cousin. Greene's grandmother, Martha Dana Greene, and Hale's grandmother, Anne Dana Sever, were sisters. Greene counted Hale's aunt, Miss Emily Sever, as his own aunt and was much at her home in Boston, the affectionate relation beginning when he was an undergraduate and being continued with Hale and his wife (born Miss Mary Newbold Patterson) and shown in the last letter in this book, page 294.

France's war debt. Thrifty financiers are the French, all right!

The Britisher left a little ahead of us to see to the preliminaries at his place. We did not plan to get there until the curtain went up.

Eventually we followed and joined our British friend at his Headquarters. Then we started off, our party consisting of two British Lieutenant-Colonels, one American ditto, two American Majors, one American Corporal (chauffeur), and a small dog named Dickebushe, because born at that place in the Ypres salient. He has never known a world without shells, gas, bombs, etc. We have a good Cadillac car in which we are all packed, the British car following us empty.

As we start the 'alerte' (alarm) is given. Archies (anti-aircraft guns) open up languidly, but presently they get the scent of the Kaiser's birds and commence to bark furiously from all the little hill-tops sticking up out of the blue night mist. A noisy dog is Archie. A pack of him make a first-rate row.

We hurry the old Cadillac along as fast as she will foot it. The Hun show is unscheduled; we want to make the airdrome before the fun begins.

Then!! as we happily ride along, one of the Kaiser's pets flying overhead spots us, gets on our trail with zest and chases us down the road, potting at us with his machine guns. Zip — zip — zip come the bullets at us out of the darkness. Tracer or illuminated bullets so that you see them only too plainly. Their hiss somehow suggests snowflakes hitting a red-hot stove. Damned spiteful sounding things are machine-gun

54

bullets! The plane is invisible, but you hear his engines droning away, not a cylinder missing. No —— ——s in Germany, worse luck!

We switch off every ray of light and roll on, hoping to throw old uncle Boche off our trail. Presently one of our brakes heats up and we have to stop. The chauffeur starts in to fix it; we are under some trees and fancy ourselves fairly well concealed. Dickebushe, however, who has no false pride, having been in the war too long and being an intelligent Belgian mongrel to boot, retires to the ditch. At the sound of the first gun he had sought the bottom of the car; now that we are stopped, the ditch looks good to him. Dicky knows only too well what shells and bombs do to masters, motor-cars, horses and stray dogs.

By this time a real show is on. Archie is now raving — he is coughing and barking in a frenzy all over the countryside. His starry shells decorate the night sky brilliantly. Searchlights frisk every patch of the heavens. The droning of giant mechanical bees overhead approaches. They belong to his Imperial Hunnish Majesty and their sting is sharp indeed, as we are soon to find out.

We are very close to one of the raid's objectives. The All-Highest's pets arrive; the curtain goes up, so to speak; the bombs come down. We have orchestra seats for a real performance. Bomb after bomb — flash! — crash! — flash! — crash! Each flash lights up the blinking darkness with a magnificent golden glare; each thump and crash jars poor old Mother Earth and rolls away to die somewhere in the distant night.

It is like good theatre business, with well-trained property men and the calcium flashes and the big base drum well synchronized.

The humor of the situation is that we started out to see a show launched against the Boche, and arrive to find old Fritz playing the star part.

Presently a searchlight seems to catch a giant moth in its white streak. But it is only for one flit; the next flit he is gone. He is too high. A second later another searchlight grips a huge bronze vampire, flying very low. There he is, the visitor from Germany, with his long wings, slim and sinister. The searchlight whitens every detail of the great bus. Pot him! Archie!! damn you!!! He is too low! Get him! you dummies on the machine guns!! Archie yelps frantically; there is a hysterical chatter of machine guns; but that insolent great fish of the air lunges out of the nervous searchlight ray — and is wiped out in the blackness!

We have been watching the show, as if it were a war movie. For the moment we have forgotten the fellow who chased us down the road with his spitting machine-gun bullets. When we stopped, he overran us and breezed on — night bombers are great, floundering buses, not at all quick on the turns.

But the damned old professional has known how to turn and come back at us — while we have been gaping at the fireworks — and suddenly we are petrified by the roar of giant propellers seemingly just above our tree-tops.

His first bomb lands in the field beside the road!

A seedy old moon, in her last quarter, sits atop a low hill across the field. She is too worn out to give much light, but there is enough of a glow from her red flesh to see the whole field rise up in black dust and smoke and hurl itself at the sky, a wicked thunder crash rolling out from under the tornado of rock and dirt.

'Thank God, he missed us!' we breathe.

The next instant a roaming star, travelling a million miles a minute, strikes the planet Earth and all our known cosmos disappears in a white sheet of flame and a roar heard as far as the Milky Way. We little human beings shrivel up like gnats in a blast furnace, a bitter taste of dust and sulphur staining our lungs for a moment before they burst. We are hurled down crashing cataracts of sound into a sightless and soundless void. But the core of one's Ego never loses consciousness of itself, though giant forces rip away all communication with outside things. 'The body is dying so fast that there is no pain,' it seems to say. 'Old Thing, come along, let's away to other planets; Earth is a washout...'

Ages later, it seems, the sweet night smell from a hayfield — and the hayfields of France in June are fragrant — steals in through the shattered windows of one's senses. Lord! how soft and cool and fresh!

You begin again to peer out — on a nightmarish world! Dimly you see trees dance up and down the road, bobbing at each other, while the whitish backbone of the road squirms and contorts like a long sea-serpent suffering from acute dyspepsia. Starry lights burst, sometimes in your brain, sometimes in the sky, for Archie is still busy. How unnatural that old Earth should have survived, you think. Tough old sphere, isn't she! Good old clay wench, she shook that attacking star off, didn't she! But he jarred the old girl a bit, all the same; her landscape looks like a cubist brainstorm.

You concentrate your will power on focussing your eyesight, wave after wave of nausea surging up as you do it. Now you hold that dim road and those shadowy trees firmly; now the planes of perspective are shuffled into a thousand distortions. But back you go to it, and gradually that nocturne prints itself steadily on your soft brain.

Dimly you make out the automobile. There is a figure lying on the ground, one or two others are groping about, one is clutching its head, which reddens the darkness in a strange way. A figure tries to speak to you. No use! It is dumb or you are deaf. You bend over the figure in the road. The head is a raw beefsteak, white bone showing through; the light of the pocket flashlight glistens on the slow-flowing blood. The figure tries to say something; your right ear roars incessantly, but your left ear as you turn it towards him, gradually begins to hear. Your left ear tells you that a far, far-away voice says 'Major' (he thinks he is addressing the other Major, his Commanding Officer; his poor eyes are pools of blood), 'they have got me, I am going to die.'

You lift him up by the body; other figures take the legs; we lift him into the battered car. The windshield is shattered, a front tire is lacerated, the body has been pierced from side to side, but she runs — slowly. We reach a hut, stretchers appear, our wounded are dressed by the light of a pocket flashlight — no other light because the marauders still roam the sky. We have one dangerously wounded, one rather seriously wounded, two very lightly wounded, and one just scratched, myself, with a tiny fragment, not much bigger than a pinhead, in my shoulder.

Lucky is no word to describe our escape. It is freakish. Two days later I looked at the naked tree-trunks in the vicinity, their bark blasted off, branches torn down, gashes in the trunks seven and eight inches deep where the bomb fragments had struck — and wonder why human skin should be so much tougher. Fortunately, we were all about the rear end of the machine and the second bomb landed in front of the machine (apparently there was also a third and maybe a fourth bomb — Teutonic thoroughness), so that the Cadillac was our shield. Happily it is not a proper, modern, lowhung car; otherwise our heads might all have been blown off. When you make a bulwark of your car, have an old-fashioned high-hung model!

The trench coat I was wearing is stained with blood and has holes ripped through it — but the bullets or fragments never connected with me. It makes an excellent relic of an interesting night's party.

So when next you read a 'communiqué' that describes low attacks with machine guns and 'copious' bombing of units on the road by airplanes, this poor description of mine may give you some idea of what it is like to the man on the ground.

Your affectionate cousin
WARWICK GREENE

LETTERS OF WARWICK GREENE

To General Francis Vinton Greene

FRANCE, *July* 20, 1918

DEAR PAPA:

It seems pretty certain that Quentin Roosevelt has been killed. There is a chance that he may have landed alive in the German lines and be a prisoner, but unfortunately, only a slim one. Long before you receive this letter the matter will have been definitely settled.

I had seen a good deal of him in the Air Service. First in the early days under Colonel Bolling when Quentin had just arrived from America. A little later he was supply officer at one of our big Aviation Schools, at that time under construction. Then I tried to have him sent to England in charge of a group who were to take the Equipment Officer's course of the Royal Flying Corps. He objected so strongly to non-combatant work, however, that we finally relented and sent somebody else over in charge of the party. Indeed, he always displayed the greatest ingenuity and energy in extricating himself from any duties that seemed to point to a non-combatant future.

At that time we were fairly long on aviators, but short on equipment and administration, and we needed energetic young officers for the latter work. Had he simply followed orders without striving to have them changed, he might have continued for a long while in useful but not very dangerous supply work. But, of course, with his inheritance that was not his temperament, so eventually he had his own way and became a chase pilot.

IN THE AVIATION SERVICE

I saw him several times on my last trip to the Front. Once with his squadron, where he was in charge of a flight with six dandy, spandy Nieuports under him. And in a squadron where everything was very smart and shipshape. He showed me his machines and then went off for a long 'hop' in one of them. The last time I saw him was at dinner the night we were chased in our automobile and smashed up by a German night bomber, as I wrote you.

He has died the finest death it is given a man to die, the one to choose above all others, if one had the choice. To die swiftly, cleanly, in the clear air, above this lovely land of France in its full summer-time beauty, at the tip-top of one's youth and vigor, in open combat with the enemy — who could wish a more royal exit from the world!

Quentin was a splendid boy, genial, energetic, intelligent and honest. A real American-bred youngster, full of humor, activity, 'sand,' and a force of personality that promised plenty of accomplishment later on in life. In his death, his father deserves our greatest envy, and in Quentin's death, his father, Mr. Roosevelt, seals forever, with his dearest blood, the stand he has taken in this war since the very beginning. He is now one with all the great British and French statesmen who have had the same loss and who 'carry on' just the same. Speeches, loans, enthusiasm, ships, munitions, etc., are all very well, but the ties which really bind Allies are the splendid dead, humble and great alike. The attitude of the poilus and Tommies, of the peasant women and little shopkeepers, has entirely changed since our men have

61

actually begun to die as well as to shout for the cause, so will the attitude of Allied statesmen, as the sons of American statesmen go down to the common war-green with their own sons. Until then we are par-venus, flattered in public, sneered at in private. Blood counts; blood is not only thicker than the water of the Atlantic, but also thicker than the wind of speeches and fine writing. For the first ten months after we entered the war the opinion on this side of the water was, that we were prepared to shed ink and money copiously in the Allied cause, but blood eco-nomically. And many things we did at home gave ground for this suspicion.

Now everything has changed. Europeans find that the American is a born pugnacious animal, that he enters a fight with a whoop of joy and that he dies as readily and as cheerily as the best soldiers this war has produced. That discovery has brought about a warmth and genuine cordiality of feeling towards us that is very marked as compared with the attitude of a few months ago.

If you should see Mr. Roosevelt, you might tell him that I saw Quentin a very short time before his death, that he was brimming over with the joy of life and pride in his work, that he died the death we all most wish for, and that in his personal bereavement Mr. Roosevelt has the deepest sympathy of the hosts of his admirers who are serving under every Allied flag.

W. G.

IN THE AVIATION SERVICE

*To Mrs. Charles A. Lindley (his sister, born
Edith Greene)*

AIR SERVICE, A.E.F.
FRANCE, *July* 29, 1918

DEAR EDITH:

In my many thousands of miles of travel about France I have seen the A.E.F. grow from a tiny khaki baby to a giant that is now ramming his fist right into the Kaiser's face. I have visited pretty much the whole show from the base ports (I have seen all of them), through the lines of communication and the great dépôts and industrial plants, to the front line at Seichprey and Xivray, where the American Army cut its first war teeth in Europe.

All the cinemas and Sunday Supplements you have seen and read give you no conception of the vastness of the enterprise. It is colossal — spelt with a C and not with a K! You must see it, travelling day after day and week after week, to visualize its immensity. Of course, if you back a project with the unlimited energy and money of the United States, you are bound to get something rather staggering. Some infant prodigy is this A.E.F.!

I remember the first appearance of the American uniform in Europe. How strange it seemed, even to those of us who were familiar with it from the Philippines! Then a little, thin parade of American soldiers in Paris on July 4th. One found much polite enthusiasm at our entrance into the war, with unlimited money to help the Alliance fighting Germany; but equally polite scepticism as to our value as *fighters*. We were the rich uncle who would back the boys in

63

the ring with a purse that had no bottom. But nobody seemed to figure that Uncle would actually climb over the ropes and wade in on his own account. The first few thousands of Yankees were succeeded by more thousands. American khaki began to trickle in through all the ports. But mostly technical troops and comparatively few fighters. Work went on everywhere on a titanic scale. Port works, railroads, camps, shops, dépôts, etc. Chunky American Quartermaster Captains loomed on the horizon of every French town. Paris was infested with Americans in Signal Corps and Red Cross uniforms. The Y.M.C.A. became ubiquitous. The Atlantic ports of France turned into great, rowdy, hustling American seaport towns, enlivened by Negro stevedores. Familiar undergraduate types appeared at all the French aviation schools. Familiar Broadway types, but in khaki, thronged the night boulevards of Paris. Throaty American women crowded in, their eyes shiny with excitement, ready to lap up every drop of war excitement. American cars rushed madly about the Front, filled with commissions and sight-seers in uniform — any old uniform, everybody appeared in uniform — enjoying the most thrilling of all sports — watching other people get killed. Everybody from home was 'saving dear France'— except in the trenches! The restaurants and hotels of Paris were crammed to the garrets, prices taller than the Eiffel Tower. Maxim's and the Casino de Paris were surfeited. The little cocottes found every khaki uniform, apparently, stuffed with hundred-franc notes. We had turned the war into a gorgeous Cook's tour.

Every busybody from Boston to San Francisco had come over 'for the ride.'

For a while it put a gay camouflage on grimy war. Americans did mean to enjoy it so! Even the French became a little drunk from the optimistic excitement. The French Army lay quiet in its trenches, licking its sores from the bloody days of the 1917 spring offensive in Champagne; but the French people saw a regenerating flood of money and energy pouring into the land. Naturally it brought a bit of elation to their tired hearts.

The British Army was then at the top of its game. Behind it were the victories at the Somme, of Vimy Ridge and of Messines Ridge. It thought that it had at last taken the measure of William's Army. Old John Bull had entered the war quite out of condition and had been punched all over the ring; but by 1917 he had trained the fat off, gotten his fighting wind and come back at Fritz with some nasty jolts. Now he planned the offensive against the Passchendaele Ridges, which would drive the Brute off the Belgian coast and so give a good opening for peace — with England's military prestige on the Continent restored. Yankees were useful to turn out munitions, build ships, make a great show of activity in France — and foot the bills! But British soldiers were now ready to take the burden off the French and win the war.

And what a royal army it was, those endless British battalions which marched into the Ypres salient in July, 1917. The finest, handsomest army the world has ever seen. It thrilled me to the bone as I watched them for weeks — with pride to think my forebears came from the same stock as marched up those Flanders roads, hundred thousand after hundred thousand. Marvellous chaps! Tommies, Jocks, Canadians and Anzacs. I can still hear the music of the bagpipes shrilling through the little Flanders towns; still see the never-ending procession of men, horses, motors and guns rolling forward — a tide of flesh and steel which it seemed even the Rhine would scarcely stop. The July sun flushed a warm, flat green countryside, full of shining canals and crowded with the tramping, sunburned manhood of the world's most superb empire. Day and night the guns talked in deep gutturals from one end to the other of the horizon; every mile you moved forward the sound grew more ferocious. They marked the savage jaws of annihilation into which this torrent of the élite of the English race and of the cream of all her industrial energy was pouring.

The disillusionment did not come until late fall. The offensive had failed; the stubborn Boche still crouched in his unbroken line from the sea to Switzerland. The flabby Russian giant had collapsed, the tiny Balkan States, one by one, had gone down the German Tiger's gullet — and then crack! flop! went Italy. Those were frightful days, in Paris and London, as the German stiffened armies swept across the Venetian Plain.

In the cold winter nights another nightmare came to trouble the dreams of Allied statesmen — a great German offensive against the Western Front in 1918, an offensive backed by all the power and military cunning and economic resources of the entire German Empire now that Russia and the Balkans were dead with Germany feeding on the carcasses — and Italy gasping. The alternative was peace at Christmas — a compromised, dishonoring peace, which the Allies manfully refused.

Then all eyes turned towards the other side of the Western Ocean; all hopes, reluctantly or gladly, had to be hung on what America would do. Something more than dollars, supplies and ships were needed to win the war. At last it was recognized — not publicly, of course; a nation is always winning in its own newspapers — that the war was lost unless a great American Army could be brought to Europe. Would it ever materialize or was it a Yankee bluff? That thought was searching every heart, American as well, during the long winter. Lord! what a long, dismal winter it was! The French and British Armies waited ominously; the spectre of that German spring drive looming larger every week. And our A.E.F. was going through all sorts of infantile diseases. For months it seemed to be nothing but an expanding madhouse. Natural enough, of course, when you consider how tiny was our military establishment before April, 1917, and how enormous the job that was laid on it — to create a modern fighting army in a strange land across three thousand miles of sea, with William's tin sharks snapping at the heels of every ship that came over.

Anyhow, the joy-ride aspect of the whole adventure faded. In 1917 the fear of every American seemed to be that the war might end before we had our money's worth out of it as a new sensation. As somebody said, America then acted like a woman who thought she could have all the fun and prestige of having a baby without the pain.

In 1918 it was very different. Everywhere in Allied eyes you met the same silent query. Were Americans still too proud to fight?

Meanwhile a certain leaven began to work throughout the entire A.E.F. That leaven emanated from the Commander-in-Chief and a small set of Regular Army officers grouped about him. It was the spirit of discipline, of stern, exacting, impersonal military discipline — something the average American had had no glimmering of in all his civilian experience. It seems to be brewed at West Point and kept ever afterwards by a certain proportion of officers, no matter how numbing or cramping the garrison life to which they are condemned in peace times. Slowly, but inevitably, it permeated the A.E.F. It sifted out the four-flushers, battered in the skulls of the too capricious and individualistic, prodded the inert, tempered the over-exuberant, chastised the erring, ferreted out the incompetent. It worked slowly, to be sure, but ubiquitously and in a straight line to its goal — a disciplined army. Not only was it a leaven throughout all this human dough, but it kneaded it together and prepared it for the great war oven into which it was going. It was ruthless; it crushed much individual talent and perhaps some genius; it cared nothing for individual injustice; it concerned itself only with striding towards a certain military result. It reached forth and laid strong hands on the Red Cross, the Y.M.C.A., the Knights of Columbus, the Salvation Army, the newspaper correspondents and

68

all the other uplifters and camp followers. It took the joy out of life, but it put the power-to-win in its place. It came straight from General P., who is pretty much iron all the way through. Out of an undisciplined people it created a disciplined army in an extraordinarily short time.

On March 21 the German blow finally fell. I was in Rome at the time; I can testify to the shock that went through the Allied backbone from one end to the other. Silent crowds were jammed about every bulletin board. No newspaper camouflage could disguise the seriousness of the splintering break-through, the temporary crumpling-up of the Allied resistance, the sickening speed of the drive for Amiens.

Crash number two came in Flanders — where the year before the British had the jump on the Germans and dreamt of pushing them out of Belgium. When Mount Kemmel fell, a terrifying picture of the British Army driven into the sea rose in every mind. But out of these disasters we got an allied generalissimo [1] and the speeding-up of the transport of American troops, two events which were to change the history of the world.

Smash number three was appalling. At the Chemin des Dames the Germans went through the Allies as if they were faced by aborigines with bows and arrows. The barrier of the Allied Armies seemed no better than rotten paper, which the Hun could punch through at will.

Meanwhile 'La Grosse Bertha' had lifted up her voice from eighty miles away and began to murder

[1] March 26th in fact, announced April 16th. R. W. H.

Parisians at their desks, or in taxi-cabs, or at prayer in their churches — and from a distance beyond the most fantastic dreams of any artilleryman! It was a sensational coup, all right! And nightly the Gothas crowded over and shook Lutetia with the explosion of their bombs. Nearer and nearer crept those hated German hordes until this city, the heart and brain of France, was practically in the fighting line. The sound of the guns was frequently heard and the glare of battle in the sky was plainly visible in the night of July 17th.

The situation was inky black. But, in a way, these disasters brought their own relief. They created united Allied action on everything; they aroused America to efficiency; they produced the ships to bring our Army swarming over. The trickles of American khaki through American ports turned into perfect Niagaras of the boys from home. They found the machinery of the A.E.F. already organized and functioning; the ground work had been done; by its means and with a helping hand from the British and French, the new hundred thousands could be quickly poured up to the fighting lines.

And how they did plunge in when Foch, who had bided his time, caught the Germans in their first false move and gave the signal to counter-attack! Were Americans too proud to fight? Well! they went after those Germans like lean wolves suddenly turned loose in a pig yard. They have the pure love for scrap — something which has faded out of European Armies after four grimy, gruelling years. On this side of the water the youths full of initial pep have long since been laid beneath the sod — those left are hardened, wary and skilful, but long, long ago the enthusiasm ran out. It is a survival of the fittest — and the enthusiastic don't live long. First over the top is apt to be first under the ground.

Now well over a million Americans are here. And they feel ready to wade right in and knock 'hell' out of the German Empire — for generations they have licked the 'Dutchmen,' the 'squareheads' in street fights, saloon brawls, lumber camps and the forecastles of ships. To despise them has always been traditional with the tough American. They were never afraid of 'Heinie' in a fight at home; so they don't worry specially just because they see him in 'feldgrau.' That spirit is priceless for such a counterattack as Foch has just made. It is rash; it may cost us thousands of unnecessary lives; but it is bred right in the American blood and it will turn the tide of the war.

Of course victory is not just over the next ridge — not by a long, long shot! The Kaiser boasts he rules the most capable people on earth; in many ways he is right. The strength of the German race is very deep-rooted in industry and patience and discipline, the discipline that pervades a nation from top to bottom and locks Germans and Austro-Germans into a great war phalanx of one hundred million people. We have always underestimated the effort necessary to break that phalanx — which is one of the reasons why the war has run into its fifth year.

The Kaiser omitted to boast that he also ruled the most arrogant — as far as foreign relations are concerned — the most blundering people on earth. That arrogance has finally armed against them the most naturally aggressive people in the world — they are also a hundred million strong and come in among these weary European fighters as fresh as paint.

But oh! these lucky, lucky United States of ours! That we should get off so lightly for all these military omissions and sins of ours for years and years past! That we never foresaw or prepared — and then that others had to bear and to hold during the heat and the burden of the fight while we could first make money, then make up our minds, then make war, and still have a year and a half to prepare an army for our initial fights while others held the enemy at bay! Of all the people in the war we will get the maximum results with the minimum loss of our own blood. Bull luck is with us. Now we have got to pay, because the days of the great casualty lists are before us, but it is nothing compared to what we might have had to pay.

Please excuse this odd, blotting-paper sort of writing paper. I have been spending a Sunday afternoon writing you and this happened to be the only sort of paper available.

Best to Charley and love to Vinton.

Your affectionate brother
WARWICK

From Greene's portfolio of drafts and miscellaneous writings, undated

It is remarkable how civilization has rallied to resist such a disaster as this war, how what one may call a condition of 'war normal' has come about in each belligerent country.

Three years ago civilized man was generally gathered to his fathers from a soft bed. His clay was borne to its little trench in the great mother-clay with pomp, dignity and reverence. The few who died violent deaths on colonial frontiers or in railroad or industrial accidents did not affect the general consciousness. That humbly proud deity of the modern world — the average citizen — grew up and had his career in an environment where from the cradle to the grave he never saw bloodshed. The conditions under which human life had existed from the beginning — with violent death ever at a man's elbow and sack and pillage ever hanging over the life of the normal town — had changed. Civilized human beings had come into a peaceful oasis in the history of the race. Industrial and social strife and competition were of the keenest, but life was reasonably sacred. The self-deprecating average man shuddered as he thought of the turbulent and blood-stained days of the past and admired his ancestors as men of iron to have withstood them. He never thought of himself as being able to endure such things. Civilized man was very modest; he disclaimed the heroic qualities of his fathers for himself and believed that he would prove soft and cowardly if the old conditions returned.

He read with awe in his own time of death and adventure (though until the coming of this war there was always more of adventure than of death even at the world's wildest outposts) in the Sudan, in the Klondyke, in the South Seas and in South Africa. He fancied those who took part in them as a species of supermen, souls still born in the civilized world, but not of it, heroes who reincarnated the dauntless spirit of the past. He did not think of them as in any way typical of the latent or inner qualities of the age, but rather as belated flowerings of ages of romance and dauntless living. He sighed as he thought of their splendor in his own (as he considered it) humdrum world and regretted that soon civilization would forget to produce even these rare 'throwbacks.'

To be sure, there was Manchuria and the events of 1904 and 1905, but their significance was not realized.

Then came August, 1914.

To Conrad P. Hatheway

AIR SERVICE, S.O.S.
AMERICAN EXPEDITIONARY FORCES
FRANCE, *August* 13, 1918

DEAR CONRAD:

I have just returned from a most interesting twelve days at the Front, during which I visited the greater part of the zone of operations of the recent battles between the Marne and the Vesle — Château-Thierry, Dormans, Epernay, Châlons, Villers-Cotteret, Oulchy-le-Château, Fère-en-Tardenois, Coincy, Séringes, Sergy, the outskirts of Fismes, and many another place made famous during the German offensive of July 15 and the wonderful counter-offensive of Foch beginning July 18.

I arrived while the battle was still in full progress, though the tide of the fighting was rolling swiftly northward towards the Vesle. The countryside was

such a bewildering mass of wrecked cities, smashed
military equipment, and dead horses and men — all
within two hours' automobile ride of comfortable
Paris — as no outsider can dream of. The first dead
man startles you a bit, but after two days you are
callous to everything except the appalling stink. The
entire district — especially the woods, the smashed,
shallow trenches of open warfare, and the little,
narrow valleys — simply crawls with the odor of the
dead, — man and beast piled on each other indiscrim-
inately.

I was in Soissons or its neighborhood three times —
once the day after it had been captured. All the
cross-roads near the town were choked with busted
wagons and dead bodies, but in the city itself we saw
only four French soldiers and six hungry cats. The
Germans were in the outskirts of the place, and every
now and again — Wouf! Thump! a shell from the
Heinies would blow into town and you would hear
the cracking-up of little brick houses and a column of
wicked black smoke would rise into the air over the
roof-tops to show where the shell had plumped. But
really there was very little shelling, considering how
close the Dutchmen were and how easily they could
have pulverized the place. Perhaps that was the
reason why the French, who are usually wise in their
generation, had no troops or material of war in the
town. The Germans were economizing shells and
there wasn't enough in the town to warrant any real
bombardment. Cats are cheap and the four French
soldiers we saw were very old ones. Also, the French
dominate the city and the valley from Mount Belleau

just behind the town and could pound the lungs out of any German batteries that made themselves very obnoxious against the town.

At the same time, if old Boche had guessed that two perfectly good and almost brand-new Cadillac cars were visiting that main square in Soissons, he would certainly have tried to chip a bit of the new khaki paint off them — he had already let us have a few on the fly as we skimmed along the top of the ridge along the south of the Vesle. But his control was bad and he only put a few more pockmarks in the wheat-fields.

Somewhere just back of the Front I found my young brother-in-law — the one who married Eleanor — living with the rest of his battalion in man-sized gopher holes in the reverse slope of a steep hill. On the crest were batteries of seventy-fives with American gunners and machine guns. The seventy-fives were busy after the Huns all the time we were there, so that it was very rackety. My brother-in-law is a young Second Lieutenant, looking as lean and tough and healthy as only people look who are leading this wholesome, out-of-door life of war. We were perfectly safe from the occasional Boche shell that came lumping along, as their trajectory was too flat to land them on the steep, reverse slope of the hillside, where everybody was living. The second day we were there a shell wounded three men, but that was because they were out of the protective ground of the reverse slope.

I was very glad to have a chance to see him and I cabled Eleanor immediately on getting back here.

I hope he pulls through all right, though the life of a Second Lieutenant of machine guns at the Front is not a good insurance risk. I also hope to have another chance to see him.

Love to both Mabels.

Sincerely

WARWICK GREENE

To General Francis Vinton Greene

45 AVENUE MONTAIGNE, PARIS

August 27, 1918

DEAR PAPA:

Your book, 'Our First Year in the Great War,' has just arrived and I am reading the same with very great interest. As soon as I have finished I will write you my comment, if you are interested in hearing it.

As I wrote Mamma, I spent a most interesting two weeks — the first half of August — in and about the territory covered by the second battle of the Marne. The greater part of the time I was with our squadrons, as that was my business, but I also had the opportunity of spending several days with the infantry.

Among the places I visited were Château-Thierry, Soissons, the Forest of Villers-Cotterets (or Retz) — where Foch hid his armies until the Germans had crossed the Marne and were pushing up the valley towards Epernay, and then struck his counter-blow — Oulchy-le-Château, Fère-en-Tardenois, the outskirts of Fismes, Dormans, Condé-en-Brie, Epernay, and Châlons. These, of course, were the principal places, and I have not named all the small places I went to. I managed to cover practically all of the

77

ground in the Marne salient which the Germans evacuated after Foch's counter-attack of July 18.

It was absorbingly interesting. The battle was still in progress, with the Germans rapidly rolling northwards towards the Vesle, where they made their stand. For the most part they were fighting rear-guard actions with detachments of machine guns left behind to hold the advancing Allies back as long as possible. The artillery fire on our side was much heavier than from the Germans — they were trying to save their guns and relying on the machine guns to enable them to evacuate their Army and its 'matériel.' But the Allies were pressing hard after them, and I saw a great deal of German ammunition, stores and equipment along the road and in the forests. Very well-made stuff, too, most of it — after the stories of the shortage of material in Germany it was surprising to see the powder in little silk bags, the ground for miles sprinkled with copper-jacketed machine-gun bullets and innumerable large brass containers lying about in the woods and bushes.

On the ground one could study the history of the series of operations while the prints of battle were still fresh on the landscape. South of the Marne and in Champagne you could follow the system of elastic defence in depth, where the great German offensive of July 15–18 was first checked and then smashed — principally by the armies of Gouraud and Berthelot. That was the first phase of the great battle.

Then to the west of the salient one found the Forest of Retz where the army of Mangin was so well hidden and whence, on the night of July 17–18 —

78

after a violent thunderstorm which drowned the sound of the tanks clanking to the Front — the sudden blow against the German flank was launched. You could follow the course of this blow right across the country until, to the north, it reached the uplands dominating Soissons and, to the east, it pierced the main road between Soissons and Château-Thierry. This blow may have changed the whole course of the war. It brought the German offensive movements of 1918 to an abrupt end. By July 19 the entire German attack had crumbled and by the twentieth their forces were evacuating the Marne salient as rapidly as possible.

South of Mangin's army you found the traces of the armies of Degoutte and Mitry, which retook Château-Thierry, forced the Germans northward over the Marne to the east of Château-Thierry and pressed hard on their heels as they retreated northward to the Vesle. Here the Americans had a large participation and did very well. They fairly swarmed over the country after the withdrawing German — their only fault being, as Foch said, that they were too impetuous and too eager; they had to be held back. They were constantly outrunning their artillery and taking machine-gun nests without the support either of artillery or of tanks. Splendid, of course, but expensive. But the best possible spirit on which to build a great fighting army.

Your affectionate son
WARWICK GREENE

P.S. I enclose a cut of the Marne salient on which I have roughly indicated my trips.

LETTERS OF WARWICK GREENE

*From Greene's portfolio of drafts and miscellaneous
writings, undated*

Back again from the glamour of this Front to the
grind of office, work, as regular, as confining as the
hardest-pushed law office at home. My year may
sound to you like a sort of superlative tourist party
when I am off on inspection trips, but that is only
because I write you about the bright, high spots.
These great armies that are so splendid in the field,
rest on the same hard-working foundations as any
other great enterprise. And that is the part of the
war that I am told off to do; the administrative grind.
The departmental side of the Army is the homely
hard-working old dad that keeps the brilliant daughters going.

Paris, of course, has been the one city of the world
to have for headquarters for the past year, and I have
been lucky in that. You are close to the beating heart
of this whole drama when you are in Paris. Today
she is a great capital, carrying on the life of a great
capital, at the Front, for today Paris is not only
actually, but officially part of the Army Zone. You
can leave a comfortable office in Paris in a fast car
and die on a German bayonet in less than an hour if
you are so inclined. And that gives her a character
such as no other city can have. 'La Grosse Bertha'
pelts her with shells from time to time; the Gothas
swarm overhead at night; and when I stop the type-
writer for a moment to listen, the fresh wind brings a
guttural, distant muttering that is the guns at the
trenches.

IN THE AVIATION SERVICE

To Miss Sally Fairchild

AIR SERVICE, A.E.F.
FRANCE, *October* 6, 1918

DEAR SALLY:

Your faith through all these four years is justified — do you remember how you stuck to it, without a waver, through thick and thin? How you said it was simply faith, like religion, founded on intuition and not on reason and therefore proof against the bleakest days and blackest disasters? How the incredible efficiency of the enemy never disturbed you — how you said that it was like the efficiency of ——, enormous, but that the world, being founded on better things, would always finally rise superior to it?

Well! it has all come true, or at least is rapidly coming true. Over here the wine of victory is warming every human being.

It has come so suddenly and so swiftly! Three months ago the advancing Germans were only thirty-nine miles from Paris, the city was bombarded daily by 'La Grosse Bertha' and the Gothas came nightly. Nobody who was in Paris will ever forget the night of the fourteenth–fifteenth of July, when the wind brought the sound of tremendous cannonading straight to us and the sky to the north was lit up with the glare of the guns — and everybody knew that the fifth great German offensive, or rather the fifth phase of the great 1918 offensive, had begun.

That was the offensive that Gouraud killed in its tracks, leaving the way open for the counter-offensive of Foch that began on July 18 and has never since stopped.

81

That was July — but a hundred years ago as far as psychology is concerned. Here in October the Western Front is crumbling before our eyes; Bulgaria is out and Turkey is getting out as fast as possible. On top of everything, today there is a peace proposal from the two principal sinners.

And the great danger of the hour is that the offer may be considered, that it may soften our will and weaken the great onward drive of all our armies towards Germany.

For since Germany contemptuously and insolently dragged us into the war, I cannot see how we can talk peace until our soldiers are in Germany itself. And that will take until next year, probably.

What an arrogant fool she was to pull us in! Without us the war would have ended with Germany triumphant. We occupy the extraordinary position of having saved the Allies and the world — and having done very little to earn it! Without us it would have gone the other way — and we are going to get the fruits of victory with but a fraction of the bloody sweat it has cost all the others in the affair. America is so lucky — so far — that one is almost afraid, knowing that Fate never permits unbroken stretches of luck and good fortune.

It is all too good to be true. And our fighting divisions have had a wonderful share in bringing about this complete change in the tide of the war.

But let's carry it through to a real finish.

Affectionately
WARWICK GREENE

IN THE AVIATION SERVICE

To Miss Sally Fairchild

AIR SERVICE, A.P.O. 702
A.E.F., FRANCE
November 10, 1918

DEAR SALLY:

These days are simply stupendous. One's nerves of feeling and reaction are so choked that they can scarcely register anything more. Bulgaria out; Turkey out; Austria-Hungary out; no more fighting in Italy; all of Servia reconquered and the Servian Army actually back in Belgrade; the Belgian coast recovered; almost all of Northern France regained; the British in Odessa; the Germans humbly suing for peace; the Kaiser abdicated — each minute of the day thrills with a fresh bit of news that would have shaken the world a few months ago.

It is incredible, not the events themselves, but the rapidity with which they take place. How your faith and the faith of others like you who have never been pessy during over four years, has been justified!

I was at a big aviation banquet a few nights ago. Loucheur, Minister of Armament; Painlevé; Dumesnil, Under-Secretary for Aviation and other Government celebrities were there. Also Nungesser, Fonck, and many other of the Aces of Aces were present, shimmering with decorations.

The speeches were excellent. None of the commonplaceness or clownishness of our after-dinner speaking. Of course it was an extraordinary occasion, for the rumor had run wildly over Paris that the armistice had already been signed. That had been contradicted, but it was announced that Germany

83

had asked for an armistice. So the speeches thrilled not only with eloquence, but with real emotion. They were really very fine.

The aviators were intensely admired by all present. They were nice looking French boys, of a stocky build, with candid, clear eyes, very much like the quarter-back type of our old football.

Yesterday I had lunch with the Egans and Peter and in the evening dinner with Peter, Willard Straight, a French Captain on General Pershing's Staff and a young American Captain, also on the General's Staff, named Hughes.

Peter has been promoted to a Lieutenant-Colonel, which is fine but not nearly as much as he deserves.

Willard was in fine form. He has a new job, but it mustn't be announced publicly yet, though it probably will have been long before you receive this.

It is quaint, isn't it, how the old crowd turns up and foregathers all over the globe! You have no idea how much the Philippines are to the fore in the A.E.F. even in our Air Service, where Mitchell is now a General and in command of all our fighting units. Lahm is Chief of Air Service of one of the Armies and other people we knew are to the front.

Personally I have had a very unsatisfactory time — as I suppose everybody will say who has had a departmental job during the war. I have been more fortunate, however, than many who have had to do this kind of work, in having had the opportunity to travel a great deal. I have seen the entire Front from the Vosges to the British Channel, all of France from the Front to the Pyrenees and from Switzerland to the sea, and a good bit of England and of Italy. But I have only been at the Front as a 'floater,' as we visitors, inspectors and liaison people generally are called. Of the excitement and beauty and drama of the Front I have seen a good deal, of danger I have had a little, but of the hardship and pain of the Front I have experienced nothing. My closest shave was our night encounter with the Boche plane, but that was as close a shave as one could have and ever tell anything about it afterwards.

I talk as if it was almost over. Of course it is, though a few more poor beggars must die or be maimed. But the Great War as we knew it is in its last minutes. Even if the Germans reject the terms of the armistice before tomorrow morning at eleven, the finish will be soon and is inevitable.

Affectionately
WARWICK GREENE

To his sister, Eleanor Potter

45 AVENUE MONTAIGNE, PARIS
November 30, 1918

DEAR ELEANOR:

I have just been down to see Willard Straight. He is a very, very sick man. It is a great question whether or not he will pull through. If he does, it will be due to his will power, nothing else. Everything in the world is being done for him, but the outcome is exceedingly doubtful. Even Mrs. Harriman was not very optimistic this morning. I had a glimpse of Willard for the first time since he has been sick; it was not reassuring. Long before this letter reaches

you, he will have gotten worse or better. His naturally healthy constitution and his will power are
pulling hard in his favor, but against great obstacles.
What a waste of a good man if he doesn't get through!

The pictures of you and your young one are delightful. How I should like to see her! The homeward
movement is beginning, but one does not know when
one's turn is coming. Two million two hundred
thousand Americans have to be transported back.

They came over to 'can' the Kaiser and can him
they certainly have. Who would have guessed that
the war would collapse so suddenly this fall!

Your affectionate brother
WARWICK

To Mrs. Charles A. Lindley (Edith Greene)

45 AVENUE MONTAIGNE, PARIS
December 3, 1918

DEAR EDITH:

I have just come back from Willard Straight's
funeral.

This morning the body lay in its coffin, covered
with the American flag and with his sword and cap on
top. Candles burned beside the coffin and flowers
were very simply and well arranged at the head and
the foot. Great thanks are due to Mrs. Borden
Harriman, who has done everything.

From the Crillon Hotel the body was taken to the
American Church on the Avenue Georges V. No gun
carriage being procurable, an automobile chassis was
used and did very well. An escort of soldiers marched
alongside and we came behind — Peter Bowditch,

86

representing General Pershing, General McCoy, General Jorstad, Colonel Mott, Mr. Stettinius, Martin Egan, and many others. We went slowly across the Place de la Concorde, up the Champs-Elysées, and down to the church. Everywhere the French — with that special courtesy which never fails them — took off their hats as we went by — even the men working on the monuments and the taxi-cab drivers. And all officers and soldiers whom we passed, saluted.

The church was full. Bishop Brent officiated and 'Onward, Christian Soldiers,' and 'The Battle Hymn of the Republic' were among the hymns selected.

From the Church we motored out to the American Cemetery at Suresnes, where the burial took place.

We are all so glad that Dorothy wanted him buried in France. It is the place where all the American soldiers who have died during this war should rest. Why should we bring home our dead? They have earned the right to sleep in the land on which their eyes closed, to remain forever in the soil for which they gave their lives. Their graves ensure that our work in France shall never be forgotten.

The American Cemetery at Suresnes lies on the slope of Mount Valérien, not far from the summit, overlooking the Seine River and the city of Paris. At present it is a raw piece of earth on the hillside, with rows and rows of white crosses, but when the grass grows again and shrubs and trees have matured, it will be quite beautiful.

Bishop Brent made a very short, but fine address, the customary parting to the dead was given, the coffin was lowered into the grave and 'Taps' were blown.

And so ended a real man — just as the years of greatest achievement were before him. The Peace Congress will miss his clear-headedness, his driving force, his idealism, his common-sense, his power over people. America had few men so well equipped for the problems now before her. His friends lose the finest and most generous comrade a man could have. At the grave ended warm friendships begun years and years ago in the Far East — Bishop Brent and I remarked to each other how many of the crowd that were gathered in the graveyard had begun their friendship for him and for each other in that Far East — Peter Bowditch, Martin Egan, General McCoy, the Bishop himself and others.

The day was a rainy one, but the sun came out for the first time, just at the burial itself, and turned the whole cloudy day into the most glorious, bright silver.

It will be hard to find another like Willard. He and Dorothy united more worlds, more sets, than any two people I have ever known. New York had no other couple who embraced such wide interests, who touched so many different people, who were quite such a special force in the community. And probably will never have.

Your affectionate brother
WARWICK GREENE

To Conrad P. Hatheway
February 10, 1919

General Patrick wanted me to stay with the Air Service, and I stayed, particularly as I wanted to finish out in the service in which I had started —

though I certainly have no love for the Air Service. From the time of the supplanting of Bolling in November, 1917, to the appointment of General Patrick as Chief of Air Service, A.E.F., in June, 1918, the Air Service was a madhouse. General Patrick was straight and able and put the Air Service on its feet so that it wound up creditably — but it went through a fearful period.

I enclose a copy of an affidavit made by Colonel Bolling's chauffeur, who was an eye-witness of his death. I was his Executive Assistant and very fond of him, so that I felt his loss keenly. He was a brilliant fellow, keen, capable and aggressive, and his death was to be a great loss for American aviation.

He died splendidly. Under the circumstances he might have surrendered. He and his chauffeur were not a part of any combatant troops operating in the neighborhood, had no combat duties at the moment, were practically unarmed and were hopelessly outnumbered. Under these conditions, surrender would have involved no military discredit. Instead he blazes right away at the German officers, kills his man and is in turn killed.

I had hoped to accompany him on this trip, but had just received orders to go to Italy so that I was unable. I said good-bye to him for the last time as he was leaving Paris in his car and I was going to the station to catch my train for Italy.

Peter I see quite often, either when I am at Chaumont or when he is in Paris.

I don't know how much longer my service will last, but I am hoping to finish up here early in April. But you can't be sure in military life — I may beat this letter home and I may not get there until the middle of the summer. It is all dead work now, but it has got to be done.

Sincerely yours

WARWICK GREENE

III

MISSION TO THE BALTIC STATES

To Hon. W. Cameron Forbes

AIR SERVICE, AM.E.F.
A.P.O. 702
March 9, 1919

DEAR GOVERNOR:

I have been asked by the American Commission to Negotiate Peace to head a Mission to visit the Baltic States, investigate conditions and submit a report and recommendations — the trip to take about one month.

I accepted at once and am now busy selecting my personnel and organizing the Mission. I am anxious to get one good lawyer, one financial man, one military expert and one good intelligence man, besides several officers expert in languages, especially German and the native languages of the Baltic Provinces. In this way I think we should have a pretty well-balanced Mission and one capable of submitting a sound report covering present political, economic and military matters in those provinces.

For our financial man I am trying to secure Ben Joy, who is a Major now on duty at Treves with General Smith, who is in charge of Civil Administration for our Army of Occupation in Germany. I saw Ben on my recent trip to Germany and found that the work he is doing there will be most valuable preparation for the investigations we shall be called on to make in the Baltic Provinces. But I don't know if I shall be able to get him.

For our military man I am trying for Lieutenant-Colonel Dawley and have made successful unofficial arrangements to have his temporary transfer approved — I have done this through some Regulars on the General Staff who are friends of mine. Dawley used to play polo with us in the Philippines — I have forgotten whether you know him or whether he reached the Islands after you had left. I know him quite well and have seen him from time to time during the A.E.F. — first when he was Adjutant of our detachments undergoing artillery training at the big French artillery school at Saumur and later when he was with the Staff of the First Army with Headquarters at La Ferte-sous-Jouarre. He is a nice fellow and I believe competent. He was suggested to me by the Regulars as one of the most reliable and capable officers for this work under the rank of full Colonel — as I am to be Chief of the Mission I cannot have a superior officer under me. The Mission is entirely under the Peace Commission, but as it is composed of officers and as we go in uniform the question of rank, etc., comes up. As the present military situation in these provinces will have a most important bearing on all the other matters we go to look into, it is advisable to have a Regular with us whose report on the military situation will carry weight with his profession. Dawley has been on G–3 work throughout most of the active campaigning of last summer and so is well equipped for our purpose.

G–3, I may explain, is the Section of the General Staff in charge of Operations.

The Baltic Provinces, as you probably know, are certain provinces of the former Russian Empire situated on the east side of the Baltic, running south from the Gulf of Finland. They are inhabited by three races, i.e., Esthonians, Letts, and Lithuanians, each of which has its own language and more or less of a national history. They have been dominated at various periods in their career by Germans, Swedes, and Russians, and their land-owning aristocracy was of German origin — the so-called 'German Barons' of the Baltic Provinces, of whom we have heard a good deal during the present war.

At the present time they are putting up a good fight against the Bolshevists, especially the Esthonians, who have driven them out of their country and are holding them on a fighting front on the eastern boundary of Esthonia. The Bolshevists, on the other hand, hold Riga, thereby cutting the Baltic Provinces in two. However, a newspaper despatch yesterday said that the returning German forces had captured Riga from the Bolshevists.

The Mission is a most interesting one because it will bring us into such close contact with Bolshevism. This group of Baltic nationalities, together with Finland, constitute a fringe of peoples who, along the entire eastern side of the Baltic, are trying to maintain national existences independently of the present Bolshevist Russia. At present they appear to be a real rampart against the spread of Bolshevism westward. But as they are comparatively few in number,

93

they are a thin rampart and one that must have outside help if it is to endure. At least that is their claim.

We go to England, then to Stockholm and from there to Reval, possibly through Helsingfors in Finland, possibly direct. Reval is the principal port of Esthonia, and is situated on the south shore of the Gulf of Finland, not so very far from Petrograd. From there we shall go into the interior of the country and try to work our way south. If the Bolshevists still hold Riga, we shall be forced to go by sea to Libau. When we have finished, we shall probably try to return through Germany.

I shall be on temporary detachment from the Air Service, returning to it to complete my work here when the Mission is finished. And shortly thereafter I shall hope to finish my Army career for good, as the financial support of my family will have to be the deciding factor in whatever I do after that. Army pay is very meagre, especially in these days of inflated currency. Moreover, we temporary officers have no security of tenure, future or pensions to look forward to, as do the officers of the Regular Establishment.

But I am delighted to have this Mission before I wind up. The work is most interesting and important and there is an opportunity to render some real service. And the present real problem of the world lies in the regions we are going to visit, or their neighborhood.

I had lunch with Ellen Emerson the other day. And saw Bill Poland a few days later, who said she had just been conferring with him about relief work in the devastated regions. He knows what a lot of

94

Latwijas Sargs

Eenfgaaa maffa:
a reghlu, par 1 mehnel
mk. 50 fap.
bej pefishifemsd
2 rub,

Deenas laikraksts. Pirmais gads.

Redakzija: Helenes eela, Nr. 1, runas stundas no pffm. 3—5 pehz puod.
Ekspedizija: Julianmas eeli 40, atwehrta no 6 rifti līdzī 6 wakari.

Sludinajumi.
Nweissgpmit un:teklā 70 fap;
fiabm, balt 25 fap. par
petit rinbiml.

Nr. 68. Leepajā, zeturddeen, 10. aprili 1919. g. Numurē maffā 15 fap.

Maise no saboedroteem klaht!

Thanks!

Yesterday was in the life of Latvia one of the gladdest and most hopeful days which Latvia shall never forget. Our country wounded by the bloody war didn't lose the conviction that the worlds democracies would understand its ambition to be a free and independent state in the League of Nations.

Latvia hoped. Her suffering people hoped. They hoped also for economic support. Their hope is fulfilled. Yesterday the first steamer under the starspangled American banner has brought hither the first relief. Now we shall have more bread! The whole Latvian ration now knows, it has not been forgotten.

Respectful and thankful welcome from Latvia to the starspangled banner! Greeting to the Great Allied powers working nobly for humanistic ideals!

A NEWSPAPER OF LIBAU ANNOUNCES THE ARRIVAL OF AN AMERICAN FOOD SHIP

pep and ability she has got and she will have a corking opportunity if she gets in proper relation with the Food Administration.

Peter I see pretty frequently these days, as the General is often in Paris. Peter, as usual, takes a very self-deprecatory view of his work, but I know that he is one aide in a million for the C.-in-C. On his side, he has a marvellous opportunity and has seen the A.E.F. from top to bottom in a way that it has been given to few people to see it.

Sincerely yours
WARWICK GREENE

AMERICAN COMMISSION TO NEGOTIATE PEACE
MISSION TO FINLAND, ESTHONIA, LATVIA AND LITHUANIA

LIBAU, LATVIA
April 20, 1919

Telegram

On my return, Libau, on April 16, after six-day trip to front, Balt Landeswehr troops attempted to arrest at railroad station General Missin, Lettish Chief of Staff, and four officers and orderlies who had accompanied and conducted our trip. Attempt was made while they were with us, getting out of our special car. I refused to allow arrest, asking German officers by what authority action was being taken. Shortly afterwards Rittmeister Armitstead, a Balt officer in Russian army, formally presented himself, stating he represented Committee of Safety of local front troops; that fearing Ministry of Provisional Government would turn Bolshevist they had taken steps to secure safety of front by removing these

95

ministers; that negotiations were being conducted respecting establishment of Provisional Cabinet in the interest of all classes of population without any exceptions; that the committee desired to inform the American Mission of the events which had occurred. I declined to enter into political discussion with Balt officer while armed Balt soldiers without credentials were interfering with our party in presence of German troops and officers representing the supreme police military power of General Von der Goltz, and if the government had been overturned and there was disorder, then the exclusive police power at this station. I also refused to submit to further interference or arrests of members of our joint party unless by authority of General Von der Goltz. I took General Missin to our house where he now is. I am informing General Von der Goltz of occurrence at station and that General Missin is a guest at our house.[1]

[1] Greene returned from the Front on the 16th, arriving in Libau on the 17th. Robert Hale of Portland, Maine (not a Hale cousin, though a cousin of Richard Hale's) was assistant to Greene in this mission and kept a diary.

Wednesday, April 16, he writes:

'Went to walk at three along the beach and through the town which was quiet. Called on Major Keenan about 4.00 and heard from him a rumor that there had been trouble between the Germans and Letts at the Navy Yard about old Russian ammunition. Major Keenan suggested Germans might be going to make trouble. I thought it probably nothing more than a new instance of the old friction. Returned to the house for tea and found Lt. Harrington who brought rumor that Government had been overturned and Germans in control everywhere. Walked with him to the hotel. Found town quiet but German sentinels at principal crossings, cavalry patrols with lances in the streets and fieldpieces in the square by the hotel. Returned to quarters and sent Rosenthal out with our Lettish messenger. He came back after dinner, confirming all rumors, — Ulmannis and others imprisoned, Latvian

MISSION TO THE BALTIC STATES

In Libau I found that Balt Landeswehr troops from the front, apparently mostly of Baron Manteuffel's battalion, known as Attacking Battalion, which was in neighborhood of Mitau when we first went to front, had come to Libau by train, and on afternoon April sixteenth had deposed Ministry by force. Prime Minister Ulmanis and Minister of Finance were with British Mission and three ministers were in asylum on British destroyer, and Minister of Home Affairs Walters and Minister of Supplies were prisoners. Sahlitz, Minister of Defense, who accompanied us on trip to front, had left our party at Preklum. He is now at large in interior.

Libau was heavily patrolled both by German and Landeswehr troops. I personally witnessed one scene of violence in streets by Balt soldiers who were brutally arresting an apparently unarmed civilian. But in general there was little apparent violence, though atmosphere very tense. So far as we know one Lett was killed at Government Printing Establishment, one at Navy Yard, and several Letts and Balts reported killed in fighting at Durben.

It was reported that at Navy Yard German

soldiers disarmed and confined, Latvian treasury notes distributed to soldiers and Germans supreme everywhere.'

On Thursday the 17th, he records the scene at the station. On Sunday, April 20, the date of this despatch, he writes:

'Easter Sunday. Beautiful weather and crowded streets. Almost no outward signs of disturbance. The Letts with the consent of the Balts posted a proclamation urging all Letts to keep the peace. There is no news about the new government, but toward evening a rumor was current that Prince Lieven, the Russian commander, would be asked to form a Cabinet. Mr. Burchard, the German chargé d'affaires, repeated the rumor as if the choice would meet with his approbation.'

97

Westphalian troops of Captain Pfeiffer's command insolently marched to headquarters Lettish troops with band playing, disarmed and ejected all officers and soldiers, killed one orderly and plundered and ransacked place. Letts have withdrawn to woods close to Navy Yard and are instructed not to fire on Germans. Dawley has visited Navy Yard and confirms looting and wrecking property, killing of orderly, etc., but we have not as yet positive evidence what troops committed outrage or antecedent events.

General Von der Goltz's attitude: He does not wish to interfere with interior politics of Latvia; as supreme police power he bears responsibility for order in Fortress Libau, which order he is in position to maintain.

Facts are that front troops operating under his supreme command came to Fortress Libau by military railroad and by force of arms deposed Ministry of Provisional Government interfering decisively in interior politics of Latvia and with bloodshed and violence.

We knew Balt plot was brewing, but had not expected it to break so soon. Various events related in our written reports precipitated matters. I believe coup d'état was executed, with connivance and assistance older Balts and the Germans, by young Balts, who had fought excellently against Bolshevism at front. If coup fails, rashness of gallant young hotheads will be deplored by the Balts and Germans. If it succeeds, the profit will largely accrue to Germans and Balt Barons. Young Balts say coup was necessary to save country from interior Bolshevism; that

98

National Government of Latvia continues and will be reconstituted in the interests of all parties. With a few this is genuine, but the dominant motives of Germans and older and abler Balts is to embarrass Allies and return to power the old Balt Baron régime, somewhat modified to suit new conditions, but fundamentally the same.

Deposed Provisional Government was inherently very weak. It failed to include Balt and Jewish representation, and so had their intense hostility. This failure was mistake. It was self-constituted and so its title as a popular government was defective. It failed to secure help from the Entente and so could not gain popular confidence. It asserted itself too much against German domination and so was allowed to be extinguished. But it was a de facto government and the best foundation on which to have built a stable and representative government with the necessary help from outside which was essential. Its violent overturn by young soldiers is a serious reflection on General Von der Goltz's responsibility under Article twelve of Armistice, is an affront to Allies and crime for which there should be a reckoning.

In eyes of common people of Latvia the old tyranny in all its rigor, backed by armed might of Germany, has returned in defiance of Allies and America. Lettish soldiers have been instructed not to resist, and so far have shown admirable fortitude and forbearance under intense provocation and almost intolerable circumstances. For moment people are quiet. They look westward for help from the democracies or eastward from Bolshevism. But their patience will not last indefinitely. They will not tolerate Baron dominance and will eventually resist the new régime with bloodshed. In proportion as their hope of help from west dies, they will turn Red.

We are sending full written reports covering military and political situation to Paris by Colonel Solbert, Military Attaché at Copenhagen, whom I have asked to come to Libau on British destroyer, or by Colonel Dawley. A British destroyer will take one of these two officers to Dantzig. Our cable ten, April twentieth, covers military situation with definite recommendations covering both military and political matters and will, we believe, furnish sufficient information on local situation to enable you to take action you deem advisable.

Naval forces at Libau have been increased by arrival two French destroyers. It is important that American destroyer or tender be sent.

Under present circumstances I advise against sending of further food supplies until a definite policy to meet the grave situation here has been adopted.

GREENE

To Mrs. Charles A. Lindley (*Edith Greene*)

AMERICAN COMMISSION
TO NEGOTIATE PEACE
HOTEL CRILLON, PARIS
June 29, 1919

DEAR EDITH:

Yesterday I had the luck to be one of the crowd at Versailles while the Peace Treaty was signed. Not one of the very select, to be sure, who were in the actual Hall of Mirrors, but sufficiently of the elect to be admitted to the grounds, the hallways and the terraces, there to watch the great ones arrive and depart and to gaze at the upper windows of that wonderful façade of the Palace of Versailles behind which lay the famous Salon des Glaces, where you could indistinctly see people grouped around the table. And, their names scratched on the parchment, the signers came out and mingled with us on the terrace.

We rolled out from Paris in a good Cadillac car, one of a procession of several thousand motors — British, French, American, Italian, Japanese and a string of lesser national fry that had come yelping into the war ring after they were certain that the big dogs were going to make the world safe for little yellow curs as well as honest dogs — all with flags fluttering and crammed with uniforms.

Up the Champs-Elysées, out through the Bois de Boulogne and so on to Versailles. A very gay and cheery route, lined with people and enlivened by French soldiers stationed every few hundred feet, waving red flags. Ostensibly they were traffic regulators. But no Frenchman will ever allow himself to be regulated by any power except the woman he is temporarily in love with, nor will any American in France since he has learned true democracy from the French. In France the mere hint of a rule or suggestion of authority is the signal for everybody to break the first and abuse the second. What was the war won for, anyhow? Why, to abolish the word 'verboten' in every language, of course! So the mere sight of blue-coated poilus waving red flags to moderate speed spurred each chauffeur to his reckless utmost. We went to the Peace signing as though it were the goal of an international automobile road race.

Through the suburbs the sidewalks were lined with the bourgeoisie sitting comfortably in front of their little cafés and shops, everybody 'en fête' and grinning good-naturedly at the democratic pomp whirling by on its way to Versailles. But no enthusiasm, except from the kids who invariably piped 'Vive l'Amérique' whenever a khaki car sped by. They have retained their first love, the American doughboy, their loyalty to him is unshakeable. Their elders have become 'frogs' to our soldiers, and the latter, to say the least, have worn the first bright shine off their welcome. Indeed, French people will tell you that they find they have invited in one set of barbarians to drive out another. There are good barbarians and bad barbarians, say the French. The Yankees belong to the first, the Boches to the second. But even the best barbarians may become a nuisance in a tight, tidy, crowded little country like France. Barbarians need a continent to stretch themselves and yell in. Cowboys are splendid against highwaymen, but a trial in the 'ménage.' Way down in their hearts the French never will like strangers or strange countries. Yet the doughboy has never lost his popularity with the froglets. Why? Well, because he is always playing with the kids. There is invariably a good time for the gamin when American soldiers are around. So the only cheering you heard yesterday as the nations of the earth, so to speak, motored out to Versailles, was very young France shrilly proclaiming its undying enthusiasm for America.

Arrived at Versailles we found ticket-holders must wait outside the Palace gates until three P.M. Yet everybody had been ordered to leave the Hotel Crillon and other Peace hostelries at one o'clock. Here it was only two and car after car whirling up and adding its load to the squirming, protesting crowd about the gate.

But an easy solution was found. One listened to the voluble and gilded gatekeeper explain that it was forbidden to enter; waited until he addressed the next in line, and then slipped by. And so the crowd trickled through the gateway; law and order were satisfied, having proclaimed themselves, and democracy was happy, having immediately broken them.

The stairway to the Salon des Glaces was the next barrier. Here red tickets admitted to the Press Gallery, and extra special tickets passed Olympians, private secretaries, and Clemenceau's lady friends to the very Treaty room itself. But certain Americans were not to be balked. One tore the crimson cover off a box of Pall Mall cigarettes, put it in the palm of his hand, where he let a flash of it be seen, and was immediately admitted to the Press Gallery! Two others were rebuffed, but shortly returned with an important-looking bundle, which they significantly showed the gatekeeper as they hurried through the gate with the worried air of being late. I suppose the gatekeeper assumed the bundle contained the Great Seal of the Republic or sandwiches and a thermos bottle for Mr. Wilson. Anyhow, the bluff worked and two Lieutenants were admitted to the Holy of Holies, the Hall of Mirrors. The bundle actually contained an overcoat hastily wrapped in paper borrowed from the concierge. Two fresh guys, but psychologists in their way!

These tricks, however, could only be worked once, and were not for the many, whom a line of very highly colored soldiers forbade to mount the stairway or go out on the terrace. But the crowd got wise, finally. It bided its time until it was an imposing mob; then pressed forward in a steady, cheery mass, brushing aside the soldiers, bayonets and all. Such buzzing, angry, brilliant soldiers! But so many flies as far as the crowd was concerned. Bayonets! why, they were made to stick fat Boches with, not Parisians 'en fête'! Great glass doors! They have got hinges, haven't they? Well! give them a good shove! And so the crowd poured out on those marvellous, spacious terraces, once made for kings and their mistresses, courtiers and sedan chairs, hoopskirts and peacocks. The French officers commanding the guard raged until the gilt on their 'képis' and decorations began to melt, to the huge amusement of the crowd, who were about to duck them in one of the great fountains, to cool them off, when the arrival of automobiles containing the German delegates distracted their attention. There was a general rush across the terrace to get a close-range view of the enemy.

What they saw were three or four sallow crows, one of them rather large and blond, a seedy Siegfried in a tall hat. Wretched dummies, sent to sign a Treaty which Germany already in her heart repudiates. Poor frock-coated civilians, so different from that arrogant and blazing military array which crowned William the First German Emperor on this same spot. And so different, I may say, from that great martial array of Germany I have been living with in the Baltic Provinces of Russia for the past three months — sixty thousand German troops, with German staffs and German generals, not at all averse to singing 'Deutschland, Deutschland, über alles,' as they marched through the streets at night, giving a little 'tiger' at the end as they passed the buildings where the Allied Missions were housed.

But back again to Versailles! What a pageant it was! The Palace of Versailles is superb, though it is now the fashion to decry it as pompous and grandiose. But palaces are not intended to be temples or churches; you don't want the pure or elevated style. They are the lounging halls, bedrooms and offices of kings and their courts. You are satisfied if they are rich, splendid, urbane. There is a beauty appropriate to pomp and it can be a very real and satisfying beauty. Louis the Fourteenth, above all kings since Solomon, knew the glory that was a king's and how to have it expressed in palace and park. I fancy he was very exacting to those architects, painters and sculptors who finally achieved Versailles. Just as the Arc de Triomphe is Napoleon, so is Versailles Louis le Roi Soleil. In either case mere architects prepared the plans, but their great masters looked them over, criticized, and pointed out changes; then what was merely academically and artistically good became immediately great, stamped forever with the impress of two giant natures. Versailles is the gorgeous shell

Louis the Fourteenth left behind him when he quitted the earth; the Arc de Triomphe is the spirit of Napoleon in enduring stone.

Yesterday Versailles shone in its best glory. It was designed as a stage for great events, not for tourists to gape at, and yesterday was an event to its liking. True, it looked down contemptuously, from its regal and colorful beauty, on the frock coats and tall hats — which have survived this war that was to abolish all tyranny — of our statesmen, who seemed more than ever like white-faced crows, thin or fat as the case might be, stalking about amid splendors which had once known statesmen costumed in harmony with the surroundings of palace and park. But luckily they were only a black, gawky minority in the blaze of uniforms which lit up the interior of the Palace and framed in the setting of the grounds and the terraces. For yesterday the French troops were back in their brilliant before-the-war uniforms, though there were enough poilus in horizon blue to show the stuff which won the war.

So everything was lovely, everything a-glitter. The weather was just what one would have asked from the gods for the occasion: a day of massive clouds and glowing sunshine, the latter from time to time cut off as a cloud mass rolled over the sun, only to shine forth again with fresh fire as the mists dragged themselves off his burning face. And this sunshine burnished magnificently the great forests which seem to surround Versailles and which the drought had already touched with faint autumn gold, although it was only June. Overhead airplanes played with one another, the drumming of their fiery little hearts coming and going all afternoon. The ivory façade of the Palace, in all its vast length, drank in the rich sunlight and radiated back on terrace and crowd, a delicious warmth.

And then, midst all the gleam and glory of this beauty and the pride and stateliness of the great ceremony, one became aware that the French, with their unfailing dramatic instinct, had placed their death-heads — in the shape of war 'mutilés' who had been given prominent places — in the Hall of Mirrors. There they were, the legless, the handless, the armless, the shell-shocked — members of that ghastly legion the war has left who are neither of the living nor of the dead. And face cases! Faces as livid as raw beef, with coarse, rudimentary openings for mouth and nose; faces which steel and fire had wrought on until they seemed the buffoonery of some drunken, obscene creator who with clumsy hands had made them of foul clay and then spat in their nostrils to give them the breath of life. There they were, in all that mellowed beauty Louis the Fourteenth had left us, side by side with the white faces of statesmen and the ruddy faces of soldiers. Living gargoyles, fashioned by that terrible, filthy, sublime sculptor, War; breathing gargoyles, who leered at the statesmen and at the parchment whose signing as victors they had made possible. Behind each fleshy mask of horror was an ordinary 'poilu's' brain, simple, fundamentally honest, rowdy, affectionate, loving women, loving wine, loving children, loving domesticity, loving work (but not too intensely) — yet forever doomed to turn on the world a mask to revolt women, frighten children and repulse mankind.

In due time Peace was signed. At once the guns began, joyful, blustering guns, booming out from the foot of the great stairway which leads to the lake. The fountains followed, leaping forth in froth and frolic, tossing their glistening spume high against the glad blue of that summer sky.

Then Clemenceau, Lloyd George, and Wilson emerged and tried to stroll about and watch the fountains. Instantly the crowds closed in on them, jostling, hustling and mauling them this way and that. But everybody was happy, including the three Deities their Masters the people so gleefully and playfully horsed about.

Extraordinary to think that for the moment the Will of the World walked about in those elderly, frock-coated gentlemen — Clemenceau, the Mongolian Tiger, whose claws drip with German blood; Wilson, true son of that elder, calculating, austere American world; Lloyd George, robust, eloquent, slightly ridiculous.

Finally Democracy hustled its dolls down the stairway and, amid a great jostle of civilians and soldiers, tossed them into a common limousine, together with a huge bouquet, and shot them off with cheers and good-will, Admiral Grayson clinging to the outside of the limousine which carried the world's Trinity; Pershing, Bliss and others following in their cars.

And then, if you were fanciful, you could hear the curtain of Fate creaking down on the heavy, bloody melodrama which began with the murder of an Archduke five years ago to the day. What crimson centuries of history have been packed into those few years! Down to the ash-heap have gone dynasties, kings, and principles; and beside them, on the red, red ash-heap, lie the dead youth of the world. Lord! if the splendid dead could rise, millions on millions of them, how they would have thronged those radiant summer skies above Versailles!... how the beat of their generous hearts would have made splendid music for the scene!... how their cries of pain and despair, of death and defeat, of victory and glory, would have challenged the statesmen who are building a new world on their bones! What a vast Valhalla, somewhere, those ardent souls must people! How the old Valhallas must shrink, how the elder warriors wither as these many millioned legions tramp into the new halls, shouting their new songs, recounting their new exploits, dragging with them their new weapons!

Yes! the crash and flame of modern battle must jar the simple old fighters; the uproarious, prodigious hubbub and the gorgeous, tragic spectacle of the war of races and continents must belittle the ancient heroes. And how its amazing and lavish paraphernalia must humiliate those who fought with such clumsy and meagre equipment! Banal writers tell you science has taken the romance from fighting. In truth, it has multiplied it a hundredfold and given war a fresh and burning magnificence. Science has furnished it with arms of precision whose terror and splendor were unimagined; it has camouflaged weapons, ships and buildings with colors more vivid than those of Asia; it has carried war under the sea and into the air and made night, when former armies rested, lurid with artillery, flare and bomb; it has propagated and propagandized war, thanks to the telegraph and the modern newspaper, until it infected the entire globe; it has drained the young manhood of the wide world, thanks to railroad and steamship, and poured them unceasingly into the two red battle lines of Europe, where battle never ceased from year end to year end and where gallant blood and brains were squandered as though earth's cheapest and most abundant products. What were the pigmy armies and tiny battlefields and short-breathed battles of other wars compared with the titanic and blazing epic of the war which began at Sarajevo and ended, if God is gracious, yesterday at Versailles!

Your affectionate brother

WARWICK GREENE

From Greene's portfolio of drafts and miscellaneous writings

The Peace Conference, Paris, 1919

Wilson: singular and angular, descendant of all the shabby generations of non-conformity; the 'poor white' come to the seats of the mighty; archtype of the unknown millions of Church Elders and Deacons who in their obscurity were the moral reënforcing of America; the plain people's self-appointed Messiah —

House: that Texas Colonel, running in and out of

THE AMERICAN PEACE DELEGATION AT PARIS
Left to right : Mr. House, Mr. Lansing, President Wilson, Mr. White, General Bliss

the international wainscoting of Diplomacy, mouse-
like; nibbling here, nibbling there, scuttling to cover
at every unusual sound —

Lansing: autocratic Chief Clerk, Departmental expert draftsman of documents; without ideas, imagination, or personality —

White: that pleasant bag of soft flesh and softer
mentality in a frock coat, modestly uncomfortable on
the Peace Commission throne —

Bliss: hard-boiled old Regular Army General; a
grey-haired walrus drinking the blood of enthusiasts
and crunching the bones of each new idea —

These were the manikins that America, holding the
keys of the world in her lusty hands; her newly raised,
vast armies, seething with youth and strength, behind her; the world's gold and food piled up on
America's fee-simple — *these* were the mediocrities
that she sent to the most tremendous council that ever
sat among the sons of men!

Hoover: coming to the economic rescue of the civilization of Europe, like a Gothic King, who had already ransomed Rome, to bar Attila and his Huns
from further inroads on the venerable wreck.

Lenin seems to be that combination of cold intelligence, iron will, and passionate vision and direct
action, which mark the greatest leaders of destruction or of construction.

What place will history give to that monstrous
nation from over the seas; that precocious child of
old Europe's of one hundred million people at the
time of the great war; who so noisily intervened in
the affairs of the old house?

What indeed!

Across the seas there had grown up that raw country, that strident civilization, so forceful, so threatening to the whole world.

Lightly Europe asked these children to intervene in a new phase of her old national wars; noisily the children from over the seas came — and forever changed the destinies of beautiful Europe.

Since the morning of mankind, Europe had looked to the East for her barbarians, for her invasions, for her destructions, for her new blood and new life.

Westward had ever lain the great ocean, ending the world. Those thousands of miles of grey and blue seas were Europe's surest ramparts.

And now, eastward across that Western Ocean came the new armadas, the new invasions, the khaki-clad Yanks. Ship on ship, fleet on fleet, men by the hundred thousand.

Their barbaric yip startled the shores of the Old World; their coarse jargon beat up from the streets of the little French seacoast towns; their humor, their impatience, their blasphemy, their mad energy, their carelessness and restlessness, their resourcefulness and rude intelligence shook the very soul of Europe. Turned into battle they were savages, illy led by their meagre, austere Regular Army officers, but ferocious and not to be denied. The philosopher saw that old gods — and beautiful gods! — were falling in Europe and that the grinning face of the Yankee was emerging through the ruin.

MISSION TO THE BALTIC STATES

To General Francis Vinton Greene

AMERICAN COMMISSION
TO NEGOTIATE PEACE
HOTEL CRILLON, PARIS
July 27, 1919

DEAR PAPA:

As you know, I was asked if I would organize a Mission for the American Commission to Negotiate Peace and take it to the Baltic 'States' to investigate and report on military, economic and political conditions in those regions.

I accepted and left Paris shortly after the middle of March as Chief of a Mission to Finland, Esthonia, Latvia and Lithuania. The maximum strength of my Mission was fourteen officers and men — no limit was put on the number, but at one time and another we had that number on the list.

I sent most of the Mission ahead, leaving myself with Lieutenant-Colonel Dawley (a Regular officer, West Point graduate, who was detailed to the Mission in response to my request for a Regular to be military adviser and expert for the Mission) in a Cadillac car in which we made a run up through the Château-Thierry district, Soissons, and then westward along the Hindenburg line, the battlefield of the Somme, etc., straight to Boulogne and thence to England.

From England we went to Copenhagen, where I had the good luck to run into Admiral Cowan commanding the British fleet in the Baltic, who ran me up to Libau in his flagship, H.M.S. Caledon. Admiral Sir Walter Cowan, K.C.B., M.V.D., D.S.O., etc., is a quiet, soft-spoken man who is one of the great fighters of the British Navy — he commanded one of the battle cruisers at the battle of Jutland. He is a very agreeable fellow and was more than kind to me, insisting that I occupy his Admiral's cabin on the trip across the Baltic and in every way showing me a very warm-hearted hospitality — not only then, but during the entire length of my stay in the Baltic. He was always willing to help our Mission in every possible manner with the ships under his command.

So I arrived at Libau on April second and remained in the Baltic regions until June thirteenth, when I left for Paris, reaching there three or four days later.

Since June seventeenth I have been in Paris, in constant conference with various branches of our Peace Commission organization and also attending sessions of the Inter-Allied Baltic Commission at the Quai d'Orsay. In our Peace Commission I have had most to do with General Bliss, though also somewhat with Mr. Lansing and Mr. White. Yesterday I sat in at one of the sessions of the Big Five at which Mr. Clemenceau presided. A Baltic question came up and was discussed for a time, principally by Mr. Clemenceau and Mr. Balfour. The President of the Baltic Commission, Marquis della Torretta (an Italian), and Mr. Pichon also spoke. It was interesting and instructive.

I am now returning to the Baltic, leaving Paris tomorrow or the day after, and travelling across Germany. Riga will be my first objective, where I will meet Colonel Dawley. I hope that then it will be possible for him to return to Paris and later to Washington, to post the War Department on the tangled and dangerous situation in Western Russia. He has studied the entire anti-Bolshevist Front from Poland to Petrograd and I believe that today he is the best-informed military man in Europe on that situation.

I hope to be able to wind up my work by the end of August and then either terminate the activities of the Mission, or be relieved by a Regular Army officer in case it is decided to continue this Mission as a military observing mission.

My experiences in Russia have been interesting and at times exciting. How worth-while they have been to me only time can tell. In any case what I have seen there will leave an indelible impression on me. It is a nightmare of disorder and bloodshed. The foundations of social and political life — not to speak of religious — have crumbled. Something will evolve out of the chaos, but what it is difficult to say.

As soon as this work is finished, I shall hope for my return home and demobilization. I am homesick to see you and Mamma.

Your affectionate son
WARWICK GREENE

Clipping attached to July 27, 1919, letter
SPECIAL U. S. MISSION
GOES TO BALTIC LANDS
*Lieut-Col. Greene in Charge of
Investigators*

LONDON, *April 9.* — A special commission representing the American peace delegation has begun an investigation of conditions in northwestern Russia, a news agency despatch from Helsingfors reported today.

Before leaving for Libau, the commission, composed of Lieut. Col. Warwick Greene and five other officers, issued the following statement:

'The United States considers that no world peace is possible until the Russian problem is solved and satisfactory Governments established in Finland and the Baltic provinces. With the object of facilitating the work of the United States peace delegation in Paris, a special American commission has been appointed to visit Finland, Esthonia, Lettland and Lithuania to study political, economic and military conditions.'

The British War Office today reported successful operations against the Bolsheviki in Northern Russia by anti-Soviet Russians. The North Russia rifle regiment occupied the village of Gapnavalok, on the eastern shore of Lake Vigozero, capturing a Bolshevik patrol, it was stated. Finnish troops, attacking a post south of Segeja, were twice repulsed.

A wireless despatch from Moscow announced that Bolshevik forces have captured Odessa.

A news agency despatch from Paris today said the Allied evacuation of Odessa had been confirmed.

The Bolshevik official communiqué stated:

'After artillery preparation, we launched a decisive attack on Thursday against the fortifications of Perekop (on the Crimean Isthmus, 150 miles east of Odessa), and after violent fighting captured the town. The next day the enemy withdrew to Armjanskibasar. Pressing the enemy, we entered Armjanskibasar, the enemy fleeing in a panic toward Simferopol, abandoning machine guns and wounded. The road into the Crimea is now open.'

MISSION TO THE BALTIC STATES

Green's Diary of the trip, Paris to Revêl

PARIS, *July* 30, 1919

We shove off from the Hotel Crillon about eight
A.M.; destination Russia! It is the brightest, choicest
July weather, with Paris at its very best.

Our Cadillac has seen much service, but runs
sweetly and is ready for much more. On the running-
boards are four extra gasoline tanks, and there is another in the tonneau. So we have six tanks in all. We
shall need them crossing gasolineless Germany. We
have many spare tires, much baggage, and innumerable cartons of cigarettes, which latter are to lift us
through tight places in Germany and Russia. We
are three: a lieutenant, an enlisted driver, and myself.

From Paris we roll the old car through Meaux and
Château-Thierry; then along the south bank of the
Marne where the last German offensive (that of
July 15, 1918) failed; up over the sunny hills and
vineyards north of the Marne; and so into Rheims.
Familiar ground, all of it; dozens and dozens of times
have I Cadillacked over it.

In the high noon we walk about Rheims, whose
ruins are vivid in the blazing sunshine. Against a
hot, blue sky the mutilated Cathedral rises over the
shell-pitted square and fills one with anti-German
rage. But what a structure! Hack it, batter it,
splinter it, burn it — and still the shattered stone
carcass is incomparable.

From Rheims we strike northward, cross the upper
end of the Argonne Forest, eventually get through the

'badlands' of the War and come into the smiling, unspoiled country north of the devastated belt.

Presently we are stopped by guards in Belgian uniform, who examine our passports and passes languidly, take a package of cigarettes with alacrity and wave us over the frontier into Belgium.

Half an hour later, more chocolate soldiers at a frontier post, more perfunctory examination of passes and we are in Luxembourg — in this part of Europe you can scarcely let a Cadillac out between national boundaries! Like Belgium and Southern Germany, Luxembourg is a clean, clean land — trim fields, neat villages, immaculate roads.

And so into the town of Luxembourg, where we stop an hour or two; then out across the delightful mediæval bridges which span the high ravines surrounding the city; down through miles of parklike forests; then another frontier — this time Germany — and we are on the Moselle, its green waters rolling north to join Father Rhine at Coblenz.

And northward down that valley we go too, our destination likewise the Rhine.

Dusk finds us at Trèves or Trier, where we are to put up for the night. A clean town, charmingly situated on green bottom lands. The Moselle flows out of a cleft in the hills to the south, washes by the foot of the city under many bridges, and disappears again to the north through a rift in the hills.

I have been here many times. Last time it was still packed with doughboys; but this July night only a sprinkling remain.

GREENE'S CADILLAC USED FROM PARIS TO REVAL, JULY 30, 1919

MISSION TO THE BALTIC STATES

A late start. It is after eleven o'clock before we drop Trèves.

From Trèves to Coblenz the valley of the Moselle is lovely beyond belief or description. First there is a joyous green river bubbling gaily northward through steep hills and filling the air with its freshness. Then the slopes of these steep hills are copper-green with vineyards (whose grapes will be bottled as sparkling Moselle), and their little craggy peaks are topped with castles, as is proper in a tourist's country. Along the shores Old-World villages lie thickly, their stone underpinnings rising from the lapping waters. In the nooks of the hills gleam fields more vividly green than the young rice paddies of the Philippines; and the ravines are choked with glossy woods. Far above lie wide upland pastures dotted with red and black specks where cattle graze. A bit like stage scenery, perhaps, but frame the picture under a blue sky, gild it with a July sun — and God bless the patriot who bought the Liberty Bonds to pay for our Cadillac and this summer joy-ride, say we three!

Two hours of this and our jaunty Moselle runs slap into the deep Rhine. At the juncture stands the big, well-scrubbed city of Coblenz: Headquarters of the American Army of Occupation!

At the sharp end of the triangle, the waters of the two rivers sliding swiftly by to run together in a splashing embrace, there rides forth, on a bronze horse, William the First, also in black bronze. His horse stamps massively on a granite pedestal, and rider and horse are framed in a semi-circular, squat monstrosity of granite, a sort of heavy hymn to "Blut und Eisen" in granite and bronze. William the Second delighted in this kind of art; so his obsequious sculptors begot them throughout the length and breadth of Germany.

Today doughboys swarm over this elephantic shrine, chewing gum and taking snapshots. One would expect Wilhelm der Grosse to tumble off his bronze carthorse with rage!

I visit Headquarters, only to learn that passes into unoccupied Germany take three days. This will never do! So I search the Headquarters Roster for Pasay Polo Club names, and soon find plenty of them. In less than two hours I am provided with passes, permits, authorizations, etc., enough to satisfy even an American A.P.M.; Forbes Field, Pasay, why, the A.E.F. began there!

Five P.M. sees us over the old Father Rhine, by the pontoon bridge which runs straight to the foot of Ehrenbreitstein. And from the top of that craggy pile streams Old Glory against the German sky. The Stars and Stripes across the Rhine! No, the 'idiotic Yankees' couldn't fight! Doughboy sentinels on Ehrenbreitstein prove it conclusively!

Across the Rhine we bear to the right and run into the French sector; then turn northward through one of those charming little valleys which open out of the Rhine gorge. Up we mount, now in the shade of the clean forest, now in the sunshine of little dappled fields, always following upward a splashing brook.

Presently we crawl through an old stone village behind a company of poilus marching along the main street, preceded by their trumpeteers playing a joyful, insolent fanfare on their clarions. Old Germany has retired within its houses and shut all doors, windows and blinds, not to see the hated sight; but all young Germany follows gleefully at the heels of the blue soldiers and those entrancing men who blow their clarions so gaily and then reverse the flashing brass with such chic. Jauntily the blue columns roll along the street; triumphantly the brass clarions and the rolling drum mock Germany! France across the Rhine, the Gallic Cock crowing in Deutschland — how the million and a half French dead must cheer from whatever Valhalla they have reached!

The sun is low and burning red through the summer dust when we come to the end of the Bridgehead area. Logs across the road, machine guns and a group of poilus mark the end of occupied Germany. Our passes are found in order and we pass into unoccupied, unadulterated Germany. For hundreds and hundreds of miles now it will be German food, German talk, German uniforms, German everything! For we are to cross Germany from her furthest western to her furthest eastern frontier.

At dark we pull into a little town called Wetzlar. We find a shingled inn in the tangle of mediæval streets, lock the Cadillac up in a cow-barn (from which all cows have long since vanished) and go in to dinner, which we eat in a gloomy dining-room, beneath oleographs of Hindenburg and Ludendorf. Sunny faces those two!

121

Dinner is meagre. As it will not vary in hundreds and hundreds of miles I shall give it to you: cabbage soup, stewed horse with cabbage, potatoes and turnips, a bright pink and cobalt blue dessert, and 'ersatz' (substitute) beer. As a great delicacy black bread is brought in with a special order of cheese, and offered like cake! There is no butter, no milk, no tea, no sugar. Every other diner has the same meal; it is stereotyped, and we are to meet it in each small town in Germany. In Berlin it is different; different, that is, in the big hotels and restaurants, where money will buy anything. Elsewhere in Berlin you would find the same meal.

So you eat to live, not live to eat. For a few days your stomach kicks, then settles down to war discipline. What a weapon is blockade! Think of our South in 1866; of Germany throughout the war and even to-day; of Russia at the present time!

In the low dining-room the other diners munch heavily away, growling to one another in gutturals. The skin sags from their faces, the clothes hang loosely from their shrunken frames. Only the fat Field-Marshal and the fat General on the wall recall what Germans once looked like.

And you could chop the gloom — human gloom — with an axe.

Through the windows the later northern twilight shows an apathetic crowd wandering listlessly about the streets.

The proprietor chats sadly with us after dinner. 'Ja! Deutschland ist ganz kaput' (Germany is completely done for) is the burden of his dirge.

MISSION TO THE BALTIC STATES

In the smoking-room a bust of William the Second, moustache fiercely upturned, presides over the mantelpiece — yes, the same William who ran away and left his loving subjects to shift for themselves when the 'débâcle' came.

In the bedrooms we find windows tightly closed, and mountains of feather mattresses under which we are supposed to sleep. No danger of the chill of a July night penetrating; nor of that great menace — fresh air!

WETZLAR, *August* 1, 1919

Up bright and early. Breakfast consists of one cube of black bread, one goose egg (from the very goose that laid the golden ones we find when the bill is presented) and cocoa, the latter from our own stores.

We wake up the good old Cadillac, lead her out of the cow-barn, hire some idle Heinies to help change two soft tires, and eventually roll away; all the establishment and half the town assembled to see our departure.

And so good-bye to gloomy little Wetzlar. I am not vindictive now that Germany is licked; I hope for better days for Wetzlar. An idle wish, however, for darker times still are brewing for Germany.

Out in the country we find a resplendent July day, with rich sunshine and bright skies — how dare German skies be so bright and gay, one thinks! The power of the sun is tempered by a crisp wind from the north, into the teeth of which we push, chasing that elusive northern horizon 'over the hills and far away'

— for we are still in the hill country of the Rhine.

The roads are excellent, though a bit winding. As we are beyond the Bridgehead areas, I drive, turn and turn with the chauffeur.

Through Hesse we find the peasants still in costume — a rare sight today in Europe, where democracy is sweeping all the world into the same drab uniformity of cheap and ugly modern clothes. The cheery colors of native costume are vanishing, just as we saw them in Mindanao as 'civilization' crept in.

So these simple-looking blighters who scramble so quickly out of the road when they see our car coming are the 'Huns' of our revolutionary day — the terrible Hessians that England sent to America to practise 'frightfulness' on our ancestors! Well! They probably did it just as supinely for George the Third as of late for William the Second — so let them hustle down into the ditch at the sight of an American car! There has been a long delay in settling that old account.

Now we leave the hill country and come down into the great German plain, which is to stay with us right through to Russia. The roads straighten out and we roll the old Cadillac along fifty-five, sixty, sixty-five miles an hour — on down grades the speedometer jazzes around seventy. We have a picked car with a specially good motor, and we are overdue in Russia!

Luncheon in the University town of Göttingen — same meal, same gloom, same lithographs of Hindenburg and Ludendorf. But the town is attractive, and the windows bright with geraniums, though cupboards are bare, and nobody, evidently, has smiled for many, many moons.

All the long summer afternoon we romp northward through big cities — Magdeburg, Brunswick, Brandenburg, and Potsdam. Everywhere the streets are filled with idle, despondent crowds; little work is going on. If the old adage is true, Satan will yet brew plentiful mischief out of Germany. What pothering fools are the Old Men of Paris! Disarm Germany and put her to work as quickly as possible; if they continue to throttle her economically, they will reap a monarchist or a Red whirlwind.

The character of the country has changed: we have left the charm of the Rhinelands, and are unmistakably in Prussia. An austere landscape; a harsher, stronger people.

Dinner at a little town, with the glare of Berlin already lighting the sky. Same dinner, same horse, same chemical dessert.

Then the spreading suburbs of Berlin swallow us up; we pass through the leafy Tiergarten, under the Brandenburg Tor, and down Unter den Linden.

Three hundred and fifty miles shows the speedometer for the day's run. Not bad in a new country over strange roads.

To bed in the Hotel Adlon, swarming with Allied and American Missions. No, there were no British, French or American uniforms when I was last there in 1916. Times have changed since the Kaiser took a villa at Amerongen. He would sleep badly could he see his Berlin now — especially his own palace, its face battered by revolutionary shells.

During the morning the Cadillac is groomed and given a huge feed of gasoline and oil at the American military garage, and my lieutenant talks the garage sergeant out of a complete new set of tires all round — every wheel is freshly shod with Goodyear's best, and every weak-looking spare replaced by Goodrich's soundest — on the plea that we are bound for darkest, reddest Russia, where any inopportune blow-out might give the Bolshies a new Cadillac staff car.

Meanwhile I pay calls and stroll about the place, dodging Cadillacs and Tin Lizzies rattling through the Kaiser's sacred portal in the Brandenburg Tor — for no doughboy chauffeur would dream of using any other entrance.

About three P.M. we get under way. Down Unter den Linden, past the huge central police station in Alexander Platz, spattered with the marks of seventy-sevens and machine-gun bullets, through miles of dull suburbs, and so finally into the open country.

The roads are straight and good; we plough east at a fast rate. There is nothing sleek-looking about this country; the soil is poor and sandy, but every inch is worked for dear life. If unsuited to ordinary crops, it is set out to wonderful pine forests, which are raised as crops, planted in rows like corn, thinned out each year as the trees grow, and at the end of thirty years harvested in one clean cut, and then the area replanted. Everything is immaculate — houses, towns, roads, railroads, occasional factories — and it is still the home of a grim and formidable people. Their hope lies in the direction towards which we are hustling — Russia. For their sins we have put them in a stage prison, with a great show of guards on the Rhine, and the British naval Titan as their jailer on the high seas. The jail has an imposing front — but no back! Eastward the world is wide open to Germans for thousands and thousands of miles with nothing but a litter of snarling, new-born puppy republics to say them nay. A firm union between German energy and German intelligence on the one hand and Russian raw man-power and Russian raw materials on the other — and, good Lord, what a behemoth we should have to handle! 'We lost the war in the West, only to win it in the East with the coming generation,' as I have heard Prussian officers mutter.

We cross the broad Oder and come into the fortress town of Kustrin, a huge advance bastion for the defence of Berlin — against the Russian steam roller which never rolled, except backward!

The town bristles with bayonets and steel helmets and for the first time in unoccupied Germany we are stopped by sentries and asked for passes. Curious transposition: In Germany, where before the war everything was 'verboten,' now everything and any-thing goes; whereas today in the Allied countries you can't blow your nose unless your passport is specifically visé'd to the effect, and in any one of Mr. Wilson's thirteen hundred 'self-determination' republics you would be instantly arrested as a Black Reactionary, the aristocrat in you fatally betrayed by the public use of a handkerchief. In conquering Germany we caught the 'verboten' microbe; it is now having a riotous epidemic throughout the rest of the world. But in Germany we have travelled five hundred miles and this sentry is the first German to bother his head as to who we may be.

We hand out our papers. They are all in order. The Prussian officers eye the big American car and its occupants with some curiosity, but are quite polite and correct.

Up to Kustrin no German official has questioned us. But martial Kustrin is a foretaste of the atmosphere down east beyond Berlin; the deeper we get into that region, the more we are to find the old Prussian spirit in evidence. We are approaching the Eastern Marches of Germany, the home of the real Junker, the last stronghold of German militarism. Beyond lie hostile Poland and Russia; they help to keep the fires of Junkerism and Militarism burning brightly in eastern Germany.

Kustrin behind us, we hammer eastward over wonderful roads, shedding a big sheaf of miles behind us every hour.

For the night we bunk down at a little town called Jastrow. It is the first time Jastrow has seen Allied or American uniforms. They take it calmly and with no outward signs of hostility.

Dinner is the same. The cabbage perhaps a little ranker, the horse stringier, the beer more resiny than ever. Luckily we are far from the dye and cellulose factories, so there is no dessert. The same pessimistic proprietor—Deutschland is 'ganzer kaput' than ever.

After dinner we stroll about the streets. We are well to the north and twilight whitens the sky until

after ten o'clock. The people seem utterly depressed
and listless. There are no young men about — many
have gone to join Germany's two million under the
sod, most of the survivors are with forlorn military
adventures in Russia. We are in the midst of a
beaten and morose race, yet supporting their sorrows
with a certain dignity.

Again the Cadillac hits the hay in a cowless cow-
barn, and we in a smother of feathers.

August 3, 1919

Off again in good season. We plough through the
outskirts of Pomerania, where the funny bow-wows
come from.

And then, insensibly at first, but more pronounced
as we go on, a Polish flavor steals into the countryside. Polish signs rub elbows with German signs;
Polish names appear over shop-windows; we hear the
peasants talking that sneezy language. We are in the
section of West Prussia which the Peace Treaty gives
to Poland.

We measure the gasoline in our tanks and find we
shall not have enough to carry us through to Riga;
so we make a side trip down to Dantzig, and finally
locate an American destroyer and have our tanks
replenished. And we have lunch in prim Dantzig.
This détour kills the best part of the day. It is late
afternoon before we are back again on the great highway to the east.

Now we come to the many mouths of the huge
Vistula, spanned by great iron bridges, their entrances
flanked by Hohenzollerns on horseback. They are

heavily guarded and we are constantly challenged. We produce our credentials and demand that they be examined immediately, as we have no time to waste. The Prussian officers are invariably polite and punctilious; our passes are immediately inspected, and in a few moments we are again on our way. No words are wasted on either side. In my experience there is no difficulty dealing with German officers if you confine yourself to the military business in hand. As the police authority of the region, these officers have the right to examine the papers of all people passing through; being on the winning side, we have the right to a minimum of delay in these formalities. On this basis my Mission spent months in regions occupied by the German forces without a row. We don't like to boast, but other Missions were not so fortunate. By confining ourselves strictly to the business in hand we saved incidents.

We dine and sleep in Königsberg. Same dinner, same pictures of Kaiser, Hindenburg and Ludendorf — plus a bust or two of little Willie, whose picture has vanished from other parts of Germany. For in Königsberg we are in the very heart of irreconcilable Junkerdom, and die-hard Prussianism. In Königsberg was organized the movement which finally swept Napoleon out of Germany, after he had all Germany under his heel, except this nub of intransigeance down on the far Baltic. When he lost out in Russia, East Prussia was immediately at his flank. And from Königsberg the reorganization of Germany began.

So today the Prussian officers who crowd the streets of this town dream, from subaltern to general,

130

of history repeating itself. At the same time the
proletariat dream of stretching hands across the thin
strip of the Baltic provinces and joining with Trotzky's Red Armies. The fun will begin when they
commence to carve up East Prussia à la Peace
Treaty. East Prussia is loaded with political T.N.T.,
and the Treaty may be a first-class detonator.

August 4, 1919

Leave Königsberg by the Brandenburg Tor. It is
still early. The sun has come up out of Russia, now
close at hand, and climbs over the yellow rye-fields
with genial warmth, but a keen breeze sifts in from
the Baltic with wisps of fog, and keeps the August
heat well in hand.

The roads are wonderful. Half the roadway is
macadamized, half soft for the passage of cavalry
which occasionally we see. Automobiles have vanished from this world. Save for an occasional military detachment, huge farm carts constitute the only
traffic, each drawn by two spanking Percherons or
Clydesdales — or whatever the Germans call these
breeds. In their off-time they evidently pose for
German sculptors to be reproduced in bronze, carrying bronze Hohenzollerns!

The country looks dry and hard, fit lair for the
Prussians. Yet it is relieved by patches of dark
spruce forest, edged with shining birch, forerunners of
Russia, towards which we are hustling at fifty miles
an hour. Also it gleams with the deep Prussian blue
of little lakes, fringes of the great Mazurian Lake
system to the east.

131

We are on historic ground. Here in 1914, Hindenburg and Ludendorf took charge of the smashed German armies (just as the Russian Bear was about to lay a heavy paw on Königsberg), swatted the old Bear twice across the snout, once at Tannenberg and once at the Mazurian Lakes, and drove him bellowing back to his own country.

I have recently read Ludendorf's book; so the country is doubly interesting to me. I can picture those two fat-bodied, hard-minded old men lumbering about the country in their limousines, organizing victory on the Eastern Front, only to lose it again on the Western. The old Bear was soft pickings compared to Germany's enemies in the West.

But those old men never drove their Mercédés and their Benz cars faster than we our khaki Cadillac. How we spank the old girl down those long, long roads, the chauffeur and I alternating at the wheel!

We cross the Niemen, pass cordons of sentries at Tilsit, meet troops of cavalry and trains of artillery returning from Russia, and soon are at the Russian frontier. We entered Germany by her western extremity; we are leaving by her eastern.

There is a guard-house, a wooden gate across the road, and a German detachment with a German sergeant-major in charge. The Heinie 'Top' says he has strict orders to allow nobody to pass into Russia unless telegraphic instructions from G.H.Q. at Bartenstein have been sent. He is a good-natured fellow and shows us his instructions.

'There are so many Bolshevists about,' he adds apologetically.

'Travelling in American uniform and American army car,' we answer.

But humor, cheap or otherwise, is quite lost on that Boche non-com. A package of American cigarettes, however, brightens him up wonderfully, two more make rules and regulations fade into fine print, three (plus a bit of telephoning) remove all taint of Bolshevism from us and raise the gates.

And so we pass from orderly and highly organized Germany — clean villages, good roads, well-built houses — into shaggy Russia — filthy villages, vile roads, dilapidated houses. The transformation is not gradual; it takes place a yard from the frontier. I am merely observing what I saw, not commenting.

I have said that most Russian roads are bad. They are; unspeakably so. But there are a few great military highways and they are magnificent. We are on the one that runs from the German boundary to Petrograd — a marvellous road shooting cross-country straight as an airplane flies; a road built like a railroad, with huge cuts and fills and few grades. And metalled with a tremendous depth of macadam, which, though a little rough from neglect, is solid even through a Russian spring thaw.

Soon we plunge into a big forest, a story-book forest where in winter you can picture wolves chasing the sleighs and devouring babies thrown to them to gain time. And in this same forest, on our return trip some weeks later, we are to have an encounter with outlaws.

We emerge from the forest into fertile Lithuania, a land actually flowing with milk and honey. Unfortunately, transport is too broken down to take these products to the starving regions. Besides, political conditions are too disordered.

Yes, a real land of Canaan this Lithuania. Ludendorf's eyes must have gloated like a fat Joshua's as his 'feldgrau' armies marched in and took possession.

And for a time Ludendorf really thought he had carved off a juicy steak for Germany from the Bear's fat flank — together with a few cutlets in the shape of the Baltic Provinces of Courland and Livonia. And no Prussian Junker has yet given up the idea that if not he, at least his grandchildren, will dine off these steaks and cutlets.

Nature has made a beautiful land of Lithuania, but man caring for it has been slovenly. The rule of the Czars, like the rule of the Turk, is known by its blight — broken-down wooden fences; log cabins thatched with dirty straw; all dogs curs; all children dirty; all horses shaggy; all wagons rickety. Under the warm August sun — it is now high noon — swarms of flies and fleas rise from every hamlet. If you stop and go into a peasant's home, the smell knocks you down and then the vermin pick your bones — I have tried to sleep in these cabins — I know!

The good Lord has kept his head throughout the war. First the Germans licked the Russians to show that efficiency is superior to slovenliness. Then the Western nations licked Germany to demonstrate that a free and tolerant civilization is superior to a brutal and autocratic one, no matter how efficient the latter. Then Lenin raises his sinister head, as a warning to the Elder Statesmen of the Western World that they

134

had better be honest in fulfilling their war-time ∠
pledges for a better world — or Hell will break loose
everywhere.

Apart from the smelly villages, the country entrances one. Off it goes, roaming away in great waves
towards the heart of Russia, and beyond that Asia;
checker-boarded with blue-black squares of pine
forest and brown-gold squares of ripening barley and
rye, threaded with blue rivers, all burnished under a
magnificent sun. We have left crowded, carefully
cultivated Europe, and have reached a rough land
of huge distances and free horizons like our own
Western plains.

If you are American, you want to give three cheers. ∠

For once more you are in a land where man is care-
less and Nature allowed to romp. No carefully
planted rows of trees along the road to cut down the
view, no lovely little towns, farms and churches to
hold the attention to details, no meticulously trained
fields and artificial forests to show how thoroughly
Nature has been tamed. Just a big, free, splashy
country, where everything is yet to be done. Untidy
fields, rough natural forests, a vast domain running
from the Baltic to Vladivostok, waiting for men with
brains and energy to take hold of it.

Even the Cadillac feels more at home and kicks up
her hind tires and snorts down the great military road
as though she were a young Lancia racer.

It is past lunch-time; so we cast about for some
flea-less, bug-less eating place. Presently, as we
bowl over a ridge and spread the country for miles
about us, we spot the tiled roof of a large manor-

house in the midst of a green grove far off in the mellow Lithuanian landscape.

Soon we wheel into the grass-grown and weed-choked driveway to demand, in the free and easy way of military life, lunch. The place smells clean and no flies or fleas swarm out to greet us; so we go in.

We find an old lady with her daughter and a niece. Her name? Well, quite simple; just Countess Gabryela Przeciszewskich Grusewska! I dare you to pronounce it — I can't! A fine old soul, looking very much as I remember old Mrs. Hallowell; Quakerish, but full of pep, humor and decision. Her husband's ancestor built the manor-house some six hundred years ago; she came of a really old family from Grodno.

The Countess's husband was dead, and her son off to the new pigmy wars in the Polish Army. All other males seemed to have vanished in the war — absorbed in Russian, German and Austrian armies, or gone down the red gullet of the Bolshevists. So the women live alone in the manor-house, where the roof begins to leak, the shutters to hang on one hinge, and the lawn and garden to grow into a jungle.

The Countess is a good sport. Our arrival upsets her not in the least. Of course we shall have lunch!

By and by it is spread on the hard-wood table. Good coarse white bread, the grain grown in the neighboring fields and ground in the windmill creaking near by; marvellous butter, just out of the churn; broiled chickens, such as would command a fantastic price in Paris; potatoes, carrots, lettuce, cucumbers, and as many other vegetables as we wish; berries, with the thickest, richest cream, such as existed before the war, but is now only a memory, at least in Europe.

Heavens, what a meal to put before people who have just come from Germany! We are liable to eat ourselves to death.

Lunch over, we dive deep into the hold of the Cadillac and pile the table high with tea, coffee, sugar, cocoa, cigarettes, and soap in payment for our lunch. All of these things are welcome, being non-existent in the country, but when the soap appears — just ordinary, commissary, Ivory soap — the ladies squeal with delight. SOAP! Mon Dieu! Gott sei dank!

Then we sit about the large, clean rooms, with their hard-wood floors, the ancestral portraits, and the big tile stoves, while the Countess tells of life at Kielmy during the war.

First, the hot days in August, 1914, when, after a hundred years of peace, the great highway over which we have come smoked with grey dust from horizon to horizon and from sunrise to sunset. All night long, too, the dust choked the stars, and the tramp of feet, the singing of the soldiers and creaking of the wagons never ceased: Rennenkampf and his Russian armies marching to their first easy victories, and the devastation of East Prussia, his forces converging on East Prussia from all directions.

'Yes,' said the Countess, 'the old Bear went south in great style, thinking he would lope right along to Berlin while Von Kluck was loping to Paris.'

Then Tannenberg, like a bolt out of the blue; fol-

137

lowed by the bitter winter disasters of the Mazurian Lakes. Down went the Bear's tail, but he kept his claws dug into the Niemen.

The spring of 1915 came with the sound of guns ever creeping nearer to Kielmy. Soon great columns of smoke began to stalk the southern skies by day; at night the western horizon glowed red. Then a sudden day of alarms and excursions and through the forests burst grey uniforms and spiked helmets riding hard on hot horses. The waves swept over the manor-house and passed on — a big German cavalry raid, two cavalry divisions having broken through for a foray into Courland. The Russians, however, rallied and the fighting swayed to and fro about the manor-house; but it was the Bear's last spasm in Lithuania. By June he had lumbered off, never to return.

Soon the great highway smoked with the dust of William's armies...

The Countess and her family settled down to three and a half years of German occupation. Prussian officers clicked about the manor-house, German soldiers were billeted in the barns. No mail, no newspapers; they were cut off completely from the world. German military administration, stern but efficient, took control of the country. So far as Kielmy knew, Germany had conquered the world. Deutschland was indeed 'über alles'; and the Army 'über Deutschland'...

Then the fall of 1918. The German 'Ost 'Army suddenly cracked and fell to pieces. Soldiers jeered their officers and plucked the insignia from their haughty shoulders; they plundered military stores and set up Soldiers' Councils. Soon the German Army, which came into Lithuania shining like the hosts of the Apocalypse, the Kaiser's very dream of an invincible army, was a marauding rabble, without pride, without discipline, without spirit.

It melted away from Lithuania. On its heels followed the Red Armies of Russia, more dreaded than ever Attila and his hordes were, buying territory and munitions from the Soldiers' Council of the rotting German Army. For our lonely ladies it was merely anti-Christ driving Lucifer out of the land . . .

The Reds came to the manor-house and held it for twelve hours; then the Germans rallied, reorganized and came back, cracking the Red brigades to bits and driving them out of the country, with some languid assistance from the Lithuanians . . .

And since that time a sloppy German Army, a shadow and mockery of its former self, has kept a semblance of order in the country while everybody waits for the conquerors, through their old, old men at Paris, to arrange things.

Yes, the Countess makes a good story of it, as she sews away, a lone canary still chirping in its cage and some window plants turning glossy leaves towards the sunshine. She has seen Russian and German and Bolshevist hosts come in their pride and melt away in their ruin, and still the old roof is over her head. She counts herself lucky, for in Russia today few countesses still sit by their old firesides.

'What will the Allies do with us?' she asks. 'Create an independent Lithuania? Let Germany hold us? Give us to Poland? Allow Russia to reabsorb us? Or abandon us to the Reds?'

My dear lady: the Allies will do *nothing*. Of that you may be perfectly sure. Their Old Men at Paris will squabble with one another in secret council; they will frantically agitate 'Hun' and 'Bolshevist' bogies to frighten their publics; they will make faces at the increasing chaos of Central and Eastern Europe and threaten now this, now that patriot who attempts to take the leadership in these desperate regions; they will jabber like simians at the Hoovers who try to point out the right road for the economic reconstruction of Europe; they will egg on an obsequious press to beat the drums of hatred, to manufacture 'atrocities,' to puff up this cause with shouted lies, to howl down that cause with slander; and in the slow course of time the common-sense of the great crowd will retire them from public confidence and then from office, one by one. If it doesn't, the night of a new Dark Ages is closing in on Europe.

In the mean time Lithuania, like the rest of Central and Eastern Europe, must find its own salvation from within as best it can in the face of wicked blockade and ineffective meddling from Paris.

But I don't tell the old lady any of this. Missions must be discreet!

We go out to find German soldiers clustered thickly about the automobile, our doughboy chauffeur growling at them. Good-natured Fritzes for the most part, curious, shiftless, slouchy. Nearly all are boys or oldish men. Rather honest and intelligent faces, but evidently quite at sea since the fall of their army and their country; their mental and moral bearings lost in an upside-down world.

Presently they stroll off, heaving a few brickbats into the Countess's apple trees as they go. A pack of wanton, aimless boys, they disappear chewing her apples.

We leave pleasant Kielmy behind us and bound away northward. It is a rich, warm afternoon: crops are being gathered in the fields; the road swarms with farming traffic; and an occasional patrol goes by. In a pleasant green meadow German soldiers cluster about a field kitchen for a late dinner, while three young pigs roast over a pine fire and peasant girls barter baskets of apples and bottles of Schnapps. Immense shouts of laughter from everybody as the bartering goes on — the first merry Germans we have seen. In a neighboring field German soldiers chase lithe young Lithuanian horses — before the war Lithuania was a famous horse-breeding country. From a German army wagon near by comes the cackle of geese and of hens, trussed up and very indignant. A pink sow squeals from the bottom slats of the wagon, mourning her roasting offspring.

Bucolic to a degree! Of course Fritz does not want to leave this fat land and go back to lean Germany; no wonder Von der Goltz's soldiers bite and scratch as the Allies try to yank them out of Courland and Lithuania!

Presently we come to the smear of yellow and red brick in waste fields which mark where Schaulen (or Shavli) once stood — a town as thoroughly destroyed as any in northern France.

The ruins swarm with a medley of Russian, German and Lithuanian troops. The Russians are of a pro-German corps under Colonel Bermond (also known as Avaloff), who are presently to fill the headlines of all papers as they take the field against the Letts and the British Navy at Riga.

Over the town hovers a German plane from a near-by airdrome. It is burning benzol and so sounds like a threshing machine jazzing. But one rather envies him, up above there, looking out over this wide, wide Russian country.

Our military highroad bisects the blister which is ruined Shavli and then shoots northward straighter than ever.

Lord, what a road! As far as the eye can see ahead and never a curve; as far behind as the last ridge on the horizon and never a bend. Romans never built a more Roman road. If you dressed up the surface a bit again, it would be the most marvellous automobile speedway in the world. Wide as three or four state roads; not a tree on it; no blind corners; a peasantry well-trained by former Grand Dukes and German Staff Officers to hunt the ditch with their wagons as soon as they see or hear an automobile — yes, too bad it's so far from Detroit and that the Red Armies hold half of the stretch between Germany and Petrograd!

Now we cross from Lithuania into the old Russian Province of Courland. Today that means passing from the wild-cat republic of Lithuania to the wild-cat republic of Latvia or Lettland, neither as yet recognized (de jure) by the Allies. They can quote Mr. Wilson by heart: 'Doctrine of self-determination,' 'Right of peoples freely to dispose of themselves,' 'Rights of small nations' — 'That's us!' cry Letts and Lithuanians.

142

Perhaps they will make a go of it. There is much stubborn strength in these small peoples of western Russia and a lot of honest purpose in their effort to get on their own feet. They are vigorous and hard-working, and they can fight.

Far more likely, however, that when the old Bear revives there will be some piteous squeaks on the Baltic — just squeaks, followed by silence.

To vary the metaphor, the Russian steam roller, which never could make the grade against the Germans, will get up steam once more and roll out these little republics so flat that you will never be able to peel them off the Russian map again.

Or Germany, throttled to death by unwise economic pressure in every other direction, will burst her paper bonds to the east and swarm into the Russian ruin, trampling the little peoples into the Russian mud. 'Then,' as a German General said, 'there will be an end to this chatter of self-determination; only the compulsion of the conqueror will prevail.' The old Prussian doctrine which has made them so popular everywhere!

Lithuania and Latvia are curiously different. In Latvia the peasants and petit bourgeois are Letts, the aristocracy and upper bourgeois originally of German blood, and the religion is Lutheran. In Lithuania, on the other hand, peasants and petit bourgeois are mostly Lithuanian, the aristocracy is Polish, and there is a huge infusion of Jewish blood in all the towns. Except for the Jews, all are Catholics.

Now we come to Mitau, captured by the Germans

143

in 1915. In his book Ludendorf says: 'We [the All-Highest, Hindenburg and himself] also went to Mitau. I shall never forget how German everything seemed there... here was a piece of our own native soil [sic].'

Well, old boy, it isn't yours yet, all the same!

We brush rapidly through the city, which I know well, too well! It is the Headquarters of General von der Goltz and is occupied by the German Iron Division.

Then out along the road where last April the Bolshies sniped us as we went along. And over the bridge where we cuddled down close beside the German machine guns and watched Trotzky's Red Boys slinking across the road six hundred yards away — and never a bark from the machine guns beside us, not even when a Bolshevist automatic began to pepper about us. Mighty soft iron was that Iron Division!

But this August day all is peaceful.

Now comes the great stretch of swamp and forest, interspersed with big meadows, which stretches from the Courland River Aa to the Dvina. A few manor-houses — rather their blackened ruins — are scattered through this area, but mostly it is wild and shaggy. Here before the war elk are said to have been hunted.

We have come from the Western Front to the Eastern and are now in the region where the war squatted from 1915 to 1917, when the Russian Revolution let down the Eastern Front. At far-away Rheims the Germans faced the west; here in front of

144

Riga they faced the east. We find a mass of trenches, gun positions, dug-outs (some of them magnificent concrete affairs), wire-entanglements, etc. Somewhat like the Western Front, yet the Eastern Front had a character of its own, vaster, more primitive, more straggling, more casual, more sloppy than the Western Front. This was the western end of a line that by the fall of 1916 stretched without a break from the Baltic to the Black Sea. Today a rotting waste of trenches and wire. Abandoned motor trucks and guns still moulder in the swamps beside the slimy corduroy roads.

Twelve miles beyond Mitau we encounter a German guard with machine guns and logs across the road; it is the last German outpost. Our passes are examined and we roll into the neutral zone of three miles between the Germans and the Letts. Last spring they were fighting together (though snarling and growling at each other) against the Bolshevists; today they are ready to spring at each other's throats. (And, to look ahead a few weeks, soon they will have sprung; German and pro-German Russians under Bermond against the Letts backed by the British Navy at Riga.)

Six minutes run and we look into the muzzles of Lettish machine guns, manned by country boys, with a student officer in charge. They are friendly and respectful to the American uniform. We hand out cigarettes with our passes and push on.

Heavens! How tired one gets of all this military rigmarole! Here is Eastern Europe a seething, starving mass of trouble and throat-cutting, crying for

145

bread and peace, and forever being handed a stone and a dirty gun. And the root of the trouble at Paris. From the Baltic to the Black Sea we have not only overthrown the governments, but also all government and all authority. Eastern Europe that is not Bolshevist is now Balkanized, as Winston Churchill remarked. Everybody at his neighbor's throat — German and Pole, Pole and Lithuanian, German and Lett, Esthonian and Russian, Pole and Ukrainian, Roumanian and Hungarian, Ukrainian and Denikinite. And all of the above at the Bolshevist throat and the Bolshevist at the throat of all of them. And when there is nothing else to do, then Jewish 'pogroms.' No production, no industry, no commerce. Everybody lying, thieving, raping, fighting, hating — Lord! what hating, murdering and plotting. Alice in Bloody Blunderland, from the Rhine to Vladivostok. We have poured the wine of 'self-determination' into these rotten old bottles; they have all burst and the mess stinks to Heaven. 'Let us curse the Peace Conference and die,' says Eastern Europe. 'Give us again the Emperors or Lenin. At least these know how to rule.'

Suppose in 1898 we had chucked Spain out of Cuba and the Philippines and then dropped the matter, as if what followed in the islands was none of our concern. Well, that is what happened, on a million times larger scale, in Eastern Europe.

If there had only been a touch of T. R. at the Peace Conference!

So we pass our Lettish guards — who ought to be in the fields harvesting the grain and flax for which

Europe is howling, just as the Iron Division ought to be in northern France, restoring that war desert — and straighten out for the last dash to Riga.

Soon the black towers and steeples of that old town of Teutonic Knights and the Hanseatic League appear, picked out in gold and sharply etched against the sky.

We are in familiar surroundings; along this same road we came last May, just after the city had been taken from the Bolshevists. Then the highway was thronged with a motley of soldiers, prisoners, and refugees. Dead bodies of Bolshies and near-Bolshies lay beside the road, children playing unconcernedly about them. Great columns of purple smoke mounted the clear sky from the burning farmhouses that marked the eastward progress of the fighting.

But this August day all is calm. The squalid war with the Bolshevists is almost forgotten; a new squalid war between the Germans and Letts is about to begin.

As we rumble the boards of the long bridge over the Dvina, our speedometer clicks fifteen hundred and two miles from Paris. On the map a straight line is shorter, but that is the road distance we have covered. And it is only the evening of the sixth day. Moreover, we lost much time at Coblenz, at Berlin, and at Dantzig.

On the bridge are more guards to be satisfied, more cursing at the military anarchy of Eastern Europe.

We roll into Riga and up to the two huge flats which my Mission occupies on Georgenstrasse — for a monthly rent of nine dollars when you reduce it to dollars. And the owners would be glad to pay us to occupy them, such is the protective value of an American Mission.

The Cadillac shakes the dust of four real countries and a swarm of make-believe ones from her tires, and rolls off, ready to start on another fifteen-hundred-mile jaunt next day if we say so.

The next three days are spent in Riga on Mission work — conferences, discussions, reports, all the usual futilities.

August 8, 1919

We trot the Cadillac out of the Lettish Government garage bright and early and start off again.

Once clear of the city, we settle down on the same great highway which brought us from Germany, passing through pine forests and a desolate country. It has been raining for two days and the world is mournful. The black bones of murdered manor-houses stick up here and there in the dreary drizzle, and the cellars of vanished farmhouses are pools of stagnant water. Bully while it lasts, *War*, but it certainly does leave a mess!

Soon we must part from our gilt-edged highway — it runs into Bolshevist positions at Pskoff — and start north over really Russian roads. As far as Wenden and Wolmar — little prim towns, Germanish, yet with a touch of Russian — they are fair.

Beyond that, my Lord!

Says Ludendorf about the roads in the 'Ober-ost,' 'At the season when the snow was melting they were transformed in places into a slough in which horses were drowned if they happened to fall.'

We have late lunch at a big manor-house. The Baron and his family are refugees somewhere in Scandinavia, but the superintendent is still on the place, and his wife gives us a good lunch. A tall, lean, rather good-looking woman who has many tales to tell of war and of Bolshevism in these parts.

The estate has a big dairy installation, and after lunch we go through the cow-barns. Wonderful affairs of blue and grey stone with tile and shingle roofs. How many cows they once sheltered I could not tell you. I counted eighty sleek cows in one barn which had plenty of room to spare. The other barns were empty.

'Yes, our herds have dwindled to nothing at all,' says the superintendent's wife. 'Russians, Germans, Bolshevists and Esthonians, all have stolen and requisitioned.'

'What do you do with the milk, cream, and butter?'

'Nothing much; dispose of some of it in the neighborhood.'

'Why don't you send it to Riga or Reval or down to Germany? In the cities the babies are dying for lack of milk.'

'Because both Esthonian and Lettish Governments claim this territory since it was recovered from the Bolshevists and neither will permit export. Furthermore, if they know we have these cows, either side or both sides may send here and requisition them. And if both come at once, there may be a fight — and we should suffer. In any case we don't want to exchange these good cows for worthless paper money. And even if we could arrange matters with one of these new Governments, the railroads are broken down. If we send by wagon, soldiers and outlaws, anybody in fact with a gun, would plunder the wagons.'

How do you protect yourself locally?'

'You see, the peasants expect to get this estate, either from the Esthonian or Lettish Governments, or by just taking it. In the mean time they don't want its value diminished. They know my husband's value as an agricultural expert and they say to him, "Keep the estate in order for the old Black Baron, Child of Hell that he is! If he comes back, we'll kill him. Presently we shall be Baron and then our Soviet will employ you. Yes, we are going to hold on to some of your "Bourzhui' (bourgeois) just like the pedigreed cows, for the milk you give us. So keep the 'Gut' (estate) in order for the 'Baron'!"

'For self-protection,' continued the lady, 'the peasants have organized themselves into Green guards, which is the name and color the local defence guards have taken throughout Russia, as distinguished from the Reds, the revolutionary troops, and the Whites, the anti-revolutionary soldiers. The Green guards are for the defence of the village or the commune against all comers. When White or Red guards come to this neighborhood the Green guards drive the cows to hiding places in the swamps and then take to the woods and snipe the Whites or Reds when they start to plunder or requisition. As a matter of fact, it was really the Green guards who drove the Bolshevists out of this area. They would do the same and quicker to any troops of a reactionary Government that came here. They are none too friendly to Esthonian or Lettish national troops, though as time goes on they will recognize one or the other of these two Governments, provided it doesn't interfere too much locally.'

And there you have Eastern Europe — a general 'sauve qui peut'!

Unfortunately, a return to tribal warfare and the Dark Ages leaves our modern congested cities, dependent on railroads and a highly organized industrial life, stranded. When there is no authority, no law and no order, the peasant survives, but the city population perishes. With every man's hand against the other, the farmer hides his grain in the ground, but the city dweller dies of starvation. The country produces food and almost always has enough for itself; the city merely consumes. Cut off from the country, it dies like a stalk severed from its roots. In short, the country can do without the city, but the city cannot do without the country. Destroy the complicated modern economic and industrial organization and the crowded cities which have been built up thereby come to an agonized end. Witness the present state of Petrograd, Moscow, Riga, and Vienna, not to mention scores of others.

For everywhere in Central and Eastern Europe the cry of the starving cities goes up to Heaven, while in the country the peasant refuses to sell good food for poorly printed paper money and hides his produce in swamps, forests, caves, and underground. If a stranger comes nosing round after food, the owner climbs into a hayrick and pots him with a rifle which is a legacy of the Great War. If strangers come in force, the entire neighborhood lies in wait for them in some cross-roads ambush, peppers them with a few rounds of bullets, and disappears in the dark forests!

Last June we would automobile out from Libau, Riga and Reval (the great ports of Baltic Russia), and in less than two hours reach districts where the farms were full of food; then we would return to the ports to see Hoover's ships loaded with flour steaming in past the huge deserted grain elevators which are such a feature of these Russian ports. Before the war these ports exported millions of tons of grain, butter and eggs. This year the crops are splendid; yet millions of dollars' worth of flour are coming from America.

And these Baltic Provinces are the most civilized part of Russia; their non-Russian peoples are the sturdiest of all the races that made up the agglomeration of the old Russian Empire. If they are so badly off, what must the interior cities of Russia be like!

No wonder money exchange is topsy-turvy and Central and Eastern Europe crumbling to ruin, dragging Europe after them. If you sin against economic laws, you suffer just as if you violate the laws of nature.

One feels that the Conference at Paris sowed such a crop of economic wild oats as the world never saw before. Already the bitter reaping has begun.

And one thinks that it might have been so different under T. R.'s practical brain and vigorous hand. Then we might have had: Germany and Austria disarmed, punished (justly but not vindictively, and openly, not secretly and under pious verbiage), but immediately allowed to resume their economic life; order enforced in the Balkans and Baltic Russia (as in Cuba and the Philippines); Bolshevist Russia handled robustly, either on an effective intervention basis, or on a strict non-intervention basis.

Eastern Europe and Russia are the natural bread-baskets of Europe. At present so many cats are fighting above the basket that nobody can get at the bread. Result — too much of a pull on the American and Argentinian bread-baskets. And so economic trouble throughout the world.

The catnip which has set all these cats mad is of two brands: one Wilsonian, labelled 'self-determination'; the other Lenian, labelled 'dictatorship of the proletariat.' And every day a new cat joins the clawing mass. Needed — a good rough-necked bull-dog to make all these cats take to the tall timber. Then Europe could get at the breakfast-basket.

We were told that a dog called 'League of Nations' would do the job. But when he was produced, he turned out to be a poodle who fled at the first 'Miaow' from America.

If the bull-dog doesn't materialize, a hyena called Lenin may eventually have a glorious cat-killing and then own the bread-basket.

We had a wild-cat finance in its day; now we have wild-cat politics and all Eastern Europe full of wild-cat republics. And such a clawing and yowling from the Baltic to the Black Sea as would have astonished even the Dark Ages.

Well! We finish our chat with the superintendent's

wife, take a look about the decaying gardens of the manor-house, and depart.

Mud, mud, mud. What roads! How the Cadillac kicks, having spent its young life on the smooth and perfect roads of France and Germany.

By and by hairy tramps with guns stop us. At first we think it is a hold-up, but no! We have merely reached this week's boundary between Latvia and Esthonia. The Coxey's Army which has stopped us are frontier guards and customs officials.

As the afternoon wears on, we come to a land that resembles Maine — rock-strewn pastures, stone fences, potato- and hay-fields in the bottom lands, short hills and heavy but ragged pine and birch forests. We are now well within the former Russian province of Esthonia, today part of the 'potato republic' (as the high-life Russian refugees call it) of Esthonia. Like Maine, it is a famous potato patch. And inhabited by a rugged and virile people.

Late at night we enter Reval and climb to our Mission's house high on the old citadel overlooking the town and the black waters of the Gulf of Finland. We have run up two hundred and fifty additional miles since we left Riga and we are far indeed from the Champs-Elysées and the Bois de Boulogne.

We have a lot of work before us at Reval and for a night the Cadillac will turn into a town car.

———————

From Greene's portfolio of drafts and miscellaneous writings, undated

We stop for the night in a little West Prussian town — clean, harsh and ugly. Our military car rolls off, seeking a garage, and I am seated at the table in a dreary café, smoking, reading a paper and waiting for dinner, which, from experience, I know will consist of horse-meat, sauerkraut and black bread.

It is late Saturday night and all the village 'sports' are gathered in the depths of the café, Germans and Poles wrangling drunkenly with one another over the fate of this particular bit of territory under the 'Versailles Treaty.' They guzzle their beer and pound the tables, thickening the air with guttural German interwoven with sneezy Polish. The gloom of the café is lit up by a lady in burning scarlet, with a gleaming yellow wig and flaming pink cheeks. A seedy 'Germania,' descended to the gutter, and very raucous and tipsy at the moment.

Presently there enters a German sergeant, short and squat, a miniature of the 'eisener' Hindenburg. Seeing me, he comes to attention with a snap and gives me a very smart salute; then passes on in to drink his beer — nauseous compound of resin and tannery water, to judge by the one I have just tasted.

By and by he comes out again. Again the snappy salute. Whereupon the following dialogue:

Greene: Do you know who I am?

Sergeant Hindenburg: Yes; I fought against the Americans on the Western Front and I know their uniforms and insignia; you are an American Lieutenant-Colonel.

Greene: Did you salute me of your own accord, or by instructions?

Sergeant H.: I am a soldier of the old German Army; I salute all officers whether friend or enemy.

Greene: So! Well, what did you 'soldiers of the old German Army' think of America coming into the war?

Sergeant Hindenburg: Ah! The 'Higher Ups' ['die Hohe'], the leaders and officers and all the aristocrats, said it didn't matter; that America was already giving money and munitions to our enemies; that she had no army, couldn't raise one, and wouldn't fight; so her paper declaration of war made no difference. But we, the non-commissioned officers and soldiers, we knew differently; the aristocrats had no knowledge of America ['hat keine Verbindung mit Amerika'], whereas we all had brothers and cousins in America; we knew what America coming into the war meant. The heart of the common German soldier became very gloomy ['tiefe Schmerz hatten wir im Herz'].

IV

A BUSINESS TOUR OF THE BALTIC STATES

To General Francis Vinton Greene

HOTEL PLAZA, AVENUE MONTAIGNE
PARIS, *November* 2, 1919

DEAR PAPA:

I was honorably discharged from the United States Army and have resumed civilian clothes after more than two years in khaki. My discharge is dated October 29, 1919. Under 'Battles, engagements, skirmishes' it allows short service on temporary duty in the Lorraine and the Château-Thierry Sectors in 1918. It authorizes four overseas service chevrons — gold — which I was wearing when discharged. I entered the Service as a civilian employee on August 11, 1917, was commissioned Major in the Aviation Section, Signal Corps, on September 12, 1917, assigned to active duty September 25, 1917, promoted to Lieutenant-Colonel in the Air Service as of September 2, 1918 (on which date I accepted the commission), and discharged from the Service in France on October 29, 1919.

From date of entry into the Service until March 20, 1919, I was on duty with the Air Service; on the latter date I was attached to the American Commission to Negotiate Peace, for temporary duty, and sent to Russia as Chief of a Commission to Finland, Esthonia, Latvia and Lithuania. On that duty I remained until my discharge.

157

My complete war record is as follows:

January, 1916, to June 15, 1917 — Director of the War Relief Commission of the Rockefeller Foundation.

June 15, 1917, to August 11 — The above and with the American Red Cross.

August 11, 1917, to March 20, 1919 — On duty with the Air Service of the A.E.F. — first as civilian employee, then as Major, and finally as Lieutenant-Colonel.

March 20, 1919, to October 29, 1919 — On duty with the American Commission to Negotiate Peace.

I received one slight wound from a bomb fragment which entered my right shoulder and left a small scar which was noted on my medical discharge certificate, though I never claimed a wound stripe. This occurred in the Lorraine Sector in June, 1918, when a German plane attacked our automobile with machine gun and bombs, killing the chauffeur, wounding several of the party and badly damaging the car. My hearing was considerably affected by the bomb explosion and was a long while in recovering. But on discharge the surgeon found no permanent damage, though there was a slight bulge in the ear drums.

During the course of the war I have visited the following countries:

England	Switzerland
Scotland	Germany
Norway	Austria-Hungary
Sweden	Belgium
Denmark	Italy
France	Russia

Also I visited the greater part of the Western Front during active warfare (the Belgian, part of the French and the entire British Front during 1917, before I entered the Army; the Lorraine and Château-Thierry, Soissons, Rheims Sectors in 1918) and since the Armistice I have seen the entire Western Front except Belfort, and a part of the Eastern Front, as well as a portion of the new Front against the Bolshevists.

In short, as a sight-seer I have seen a great deal. My duties as an Inspector in the Air Service took me from one end of France to the other, as well as over to England and down to Italy. I have motored many, many thousand miles. I saw the A.E.F. come to France in the shape of General Pershing and a few staff officers; I saw it grow to an army of two million men, the youngest, the freshest and the most aggressive troops in Europe; and I have seen it fade away again westward leaving only a handful of men on duty in Paris. It has been the greatest and most surprising crusade of history, this A.E.F., and few military ventures have been more clean-cut in performance or decisive in their effect on world history.

I wish we could arrange for you to have the leisure and the opportunity to write its history, which should be written by a West-Pointer, steeped in the tradition of the American Army. At the same time, a truly critical history of the A.E.F. should be written by one who was not a member thereof and who, also, at the time stood outside of the military work at home which went to support and nourish the American Expeditionary Force in France. You fulfill both requirements. If you could get back to an objective point of view, as in your former military works, you could do it. If I should have any success in making my way commercially, I hope to make it possible for you, should the scheme interest you.

To go back to my own story: I have served my country hard and I hope usefully. At the same time I shall always regret not having had service with troops. My military record is a poor one for the son and grandson of West-Pointers and Major-Generals who led soldiers in war.

My experiences in Russia were exceedingly interesting and I hope worth while, though I have some doubts. But they are a long story, which I shall hope to tell you some day.

Your affectionate son,

WARWICK GREENE

To Mrs. Francis Vinton Greene

SOCIETETSHUSET, HELSINGFORS
FINLAND, *January Eighth,* 1920

DEAR MAMMA:

Let me give my diary for the past few days:

Stockholm, *Tuesday, January* 6, 1920

A holiday in Sweden; so a bad day for doing business. Meet Max Rabinoff in the lobby of the Grand Hotel with two friends — an American named Hutchinson and a Russian named Aberline. Find they are bound to Helsingfors and Reval on tonight's boat, just as I am. Rabinoff, as you may know, is a well-known Opera Director. Among other things, he first brought Pavlova and Mordkine to England and America. Also he ran the Boston National Grand Opera. I knew him in Paris last summer.

Just before the steamer leaves, I take a hasty taxi ride out to Oak Hill to say good-bye to the Morrises, who are just back from the country and dining quite 'en famille,' Mr. and Mrs. and Miss Burleson.

Then down to the steamer, which I find a wee but rugged one, built in honest Scotland to buck the Baltic ice, which she has been doing for the past generation or two. A nice boat, painted white outside and very clean — like everything Swedish — inside.

Quickly we drop Stockholm with its million lights reflected in the black waters that everywhere rush through the heart of this city, and enter interminable narrow passages between rocky coasts and islands, for all the world like the Maine coast, but bleaker.

In my bunk, close to the waterline, it is impossible to sleep for some time owing to the row the boat makes forcing her way through the ice. Crack! Crack! Crunch! Crunch! Swish! Swish! At times it is too much for her; grinding and shivering she loses speed and finally stops, though the engines are charging her full speed ahead. The ice presses closely in on her hull: 'We've got you this time, Old Girl!' it seems to say. But she backs quickly away before freezing in; and charges the barrier full speed again. Sometimes it takes several charges; but eventually she gets through.

From the porthole one looks out on Antarctic desolation.

How the hulls stand it, I don't know! Built for the purpose, I suppose.

Morning finds us steaming through a mess of rocky islands and islets — the famous Äland (pronounced Ōland) Islands stretching across the mouth of the Gulf of Bothnia from Sweden to Finland. A bleak group, but important strategically so that Sweden and Russia have forever been growling and bristling about Russia's right to fortify them. During the war, Russia finally fortified them to keep the German fleet from going up into the Gulf of Bothnia and shelling Russia's only railroad connection with the Western World. There was tremendous snarling — but Sweden remained neutral.

Often and often had I heard the Äland Islands discussed beneath some of the most marvellous tapestries in the world — at the Quai d'Orsay in Paris, when I used to attend meetings of the Interallied Baltic Committee — and always laid aside at the end of the meeting with a sigh and nothing decided, as though too difficult a subject for human wisdom. And here they were! in all their icy actuality — in all their rocky nakedness — just a desolate string of brown nubs in that vast ice prairie which people said was the sea. Why! one of those priceless tapestries could have paid for all that junk of rock, ice and scrub-pine which straggled along the cold skyline!

From time to time we stop at the scanty settlements. The houses are frame, again emphasizing the likeness to the Maine coast. The inhabitants come down to meet the steamer in tiny sleighs drawn by shaggy ponies. Finnish officers, in their new uniforms, ride about among the work-a-day folk.

Through a sea frozen tight as white granite about these islands, the lane from Sweden to Finland is kept open by the passage of steamers, which tread and retread the same narrow pathway of broken ice each trip; on either side of this pathway the frozen sea seems as firm as terra firma itself. Occasionally winter lays a specially paralyzing hand on this lane, glueing the broken ice together into a frozen macadam in which ordinary steamers are helpless until the big ice-breakers have come and smashed the passage open again.

Once or twice, however, we come on open stretches of water in channels where the currents run strongest; there rowboats await us and hail us like a passing street-car. We stop and hoist passengers and goods aboard and lower down other passengers and goods to take their place. And down into one boat goes a magnificent keg of beer, amid great interest from the passengers — Finland is a brand-new, virtuous Republic with prohibition, quite unlike experienced and wicked Sweden; evidently, however, the Åland Islanders practise self-determination with reference to liquor.

In these northern latitudes daylight slips away almost as soon as the dishes are cleared away after lunch. Thereafter we make our way through the wintriest kind of a night, the lane of broken ice lit up by a blazing searchlight forward.

Suddenly we turn and ram the solid ice prairie,

with all the energy of our stout Dundee engines; we cram and crowd our way some hundreds of feet into the ice until we come to a jarring stop. Then we whistle; very loud and hoarse it sounds in that bleak, mummified world. It is promptly answered by jingling sleigh-bells and from the shore come people in sleighs and on skis and goods on sleds. Right to the ship's side they come, produce a ladder and climb aboard the ship as though it were a building on solid ground. Fantastic sight! Out of the Arctic night the ponies trot in and out, coming so close that they rub their noses against the ship's sides. And we supposed to be at sea!

Unloading and loading finished, the whistle hoots again to frighten away the ponies; then the engines awake once more to convulsive efforts, yank the hull free from its icy bed and slide it backward into the little lane and so back to the big lane and then forward to Finland.

A little past nine P.M. we tie up at the wharf in Abo. Here we find a tedious Custom House — bad enough they were before the war, but now the limit since 'self-determination' converted Central and Eastern Europe into a crazy-quilt of tiny nationalities.

I go grandly through as I have a diplomatic passport; but it takes hours to search the baggage of the other passengers.

Outside the roomy sleepers of the five-foot Russian gauge await us — and sleepers of a most un-Russian cleanliness, showing the Swedish influence in Finland. Big cars, but drawn by a tiny locomotive with a huge stack, just like the pictures of Civil War locomotives.

And the tender piled high with wood, for they fear no coal strikes in Finland which is shaggy with forests.

All signs are in two languages, Swedish and Finnish, the two national tongues of this tiny nationality. They are as much alike as French and Chinese. Swedish, of course, is Scandinavian and Finnish Mongolian. Perhaps four hundred thousand of a population of considerably over three million are of Swedish blood; the balance are Finns, a branch of the Mongol race. Culturally the country is Swedish, as it was once a Swedish province, and up to sixty years ago Finnish was considered merely the uncouth jargon of the peasants. The language of government, of law, of commerce, of literature and of polite society was Swedish.

Then came a Finnish revival, first as a literary or cultural movement, later as a political force. This revival was really a revolt, first intellectual and political and then political and industrial, of a submerged racial majority against a cultivated and long dominant racial minority. Since the Armistice that revolt has made great strides, part of the general boom in submerged nationalities throughout Europe.

Finnish majority and Swedish minority dislike one another, but this dislike is overshadowed by a really splendid hatred for Russia, which enabled them to combine, take leave of the Bear when he fell on evil days, and set up national housekeeping together. Today independent Finland is making fairly good weather, politically speaking.

But neither Swede nor Finn will yield to the other in the language matter; so this remote small country, close under the Arctic Circle, must have its two languages — in the Diet, in the Courts, in the theatres, in business, in all official publications and proclamations, in street signs, in notices and in advertisements. As if life were not complicated enough these days! And neither language known to any foreigner.

January eighth, 1920

Arrive at Helsingfors a little after dawn — in other words, about eight A.M. Pile my belongings into a little sleigh and am quickly whisked to the Societetshuset, a modern European hotel as good as you would find in any city. My room costs me forty marks a day, which, translated into dollars at present exchange rates, means one dollar and twenty cents. The same room in Stockholm cost me four dollars and a half per diem. Meals the same way. A good lunch at the Societetshuset comes to sixty or seventy-five cents; at the Grand Hotel in Stockholm, two dollars and a half. And wonderful food in Finland; good meats, quantities of the freshest butter and eggs and plenty of milk and cream. Yes! If you want to escape the high cost of living, come to Finland and live on the exchange from American dollars.

Friday, January ninth, 1920

Find there is no steamer across to Reval before Sunday. In Finland we are in the last outpost of civilization; our difficulties and tribulations begin as soon as we try to cross the Gulf of Finland.

I have Mr. Haynes, our diplomatic representative, to lunch, together with —— and Rabinoff.

166

A BUSINESS TOUR OF BALTIC STATES

In the evening we go to the cabaret at the Fennia. Really very good; they have picked up lots of stray talent from Russia. Helsingfors, of course, swarms with Russian refugees. A melancholy lot. Rabinoff is almost prepared to pick up one or two of them — I mean, of the cabaret talent, not the melancholy refugees! — and take them to America.

I forgot to say that the preceding evening we went to the Finnish opera to see Eugen Onegin laboriously translated and sung in Finnish and by Finns. Dull! oh! how dull! Servant girls and coach-boys doing Grand Opera! And such a plain, plain audience — plain faces, plain clothes, plain thoughts. But very serious and a bit touching in their evident liking for the music. Yes! it may be a very plain world when all these submerged races have set up as nations. The greatness and glamour of the big, proud, old civilizations are evidently not to be theirs.

Saturday, January tenth, 1920

Killing time for another twenty-four hours. Take a good walk all about Helsingfors. An ugly town, mostly second-rate Swedish or German architecture, with a dash — only a dash — of Russian thrown in. But quite solid and prosperous. Having weathered the Great War and a Bolshevist régime in 1918, Finland has gotten vigorously on her legs as an infant republic and bids fair, in time, to become a fourth Scandinavian State. She has some of their good qualities and many of their defects — but I think there is enough of the staunch Scandinavian strain in Finland to pull her through these troubled times and make

167

her a tiny independent nation. She should be dull, respected and good. Nobody will ever visit Finland for its brightness or its charm. Or go wild over her chunky, estimable folk when they visit other countries. Of the charm, the brilliancy, the instability of the Slav nature she has nothing.

Yet there is a something rather attractive about her northern landscape, with its forests, its lakes and its melancholy. But it does not breed a beautiful race, this Suomi, this land of a million lakes.

In the evening call on some Russians and Finns. One lady is specially interesting — a splendid, big, vital thing married to a prominent politician. A wonderfully good talker, knowing all languages and fluent on all subjects. And even her fat — which Russian ladies acquire young — cannot wholly submerge her charm.

And then there is a Russian girl, a little, black thing, keen as a newly sharpened pencil. And Red, oh, my! she's Red! To her Lenin is the new Messiah. For him she would walk on live coals and face firing squads with a sneer and a taunt. Bristling with energy and intelligence I can see her leading Bolshevist Battalions of Death, commanding armored trains, dashing off brilliant propaganda in twenty different languages, heading Red Missions to Afghanistan, dominating a Terrorist Committee and making the prisons run with blood — for young girls of her sort do all these things. An ugly little thing, physically, and yet with a verve, a dash and an intensity that make her attractive. As dangerous as a rattlesnake in a nursery.

A BUSINESS TOUR OF BALTIC STATES

Helsingfors, *Sunday, January* 11, 1920

Sleigh down to the wharf and board the Poseidon. Ugly, miserable tub, crammed with people, in which we are to cross the Gulf of Finland.

—— takes a good look at her — and then abandons his trip. He has been steadily weakening for some days, as he has heard more and more of the dangers and difficulties of travel in Baltic Russia. The Poseidon decides him. He takes his baggage off her and remains behind to catch a steamer leaving in a few days direct for civilization.

We chunk our way out through the icy harbor and finally into the free waters of the Gulf. It is a royal northern day — fresh, cold seas; marvellous green skies; the sun hovering a few feet above the horizon and making a strange, brilliant twilight of noon. The air is indeed like champagne, of the iciest and friskiest sort! By and by the snowy shores and pine forests of Esthonia appear. The citadel and church spires of Reval stand up under the low, mild sun, whose queer light kindles them into the most alluring dream city. Dirty Reval! how beautiful you look as you hang in that golden furnace between icy seas and icy skies! Who would think you were merely the lair of these dirty, hunky, rude, stupid Esthonian upstarts!

About three P.M. we push into the ice-jammed harbor of Reval, pass three Esthonian men-of-war (Russian property, captured from the Bolshevists and given to the Esthonians by the British) and perhaps half a dozen British and French destroyers.

Ashore, another fiendish Custom-House — for we are passing into 'free and independent' Esthonia.

169

Due to the incompetence and insolence of the Esthonian officials, it takes three hours to pass the Poseidon's passengers through the miserable place. Because we come from what ought to be a little sister republic to the north, we are looked upon with the greatest possible suspicion. Finland's money — and Finland is a prudent, resourceful, go-ahead country as compared with the wild-cat Republic of Esthonia — is worth less than dirty paper in Esthonia — nobody will give us any of the worthless Esthonian marks in exchange for it.

Rabinoff is expecting great attentions from the Esthonian authorities, for he helped them greatly in Paris and was coming to them on official business, but no waiting officials, no champing limousines are on hand at the dock. After much telephoning, he finally gets the authorities and by and by an automobile carrying a worried, taffy-haired young intellectual — for a crop of high-school boys has ridden into tempo-rary power in each one of these peasant republics — appears. No wonder he is worried; the town is full of refugees and not a room to be had at any hotel, or anywhere else. Rabinoff and the youth invite me to accompany them; but I have dealt with Esthonian officials before and know them far too well. I break out of the reeking Custom-House into the frozen darkness, pick up a brigand in a sleigh, find a stout youth with a sled on which all my baggage is piled — lugged out of the Custom-House by myself, as no official or underling would possibly touch it in this land of the newly free. Then the brigand, the boy and myself go straight to the Hotel of the Golden Lion —

a filthy and mangy lion he is, let me say! Not to get rooms — I know the place is jammed with Esthonian officers, Danish drummers, American journalists and little fuzzy-haired blondes — but to interview the head porter, before whom I dangle a fifty-mark note, with the result that within twenty minutes I am lodged in a room far from the fashionable centre of Reval, but large, clean, well-heated, and cared for by civil servants, none of which things could be said of the packed Golden Lion. And the room costs me from twenty-eight to thirty-five cents a day, according to one's luck with exchange, which varies from one hundred to one hundred and thirty-five Esthonian marks to the American dollar, depending on your skill in bargaining.

Reval, *Monday, January* 12, 1920

I find that my friend Rabinoff, accompanied by the representative of the might and majesty of the Esthonian Government, spent hours careering about the town looking for rooms. Finally Rabinoff and his friend Eberline were stuffed into one small and dirty room at the Golden Lion. I chortle loudly.

Call on our Consul, who turns out to be one Captain Hurley, formerly commanding a company in the 165th Infantry and afterwards Adjutant to Colonel Bill Donovan, when I met him at Remagen on the Rhine. He is newly arrived in this Esthonian wilderness.

Nine P.M. I embark on the really frightful journey to Riga. I am supposed to have a compartment reserved, but it turns out to be merely a wooden shelf in a compartment that contains nine people before the night is out. There is no upholstery in the dilapidated cars, which really is a blessing, as wood is much more discouraging to the vermin. The car has double windows, which in addition are tightly nailed and sealed and the ventilator is stuffed with clay — in this part of the world people have a mortal terror of fresh air. The compartment fills cramful of dirty soldiers before we are an hour out of Reval. By hard scrapping I keep my shelf to myself. The air becomes so thick you can hardly push your hand through it. The only light is one candle — there is no other means of lighting the car.

And so we trundle along through the bitter winter night, bumpity bump! thumpity thump! on our flat wheels and wretched roadbed. Hours and hours do we linger at each station — for all the gossip has to be exchanged and nobody hustles, and nobody hurries and nobody worries and nobody can be spoken harshly to or disciplined — because, isn't Esthonia now a free country? Yes, indeed it is! And do free men work? Of course not! And have free men any obligations to be polite or efficient? Perish the thought! So the division superintendent can't speak crossly to the station-master, and the station-master can't speak crossly to the conductor, and the conductor can't speak crossly to the fireman, and that worthy can't speak crossly to the haughty woodcutters who bring the wood for the locomotive — as you go down in the social scale, you go up in sovereign rights. Barons, Russians and aristocrats may be abused with impunity, but beware of suggesting to

172

the wood-chopper that the locomotive has waited two hours for fuel — he would split you with his axe as quickly as a birch log! And beware of suggesting to the fireman that he is paid to keep the log fires burning brightly under the old locomotive's belly instead of toasting himself before the huge samovar in the station and chatting with the tea-girl — he would denounce you as a Tsarist! And don't hint to the station-master and the conductor to cut short their card game with the local commandant and his adjutant — because they would be perfectly jolly and invite you to join them and have a quart or so of forbidden vodka.

And then, when anybody has a mind to work, there is always a big chore of switching to be done at each station — and so short are they of locomotives that the engine of the through 'express' has to be borrowed for the purpose.

Do you wonder it takes forty to forty-eight hours to make the railroad trip of two hundred and fifty miles between Reval and Riga?

And so the long night drags through, mostly at stations. Daylight finds the air of my compartment yellow as a meershaum pipe. Long before, the one candle had guttered itself out — died from lack of oxygen in the air, I think. For six hours we remained in coal-black darkness, the nine Esthonians in the compartment howling murder at any one leaving the door into the aisle open even for a second. They love their air thick as porridge soup, these people of tumbled-down Russia. Save for a few agile fleas, my wooden shelf is still free from unwanted intruders —

again I praise Heaven there is no upholstery in the place.

Tuesday, January 13, 1920

Day, when he does come, is a magnificent fellow, cold and sparkling — outside, of course; within we might be stifling on the Congo. The lazy sun lies for a long, long while in the pine forests, kindling their brown and green with frosty gold. Eventually he gets up enough energy to hover above the tree-tops and to wink at us between the taller ones.

During the forenoon we come to Walk, a dreary town marking the ethnographical boundary between Esthonia and Latvia, though the political boundary is a bit further to the south. Esthonians, I may say, are a peasant race of Mongolian extraction, long incorporated into the Russian Empire and locally dominated by a land-owning aristocracy of German descent. Latvia is the Republic of the Letts — you will find it on no map unless very recent. Letts are another peasant race, of Indo-European stock, who inhabit the southern half of the former Russian Province of Livonia, all of the Province of Courland and the western part of the Province of Vitebsk. Like the Esthonians, they have been dominated by the Baltic Barons.

Complicated all this, I know, but you have to understand it to grasp the present situation in Western Russia. The salient feature is that all of Baltic Russia is inhabited by non-Russians — in Finland the peasants are Finns, the upper classes Swedes; in the Provinces of Esthonia and Upper Livonia the peasants Esthonians, the upper classes German; in

174

A BUSINESS TOUR OF BALTIC STATES

Lower Livonia and Courland the peasants Letts, upper classes German; in Lithuania, peasants Lithuanians, upper classes Poles. All of Baltic Russia, then, is non-Slav and was incorporated into the Empire of the Tsars in the course of Russia's irresistible push to the Baltic Sea. As soon, however, as the Tsars broke up, these countries broke loose. Today they form the republics of Finland, Esthonia, Latvia and Lithuania, to give the string from the Arctic Circle to Poland. In the three latter the peasants have seized the entire political power, suppressing the land-owning aristocracy. Except Finland, none has received even 'de facto' recognition from the United States, though Esthonia and Latvia have received 'de facto' recognition from England and France.

In short, a string of jerk-water republics, which have put up a fairly plucky fight against Soviet Russia (in their minds accent is on the Russia rather than on the Soviet), and are in mortal dread of Germany and of a revived Russia. Their greatest internal sport is confiscating the estates of big landowners.

At Walk the population is fairly evenly divided between Letts and Esthonians. The Esthonians, however, hold the city and a strip of country south of it. So the Letts are very sore. These little upstart republics, menaced on every side by powerful enemies, having every interest in common, with a most precarious future before them — for only by the extreme grace of God and the League of Nations could these tiny and ill-behaved peoples set up national housekeeping right on the very doorstep of the west-

175

ern gate to the vast Russian hinterland — have so little sense, common-sense, and ability to get along with other people, that they are already almost at war over a few wretched miles of disputed boundary!

I have plenty of time to think about all these things; for we remain six or eight hours at Walk (pronounced Valk).

In their new excess of nationalism, the Esthonians have changed all the names in the country — let there remain no taint of Russia or Germany about us! Esthonian is a poor little language spoken by about one million two hundred thousand people, estimating liberally. The majority of this population already spoke Russian or German. Today Esthonian is the official language. All names of towns and places, as well as streets and roads, have been changed. Result, every map has become worthless and nobody knows where he is at. Historic Reval, for example, now masquerades as Tallin; Dorpat as Tartu, and so on down the list.

I walk about squalid Walk, take a hike through a neighboring forest where I am held up by a tramp with a gun who turns out to be a guard.

Like every other town along the railroad, Walk or Walga swarms with soldiers, clad in every known uniform; Russian, German, British and American — yes! American, for we have sent them considerable material from our stores in France — predominating. It is odd to see the American eagle buttons on this loutish soldiery.

There is an armored train at Walk which has just come in from the Bolshevist Front, an armistice

176

between the Esthonians and the Bolshevists having recently been signed. In many places the armor — merely sheet iron fastened on the sides — has been pierced by steel-jacketed bullets.

Night soon settles down over the scene; black night, shod with bitter cold.

By and by a wheezy locomotive goes over and picks up some wooden cars which should be on the junk-pile, but are on a siding, and yanks them ill-temperedly up to the platform. We pile in, finding the usual bad air, but very cold — and cold, foul air is a trial, let me tell you! There is no light; so I produce a candle from my pocket and we glue it on the window-sill with its own grease. Rattling and bumping we travel for an hour or so; then stop. We have reached the 'boundary' between the two little wild-cat Republics. An Esthonian officer comes through, says he is the military control and takes my passport — to my great misgiving, but you can't argue with any Military, even Esthonian! Don't I know!

Presently a gentleman comes through searching for 'Der Oberst Grun' (Colonel Greene). I allow that I am he; whereupon the gentleman conducts me out of the car. He is polite — something must be wrong with him! We cross the snowy little platform in front of a log house. Groups of shambling soldiers are herding the wretched passengers of my train to and fro in the dark — from the train to the Esthonia pass-control; then across the imaginary 'no-man's-land,' where they are met by shambling soldiers from Latvia and herded into the Lettish pass-control. Poor passengers! They have committed the crime of trying to travel from one pocket handkerchief 'state' to the next — so, of course, they are regarded with the greatest suspicion. One expects to hear a squeal any moment as a 'guard' pokes somebody with a rusty bayonet. Free little republics! Heaven preserve us from this freedom! The most tyrannous of tyrannies is that of peasants suddenly raised to the seats of the mighty.

We enter the Lettish pass-control. A largish, whitewashed room, with double windows all tightly sealed and containing last summer's air, besides a huge and very hot stove. The temperature is about 99 degrees F. Over in one corner sits the Lettish Commandant — a sly-looking, sulky young man — playing cards with a lady who is wrapped in a huge padded overcoat and her head swathed in a thick shawl. Certainly she does not intend to take cold in that chilly atmosphere of F. 99. I am informed that there is a telegram to treat me well and give me a reserved compartment on the train to Riga. So I am invited to wait in the Commandant's office. I pass around some Cuban cigars. To my disappointment the padded lady refuses. The rest accept with alacrity. From time to time trembling passengers, who have successfully weathered the Esthonian pass-control, the guard-shift and the crossing of no-man's-land, appear before the awful tribunal in our room.

The temperature drops to Fahrenheit 96; so wood appears and is fed the fat tile stove. I suspect that it is wood destined for our locomotive and its diversion to keep the padded lady warm will mean another hour's delay.

A BUSINESS TOUR OF BALTIC STATES

There is a stand of rifles in front of the railing; one of the soldiers steps over to it, takes a rifle, pokes the fire with the bayonet, rams in the logs with the butt end and returns it to the stand. The Commandant takes only the most languid interest. 'Oh, the Allies have plenty more for us,' I suspect he would say if reminded that a poker is cheaper for poking fires than an Enfield rifle.

By and by there is a commotion about me and my passport; here I am, but where is my passport? Much questioning and explanations in sign language and bad German. Presently it becomes clear that I am in the Lettish pass-control and my passport in the Esthonian. This is like having the soul separated from the body. Nothing in the rules covers such a situation, and nobody knows what to do about it. The padded and muffled lady regards me with more suspicion than ever. 'I knew from the very start that he was a Tsarist refugee,' that accusing, cowlike, Lettish eye of hers seems to say. 'Why! he wanted to open the door and kill us all with the cold!'

Luckily my Havanas have made a favorable impression. A soldier is despatched across the bristling dangers of no-man's-land to the Esthonian 'enemy' and in due course of time returns with my paper soul.

At last we get through to the train. A few box-cars, one or two decrepit third-class cars and a wee second-class coach. Within we find the floor two inches deep in slime and indescribable filth. The seats are merely wooden benches, very short and narrow; there are no compartments. Besides myself there are two passengers, one a Russian manager of a British engineering concern in Russia who had recently escaped from Soviet Russia by being at Gatchina when General Yudenitch captured the place. He speaks good English, blessed relief!

We rumble along for a few miles, the car lit by my one candle. Then we stop and another guard comes thumping through the car — a Lettish officer accompanied by three or four soldiers. If only a few of these people in uniform were at work, we might have some railroad service, clean cars, etc. But these days everybody has become a member of the leisure class, particularly that portion which wears a uniform. Indeed, in Western Russia the population today falls into two main classes, the leisured and the starving.

The officer makes a great commotion about me. In the excitement of the tangle about my passport back at the boundary they forgot to visé it; the officer is very stern. But long since I learned the great rule of procedure in present-day Russia — be calm! 'There is no boundary visé on this passport; you are quite out of order,' says he in his best Lettish imitation of a Prussian officer's manner. 'Sorry your boundary officials are such neglectful fools; you should report them,' say I, lighting a cigarette, returning the passport to my pocket, putting my feet up on the bench and handing him a cigar. 'Besides, I have the only candle, and if you eject me the train will run all night in darkness.' He glares, his guard rattle their rifles; then his eye fixed on the cigar softens and his hand slips over it like the practised head-waiter's over a tip.

Imagine the United States with every county turned into an independent country with custom-houses and frontier guards and deadly suspicious of each other; that will give you an idea of the situation in Eastern Europe.

At the next station we are taken by storm. Into our wee car bursts a mob which grabs every available seat, and then crowds three on every bench — intended for two. The aisles are soon jammed. Loaded to the very roof, the train continues its ramble down to Riga. We are so packed we can hardly breathe. Imagine a subway car at the worst crush hour; imagine subway air, only ten times worse — picture the filth of the crowd and the vermin — and then try to grasp what a trip of fourteen hours under these conditions would be like! Really I never passed such a night! It is like a Chinese torture for fourteen hours without intermission. Squeezed into a narrow corner of my bench, sitting bolt upright, not even able to stretch out my legs because of soldiers' baggage piled between the seats, stifled in the unspeakable air — wouf! what a fourteen-hour stretch!

Wednesday, January 14, 1920

Sometime during the forenoon we pull into Riga. Nearly forty hours from Reval. Last summer I have gone from Riga to Reval in my Cadillac in a day — breakfasted in Riga and supped and slept in Reval. And this in spite of bad roads.

I grab a droshky sleigh and whish over to Gade's.

John A. Gade, as you may know, is the United States Commissioner to the Baltic Provinces of Russia, representing the State Department. How Esthonia, Latvia and Lithuania do gag and balk at his credentials, 'to the Baltic *Provinces of Russia,*' they who have repudiated everything Russian, sovereignty, language, culture and even the poor refugees from out of Red Russia who try to hover in their midst! Suppose a diplomatic representative arrived in Washington with credentials to the 'British Colonies of North America.' That's the way the Esthonian and Latvian 'Governments' feel about it. And nothing more touchy or conceited than these tiny new 'States' of Eastern Europe, let me tell you!

During the war, Gade was our Naval Attaché at Copenhagen. Later, at my request, he was attached to my Mission to Finland, Esthonia, Latvia and Lithuania. He took charge of half of my Mission and proceeded direct to Finland and Esthonia, while I took the other half and went to Latvia and Lithuania. He made all our first investigations in Finland and Esthonia and wrote our reports on those two.

Today he is back as United States representative in Esthonia, Latvia and Lithuania, as the new 'Republics' call themselves, or in Esthonia, Livonia, Lattgallia, Courland and Lithuania, if you followed the names of the old Russian provinces.

He is an able fellow with a splendid command of languages, which is invaluable in the Baltic.

His offices are on Georgenstrasse, across the street from the two huge flats once occupied by our Mission, but now in the possession of the American Red Cross; his living quarters in a roomy flat around the corner, which also houses the other members of his Mission — Curtiss, one of our Aces in France; Lehrs, who was with my Mission; and Chapman, who was my secre-

tary and stenographer both in the Air Service and the
Peace Commission.

RIGA, *Thursday, January* 15, 1920
Busy all day, but nothing of interest to record here.

Friday, January 16, 1920
Again busy. See Princess Anatole Lieven and her
two daughters and two boys. Of the Lievens I think
I have often written you. Him I consider the finest
all-round character I met while in Baltic Russia — so
simple, so honest, so capable. And she is like him,
except a little more shrewdness. He is now in Paris,
recovering from a desperately severe wound received
while fighting the Bolshevists last summer.

Saturday, January 17, 1920
Lieutenant-Colonel Wilson of the British Army
turns up. He was one of General Sir Hubert Gough's
principal assistants when Gough was in Baltic Russia
to carry out that illusive thing known as the Allied
military policy in that part of the world. In that
capacity I got to know Wilson, who is a very decent
chap. In 1918 he was in America on a war mission
and came to know Dorothy Straight, Mary Rumsey
and many other friends.

Wilson has come down in a private car and invites
me to accompany him back. With the memories of
that trip down still thick in my mind, I accept with a
shout.

We are scheduled to leave at six P.M. We arrive at
the station to find that the locomotive has broken
down and been taken to the repair shop, 'and may

be ready in some hours.' Wilson immediately smells a rat; he has come down in the special car of the British Military Mission behind an Esthonian locomotive; Latvia has long claimed that Esthonia owed her two locomotives — and they are worth their weight in solid gold, these days in Russia — and for that reason the Esthonians were reluctant to let it go into Latvia for fear the Letts would grab it — grab with your own strong right arm being the great game of Baltic Russia — even though it was attached to the British Mission.

So now the sudden disappearance of the locomotive into the repair shop looked very suspicious.

There follows a great hurrying to and fro, calling up of Missions on telephones, putting of secret service men on the job, etc., etc. I dine comfortably with Gade — who has set up a real home, which the fortunate visitor greatly appreciates in this land of discomfort and turmoil — and return to the station at ten o'clock to find the locomotive purring contentedly at the head of our little special train, and Lettish guards standing most demurely about, as though there had never been a thought that that locomotive ought to stay in Latvia. I send Gade's Cadillac crashing about town to retrieve Wilson. It returns with him and a certain Colonel McGregor of the British Red Cross.

And so our tiny special ambles out of the station before midnight and clatters off northward through the icy wastes of Livonia, a magnificent comet's tail of sparks streaming from our funnel, for a locomotive burning dry pine and birch makes a royal pyrotechnic display. We have our little special coach to spread out in, and each can read himself to sleep in his bunk by the light of a separate candle. In short, extraordinarily luxurious travel!

Sunday, January 18, 1920

We lose our locomotive at Walk and remain there most of the day. Towards evening we are hitched onto a shambling little local train whose locomotive grunts and groans at our additional load on its worn wheels and frail boiler, but eventually delivers us at Dorpat.

Dorpat is buzzing with the conference between the Bolshevists and the Esthonians. An armistice has already been declared and the peace terms are under negotiation. One of the British Economic Mission gets aboard and tells us how things are going.

Monday, January 19, 1920

Pull into Reval about eight o'clock. The car of the British Mission awaits us and hurries us to the Mission's house through the raging cold. Wilson is kind enough to invite me to share its hospitality, which I am glad to accept.

And here, for the time being, this diary must run down.

With dear love

Your devoted son

WARWICK GREENE

REVAL, *Monday, January* 19, 1920

From the station the motor quickly takes us to the British Mission. Wouf! but it's cold! The thermometer is far below zero and the wind keen as a newly stropped razor. Beneath the motor's wheels the snow crackles stiffly.

The British Military Mission is housed in the same dreary brick building it occupied when I was here last summer, and attended conferences there presided over by General Gough. Of General Gough and of those conferences I could write you many, many things. And I shall write them, some day. But for the moment I refrain out of regard for the Finnish censor — to whom I give my greetings if he opens this letter! Gough was a genial, delightful man and I look back with much pleasure on my associations with him here last summer.

But within the dreary brick building is all the warmth, the comfort, the hospitality of a well-run British Mess.

Above all, a splendid bathtub, swimming full with warm water, unimaginable joy after a trip in Baltic Russia!

Upstairs I have a good room, still adorned with the pictures of the family who own the house. German Balts, to judge from the portraits. Ladies of the age of bustles and tight bodices, and unmistakably German. The room belongs to the boy of the family, judging from various relics and pictures of University Vereins with youths in their queer students' caps. German names are scrawled underneath, names of the great Baltic Baron families famous in the diplomacy and the armies and the navies of a vanished Russia — Rosens, Wrangels, Kaiserlings, etc. For you know these German Balt families have been the great

186

people of the Baltic Provinces for seven hundred years. Since the Armistice, however, they have fallen on very evil days, at the hands of Letts and Esthonians as well as Bolshevists. Their estates are being confiscated; many have been killed; most are in exile.

We are, of course, merely billeted in the house — the wishes of the owners, if they are still about, have nothing to do with the matter.

How often have I been billeted in private houses during the past two and a half years — in France, in Belgium, in occupied Germany, in Russia! And how callously one camps down in these private homes, uninvited and usually unwanted guests! Frequently, of course, in France and Russia, one settled in houses whose owners were refugees and nothing but a few damaged and neglected pictures and personal belongings told of what manner of folk they were — as in the house we are now in.

It is going to take a long while to get over the habits of war.

In the afternoon I decide to accompany Wilson on his trip to Narva to see the typhus situation — stories of shocking conditions among the remnants of Judenitch's defeated army are abroad and Gade is very anxious to have them investigated.

So at nine P.M. we trundle down to the station where our private car has been hitched onto the evening train to Narva.

Ahead of our car are four or five box-cars, each with a stove. They are for Bolshevist prisoners being returned to the Reds.

Presently the prisoners come marching down the

platform, guarded by some specially selected Esthonian soldiers, well-set-up young bourgeoisie who can be depended on to guard Reds without becoming contaminated by their propaganda. They herd the Bolshies into the box-cars, with much laughter and badinage handed back and forth. Reds and Whites, both seem as cheery as possible. 'Don't crowd us so, brothers,' calls out one talkative Red, 'better look out, you know — next week *we* may be crowding *you* into the prisoners' cars!'

Finally all are crammed and jammed into the cars and the locks sealed. Our talkative friend sticks his face out of a little window at one end. The platform is crowded; he has an audience; his agitator's face beams. 'Come on, brothers,' he addresses the platform crowd, 'come on with us to the Reds! We are going straight through, you know, in these very cars; through to Petrograd and the Workingmen's Republic. Come on! give us a lift, and then we will return and give you a lift to form a Workingman's Republic in Esthonia! Haven't you had enough of working and dying for the Bourzhui! When did the Bourzhui ever work or die for you? Why do you go out in this bitter cold and snow and face the Red bullets? For Esthonia? You poor fools! For the Black Barons, for the capitalist English, for the Esthonian Bourzhui, to betray yourselves, your families, your workingmen brothers throughout the world.'

The crowd presses closer; it is not unsympathetic. The Red orator glances down at the irresolute young soldiers of the prisoners' guard. He cackles with

laughter. 'Look,' he says, 'at these pretty little play-
soldiers! I wonder if their mothers know they are out
so late! Poor little kids, if Trotzky catches them!!!'
The agitator's voice fills with crocodile tears; the
crowd laughs appreciatively; the young bourgeois
soldiers look sheepish. The Red continues: 'You see,
I am just a simple, hard old fellow from the navy; we
drowned our Tsarist officers as you drown blind kit-
tens off Cronstad and Crasnya Gorka! That was good
sport, especially with the old devils! But all those
nice, nice little boys — it was a shame! And they
could have escaped it so easily if they had agreed to
become good little Reds. Poor lads, they were so
obstinate! Had to drown all those puppies in the
cold, cold water!'

The young guardsmen shift about uneasily; their
officer, a spectacled young bourgeois who might be a
professor of botany at the University of Dorpat, pre-
tends not to hear. Rough-neck Esthonian soldiers
crowd about, grinning broadly. The young Esthonian
'Grotties' of the guard try to look soldierly, as shouts
of laughter burst about them.

The orator looks about the platform and spots the
British uniforms. He addresses Esthonia in general:
'Oh, yes! The English are brave enough when *you*
are between them and the Reds. But watch them
skip the day we march into Reval, as they did when
we marched into Riga last year; ran away in their
destroyers! Left all their Riga friends to our attentions! Went back to Old England fast as they could
go. Never mind, there will be Soviets in London and
Glasgow next year! Litvinov will be Red Ambas-

sador in London — and those fine new destroyers
that fired on the Red fleet at Cronstad will be his
despatch boats! Poor, poor little White Guardsmen
of Esthonia, who will save you then?'

The locomotive whistles; we are about to start.
The orator turns his head back into the box-car,
'Give them the Red Song, comrades!' he shouts.
From the four box-cars immediately swells the Hymn
of the Red Revolution, sung lustily and insolently,
accompanied by a tremendous drumming of boots
and fists on the wooden sides of the cars. And then,
yes! from the depths of the crowd on the platform
comes an answering cheer! And so we pull out from
Reval, into the icy, icy night, the revolutionary song
roaring up to the frosty stars from our train, a sympathetic echo following us from the station!

NARVA, *Tuesday, January* 20, 1920

Arrive about nine A.M. Then to the British Mission for breakfast. All the windows in the building
were broken by last week's bombardment, except
in one room which consequently has to do duty as
dining-room, office, sitting-room, etc. — for you cannot live in a room with broken windows during the
Russian winter.

As the British are having a conference that does
not interest me, I spend the morning strolling about
the town.

We are now in real Russia — the Baltic Provinces
are only the fringes of Russia and very much German-
ized. In Narva true Russia, inhabited by Russians,
begins.

190

A BUSINESS TOUR OF BALTIC STATES

The Bolshevist lines are about four miles away; there is an armistice, so there is no firing. And probably never will be again because the armistice will soon become a peace.

Narva has suffered heavily during the war against the Bolshevists. Entire blocks of buildings have been burned and stick their black bones out of the snow; many of the unburnt houses are shell-scarred. Yet the town is full of life and color. It is market-day and streams of sleds and droshkies pour in from the country. The market-place is a jam and jostle of every race from the wide Russias. One sees the discarded uniforms of many nations — British, French, American, German, Russian. For the Liquidation Commissions of many armies have been busy passing on their surplus stocks for these mad little wars of Eastern Europe. Occasionally an officer swaggers through in Circassian uniform — very chic indeed!

Down by the deep river gorge are two splendid castles, one built by the Swedes, one by the Russians. Across the ravine they rear their stone walls, defying one another, as Swede and Russian defied one another when Sweden owned these provinces and the Bear was girding up his loins, under Peter the Great, for his push through to the Baltic. Each built his castle to guard the boundary river. There they stand today, on the boundary of what for the moment is the line between Bolshevism and anti-Bolshevism. Undoubtedly the Red Bear, under Lenin, will shove through to the sea again, just as the Black Bear did under Peter. Red or Black, the Great Bear must cool his paws in the Baltic Sea.

The streets are thronged with soldiers. Esthonians, well armed, jostle the wretched, disarmed Russian soldiers of Judenitch's army. How they hate one another, Esthonian and Russian! Especially the officers. The underdog has become the upper dog; the oppressed the oppressor. And, as usually happens, the oppressed become oppressor, oppresses with compound interest! How truculently the Esthonian officers strut about whenever they spy a Russian, how rudely they crowd Russian officers off the sidewalk, how insolently they receive the salutes of the young Russian officers!

Poor Russian Northwestern Army! Perhaps you remember how it was formed and put under the command of General Judenitch and, aided and abetted by the Allies, made a desperate plunge to capture Petrograd, which it came within an ace of doing. Then Trotzky brought up heavy Red reënforcements, hurled them against Judenitch's flank, and chased his defeated army back to Narva, where the Esthonians halted the Reds to prevent an invasion of Esthonian territory.

Today Judenitch's army is no longer an army; it is merely a horde of refugees, without discipline, organization or morale. Of course disease has broken out, as it always does under these circumstances, and the remnants of the force are rotten with it.

After lunch we go to inspect the hospitals. And now prepare for horrors! For we are going to plunge into them — unmitigated ones!

The first building is a hospital, built as such, with good heating, lighting, plumbing, and tile floors.

With proper equipment it would be a first-rate hospital.

But that equipment seems to be almost wholly lacking. There are not even enough beds; at least one third of the patients lie on the floor with nothing but some filthy straw or rags between them and the cold tiles. Furthermore, most of the beds, although single, contain two patients. No bed has sheets, pillows or pillow-cases; few have what we should call mattresses, and many are even without pallets, the two patients lying on the springs.

In the entire hospital, not a single patient has had his clothes removed; each lies in the filthy rags in which he has been campaigning for the past several months. There are so signs of soap, towels or disinfectants — they may exist, but certainly they are not in evidence.

This hospital is bad, shockingly bad according to our standards, but the next are nightmares.

We enter buildings, miscalled hospitals, in which the sick lie by hundreds on the floor, in some rooms so closely packed together that there is scarcely room for them to turn over, and where the dead lie side by side with the living, perhaps for hours, perhaps for days, for lack of orderlies to remove them. The patients are sick with flu, dysentery, recurrent fever, frost-bite and spotted typhus. In some hospitals with four to six hundred cases there will be only one qualified nurse on duty, with perhaps two assistants — in one hospital we visit there is not a single doctor on duty at the time of our visit. Orderlies are few and far between and these not inclined to obey orders

— the Judenitch army is today merely a rabble of refugees, and the well soldiers refuse to work in the hospitals for fear of contagion. Under these conditions I leave it to your imagination to picture the sanitary conditions which exist. When you enter the rooms, especially the typhus rooms, the foul and fetid smell almost knocks you down; the filth of the patients and of the rags and straw on which they lie are, of course, impossible to describe in a letter. American white bread and bacon, the ration of the Northwestern Army, lie rotting about in the general loathsome dirt and disorder. For the most part the patients are quiet; but some groan and many rave in the typhus delirium. Others call out to us in the most appealing and pathetic way as we go by. In places you see milder cases trying to help comrades through the final phases of their sufferings. Still others point out the dead that lie near them.

Plucky, plucky girls, the few nurses that abide by their duty! Many proved slackers; they had merely accompanied the army in Red Cross uniform as the wives or mistresses of officers. Many others were sick or dead themselves — how anybody could be a day in those typhus rooms, without contracting the disease, was beyond me. The few that still stick to their job deserve all praise. One plain little woman, with a broad, honest face, struggling almost single-handed with her hundreds of patients, explains the desperateness of the situation and the unnecessary sufferings of the men so simply and so tragically to us. I was glad to leave some of my W. Cameron Forbes relief funds with the British officers to care for the doctors and nurses when they in turn came down — for the greater proportion have already contracted disease. Unless there are private funds, it appears that they fare no better than the wretches we see about us. If there are funds, they can be cared for in certain private houses. It seems to me that these women, when they in their turn catch the typhus, richly deserve at least that much help.

From the 'hospitals' we go to one of the barracks — a dark and noisome loft in which several hundred men are quartered. Not the faintest shadow of discipline or order remains — even by Russian standards — and at least fifty per cent of the men seem to be hospital cases. Sick with flu, dysentery and fever they lie about the floor.

At the entrance to the barracks we find a sled with two sick men lying on it, one apparently dying. The driver seeks admission to the barracks for the two men; he has tried the hospitals and been refused. He is also refused at the barracks. The sick continue to lie on the sled without covering except their clothes. Remember, that all about is Russia's Arctic winter, a bitter cold that pierces the thickest furs. Undoubtedly the driver will not have to wait much longer before driving them to the one place where there is no question of refusal to enter — the mortuary we are soon to see. Jack Frost will soon outstrip whatever disease they have and register their death on his own account.

From the barracks we go to another horror miscalled a hospital. I think it is the worst we have yet seen, particularly the reception 'ward' into which the sick have been thrust until there is not an inch of space on the reeking floor for another case. In this room no fire has yet been lighted and it is heated solely by the animal heat from the patients themselves. It is also unlighted. There are no doctors, no nurses, no orderlies. You step into a foul, cold gloom livid with human suffering.

Outside we go to the 'mortuary.' In the open courtyard four corpses, frozen stiff as pine logs, lie on a sled. But there is neither driver nor horse to take them away. In a low shed is the mortuary itself into which fifteen or so human corpses have been flung like dead cats or rats. Some have been stripped stark naked; all are frozen stiff (a blessing, of course) and lie about in grotesque attitudes.

At last the cold dark ends this nightmare of an inspection and we go back into the town of Narva.

Dinner at the British Mission, followed by visits from some of the Russian officers of Judenitch's crumbled force; then down through the biting cold to the train. The sick Britisher is made as comfortable as possible; the rest of us make ourselves at home in our bunks, each with a stub of a candle to read himself to sleep by. Presently our train trundles off into the night and the clean frozen fields of the country, leaving festering Narva, swarming with life, full of hatred, and bitterness, reeking with foulness and death, behind us.

But the memories of those 'hospitals' remain with us — dreadful memories, loathsome memories! The Allies aided and abetted that expedition of Judenitch's and its reckless plunge forward to take Petrograd — and now have abandoned the poor wretches that escaped the Red bullets, to this unspeakable misery. Our consciences all hurt us as we go swaying home in that little railroad coach. Individually we had nothing to do with it; but having seen those hospitals, we hate to share, even vicariously, in the guilt for their existence. What a calamity all our meddling in the affairs of Russia has been!

REVAL, *Wednesday, January* 21, 1920

Learn there will be no steamer over to Helsingfors before next Tuesday 'at the very earliest.' Am trapped in Reval for a week more. Travel in Baltic Russia these days is the travel of a nightmare, forever hurrying forward, forever getting nowhere!

Luckily I am comfortable at the British Mission. Wilson is a very good fellow and has a Mess with genial officers and good food — Bevan, a kid Major from the War; Fitzhugh, an elderly Major who used to be in Peking; Fitzgerald, a six-foot-two Captain of the best English-Irish strain; and others. The place is full of the joy of life.

REVAL, *Thursday, January* 22, 1920
REVAL, *Friday, January* 23, 1920
REVAL, *Saturday, January* 24, 1920
REVAL, *Sunday, January* 25, 1920

Four days as like one another as buttons. Each day clearer and colder, if possible, than the preceding. The mercury cuddles at the bottom of the thermometer and even at noon will hardly venture above fifteen degrees below zero, Fahr. Out of doors your cheeks burn like scarlet; if you take your hand out

197

of your glove for an instant to pay your driver, it becomes as stiff as marble. And the finger-tips ache for an hour afterwards.

Today I dine with Baron Rosen, his sister and mother. They live in a two-story brown wooden house, in a side street, for all the world like an old house in a New England town. Within the likeness is still more striking — low ceilings, old furniture, breeding and gentility stamped unmistakably on everything. And the mother and sister are extraordinarily like well-bred New England folk. Well-bred, of course, they ought to be; for they are Balts, descended from the Teutonic Knights who conquered the country seven hundred years ago and founded a land-owning aristocracy which dominated the country up to November, 1918 — and has been having the very devil of a time ever since! For as soon as the German armies melted away after the Armistice, the Red armies overran the greater part of the country. These in turn were overcome by the Esthonians, assisted by British arms, who drove the Reds out of the country and set up Esthonia as an independent country asking recognition as such from the world. England and France have given her 'de facto' recognition, but not America as yet. But this peasant Republic has no use for Balts, Barons, or town bourgeoisie. In fact, Balts are their pet aversion, much more so, really, than Bolshevists. For seven hundred years the Baltic land-owning nobility held them down; today they feel their turn has come. So they are busy confiscating the big estates of the Balts, usually without compensation. For the most part the

198

Balts who remain in the country live a hunted, unhappy life.

The Rosens fare a little better, for Baron Ernest is a good business man, who has stayed strictly out of politics and plots. So he continues to make his living, though not without anxieties.

After lunch, several friends come in. The talk is all of confiscation — and of what they shall do to keep from starvation. One agreeable lady turns up, who says that agents of the Esthonian Government appeared at her estate two days ago and it is evident that it will be seized in a few days more. It is a great estate, one of the greatest and proudest on the Baltic seas. She wonders if she can teach music or dancing and whether she can get jobs as lift boys for her two young sons, if they will be allowed to go to some city in Scandinavia or Germany.

Then they talk about the Esthonians. It seems that all the new Ministers' wives are continually sick, and the doctors tell them (the Balts) that it is because they were country girls, used to sweeping, washing, milking, churning and other robust work, who are now always ailing because they have dressed up as 'ladies' and sit around on sofas all day long, doing nothing!

Then the Balt ladies wonder if the change in methods of living will make them sick, too — whether washing and churning will be hard on ladies.

And much more of the same sort.

Monday, January 26, 1920

Another day in Reval — I am getting to know the old town very well.

The pleasantest feature is the cheapness of every-thing. Today one dollar, U.S., buys from one hundred to one hundred and twenty Esthonian marks. So one mark is worth less than one cent. And if you purchase skilfully through pounds, it is much less — sterling is always in demand in the Baltic and so commands a better comparative exchange value than dollars. Today I order the following dinner for two at a restaurant in town: 'hors d'œuvres' consisting of appetizing little fish, cold meats, cheese, etc.; good fresh fish; splendid beefsteak with potatoes and onions, plenty of good white rolls, as well as both wheat and rye bread with all the fresh country butter one could tuck away; delicious méringues for dessert and all we wanted of them; mineral water to drink (Esthonia is a temperance country); and all topped off with tea and coffee and cakes.

Price for two, including tips, one dollar!

Tuesday, January 27, 1920

Still at Reval! I know every stone in the place. I have arranged all my business in connection with this job which keeps me in the Baltic, have lunched or dined with all our organizations — Red Cross, Consul, A.R.A. (Hoover's organization) Children's Relief, etc., etc., and am more than ready to move on.

Red Cross and A.R.A. are doing a big work. The latter is feeding seventy thousand children in Esthonia alone.

The Y.M.C.A. is also here.

My last day in Reval, I hope. I know it now in winter as well as summer. Last August when I was

GREENE AND HIS CHOW DOG PETER
In front of his house at Pasay, Manila, 1911

here the weather was like the best Bar Harbor brand with the fog left out; now in winter it is cold, dazzling and glorious.

I forgot to say that the British officer — Major Craig — we brought back with us sick in our car from Narva, has developed into a bad case of spotted typhus and has been delirious ever since. The other British sick with typhus is now convalescing.

REVAL, *Wednesday, January 28, 1920*

At last the day of departure! Today a boat goes to Helsingfors. Lord! how good to get away from Reval!

We are notified to be at the dock at seven-thirty A.M. *sharp.* But at eight we are still breakfasting comfortably at the hospitable British Mission. Captain Fitzgerald, who is going over as courier, is not in the least uneasy. 'Of course the beastly thing will wait for us.'

Eight-thirty. Still no motor. We can't possibly tuck away any more breakfast; so we warm ourselves at a cheery fire. England becomes a bit uneasy. Perhaps after all the 'beastly thing' may go away without us!

Eight-fifty-five. An unrepentant driver and motor turn up. We bundle in and go down to the wharf. It is savagely cold — a cold that eats right through an overcoat that is not fur-lined (mine isn't!) and curdles the marrow in your bones. Clear, bitter weather.

Sure enough the 'beastly thing' is still at the pier. The same dirty Poseidon on which I had crossed before. But she is a ship of deliverance; she means escape from Reval; so we look at her with kindly eyes.

But it is after ten o'clock before she parts company from that wharf. The half-past seven announcement was merely psychologically correct, intended to get Russians and Esthonians down at least by nine o'clock. Then an hour to search baggage and so a ten o'clock sailing. Had ten been announced as the hour of departure, we should either have left without passengers or had to wait until twelve to gather them in.

On deck the Poseidon is a mass of stained and dirty ice; within a jam of people. So crowded is she that every stateroom is marked for six persons, though there are berths only for two. In addition the hallways and saloons are packed.

Slowly we crush our way through the tousled ice of the harbor and emerge into the open sea. It is covered with a film of pure ice clear as green glass. We rumple it up in long waves and slit our way through with little effort.

But only for a few miles. Then the clear green of the young ice changes to a snow-whitened veteran ice-field. We are now punching against old, tough, experienced ice — the kind which will soon teach the little Poseidon that she is not an ice-breaker.

For a couple of hours we make fair headway, perhaps six or seven knots an hour. But it gets harder and harder. By the third hour the Poseidon is puffing hard. We no longer seem to be sawing our way through the smooth surface of a frozen sea; instead we have come into a bleak snow-covered world, pitted with inequalities, scarred with fissures, heaped about with hummocks. Off on the horizon baby mountains of ice show their heads. There is nothing to suggest that this rugged world is superimposed on the unstable blue sea. The Poseidon seems entirely out of her element; you can no longer believe that salt water presses about her keel. She seems more like a lunatic ship that has jumped ashore and is trying to make headway across a snow-covered land-scape — a nightmare such as might come to one of Kipling's thinking ships.

By and by the Poseidon stops like a horse that is absolutely dead beat. The ice gives her a sudden squeeze — you feel it. She squeaks and jumps back-ward, managing to shake herself free. We back down the lane of broken ice we left behind us; then we try for a softer and thinner place in the ice. This time we find it; for our captain has an uncanny sense for weak spots in ice. He knows ice just as a Gloucester skipper can think like a cod.

But we stick more and more. And finally for good. For all her backings and fillings and thrashing pro-peller, the steamer cannot free herself. The captain stops the beating engines and the ship whimpers a bit at the escape pipe, like an animal that gives up the fight.

'Stuck, old girl! Stuck till spring!' exults the ice.

The passengers pour out on deck. They are glum, until the mate sings out, 'There comes the ice-breaker!' We look to the north where a black smudge stains the white horizon. Spirits rise.

By and by we make out her hull plainly, a fat solid ship with two funnels. She looks strong and efficient. On she comes, crashing through the ice. It makes you think of an axe going through plate-glass. No effort to her, this ice world! She rips and cracks and chucks the ice out of her way as though it were play. But the enormous volumes of smoke pouring from her stacks tell what that play costs in priceless coal — I have forgotten how many hundred thousand Finnish marks one trip costs. No wonder we wait weeks in Reval for a boat.

The ice-breaker comes abreast of us. On her side you read in huge letters 'Wäinämoinen.' Formerly she belonged to the Russian Government and was called after one of the Tsars. Then came the Revolution and she was rebaptized for the first Guards Regiment to revolt. Later Finland set up in business as an independent country and the ice-breaker was renamed after the hero of the Finnish epic, the Kalevala.

She passes us on our starboard, swings, backs disdainfully into the thickest of the ice-field — thus changing her direction like a locomotive on a Y — and then charges by our stern quarter so close you could jump aboard her.

There are agonized cracking noises from the ice which grips the Poseidon; then it dissolves into a turmoil of cakes and floes in the boiling wake of the icebreaker. On she charges, straight ahead of us, showing her squat stern and broad beam with a cataract of splintered ice and angry waters trailing behind her. She whistles peremptorily, as if to say, 'Come on there, my child! I have busted up the ice for you — shake a leg and get into my wake and we'll make tracks for Helsingfors.' We whistle back obediently and waddle along after the Wäinämoinen like a seal calf after its mother.

For a while all goes well and it looks like dinner — for all hands in Helsingfors. The Wäinämoinen surges steadily on, crunching furiously through the ice, spreading a huge wake behind, and darkening all that white world with smoke. Heaven only knows how many tons of coal it takes to crack the Ice King's crown!

But thicker and thicker grows the ice; colder, stronger and bitterer the wind. For all her bullying assurance the ice-breaker goes slower and slower. Her wake is an ever-thickening jumble of broken ice, in which the Poseidon was hard going. At times she sticks fast, right in the wake, too! Then she bleats pitifully on her whistle. To which the Wäinämoinen responds with exasperated hoots, but turns around just the same and comes back and cuts us out with the same manœuvre as before. 'Heavens, what a helpless child!' she snorts as she turns again to the business of hammering and splitting the ice that lies ahead of us.

The sun sets in a nest of pale and very cold gold; immediately the wind picks up fresh courage and races troops of frantic snow squalls across that bleak world. The plucky little Poseidon becomes a mummy of ice fighting vainly against Arctic forces. Her boilers still warm her steel carcass and she streams a little light out into the wild night; but for all the distracted energy of her engines she is not making an inch of real headway. The ice-breaker comes back, huge and rather mystic in the dark, and cuts around her. Renewed struggles on our part, but we can't budge. Again the Wäinämoinen comes back, after a heated conversation on the whistles, and circles us once more; all the ice as far as we can see in the dark has been broken up into an angry whirl of ice cakes and water.

It is our undoing. For on those miles and miles of ice-field presses all the force of the blizzard, while beneath obscure currents are at work. The area of broken ice and water created by the Wäinämoinen upsets the icy equilibrium; the vast ice-fields start in motion.

Out of the night the ice-field on the starboard bears down on us and seizes the Poseidon as a hydraulic press might seize a gnat...

Instantly the ship goes into a convulsion, snapping, cracking, heeling first this way and then that; below, the steel ribs and rivets screech under the agony of the strain that is on them — any moment you expect to hear them snap. The passengers rush out on deck; crew and stewardesses stream up from below; the flat ice-boats are dragged down from the superstructure; the lifeboats swung out and partially lowered, rockets brought up; the crew sound the pumps.

Looking over the starboard rail one sees a solid layer of ice, twelve inches thick, flowing down out of the night and bringing up squarely against the Poseidon's sides — you think of lava as you watch it. Lava is hot and the ice is cold, but there is the same slow, sinister march, the same sense of irresistible force. It presses against the ship's side with intolerable pressure; if she were not built for these icy seas she would crush up like an eggshell. Something must give way; so far it is the ice which with vicious growling and snapping, curls up and breaks off in great cakes which fall thumping back on the ice-field, slowly building a rampart which, if it continues long enough, will climb to the rails of the Poseidon and then overwhelm her.

The passengers huddle about the deck. Nobody gives any orders; nobody troubles to calm them. Luckily they are mostly Russian refugees so inured to trouble that one danger the more doesn't drive them into a panic. They are camels whose backs the last straw long since broke; now you can hurl boulders on those broken backs without further remonstrance.

Fitzgerald and I go to the mate, who talks English. We get small comfort from him. If there is open water to leeward and the wind continues, we shall be swept down on the rocks and sunk; if we stay where we are and the pressure continues, the ice rampart will build up until it invades the decks and sheers off rails, superstructure, funnels and masts; if the pressure increase, the hull will give and the ice will squeeze the boilers up through the decks and the ship will sink beneath the ice.

At first we think he is stringing us a bit. Unworthy thought! — for a Finnish mate doesn't joke! Moreover, preparations for abandoning ship continue; fires are drawn; the stokers come up on deck; provisions and water are put into the lifeboats (though what we are to do with boats in this world of ice is beyond me); and we howl and howl and howl on our siren. How we wait and howl; the little Poseidon just sobs her heart out on that siren!

Lost in the bitter darkness the Wäinämoinen hoots back at her, 'I don't know about you, child, but I am caught in an ice jam that is TWENTY-SEVEN FEET THICK; with all my engines and all my propellers and all my prestige as an ice-breaker at stake I can't budge a millimetre. Moreover, I am being squeezed so hard that even my stout hide and big ribs can scarcely hold out. I am surprised *you* are still alive, child!'

Then (as we afterwards learned) the panicky ice-breaker wirelessed to Helsingfors that her position was grave; ours hopeless! Luckily we were only on the edge of the ice-jam; had we been in the thick of it with the Wäinämoinen, the ice would have finished us in five minutes.

For an hour or so the passengers remain on deck. Beyond the rails of the ship you can see nothing except a racing army of billions of snowflakes; the winds howl as though the heavens were filled with packs of titanic wolves.

And then, just as the ice rampart on the starboard side of the ship has built itself up to a formidable height, the pressure relaxes; then ceases. Blessed relief! The fiendish crunching and snapping and cracking die down; the wind lets up, snowflakes fall perpendicularly, the siren ceases, the passengers troop back into the delicious warmth and bad air of the cabins. It may be only a respite, or the movement of the ice may have ceased for good. Anyhow, everybody goes to sleep. The staterooms are packed with six and seven each, mostly ladies; the passageways and dining-saloon tables covered with tired men.

I find a comfortable place down in the forward hold, snuggle in among the baggage and go to sleep. It is strangely quiet, after that inferno of noise.

About three A.M. I go on deck and take a look around; the sky is a serene and enormous bowl of bluish black, sparkling gaily with stars. A young moon slides slowly about it. Not a wisp of wind or a trace of cloud is about. Nature seems mildly surprised that we should have been so excited three hours ago. 'Really, I didn't intend to do anything bad,' she seems to say.

January 29, 1920

Morning is glorious with blazing sun and blue skies and miles and miles of glittering ice all about us. Ahead lies the Wäinämoinen, apparently in a low range of ice-hills. We climb down the side of the Poseidon and stroll about on the ice. Apparently a couple of Peary's or Amundsen's ships have been caught in polar ice and are to remain there indefinitely.

About nine o'clock there is a great business of smoke from the Wäinämoinen's funnels, followed by a tremendous thrashing of propellers at either end (she has both bow and stern propellers). Inch by inch, foot by foot, yard by yard, furlong by furlong, she enlarges the icy bath in which she lies, as the hours go by. Backwards and forwards, forwards and backwards, she slugs, each time crumbling up a slight bit more of that tenacious ice. The jumble of broken ice and water enlarges, until at the end of three or four hours it is quite a respectable lagoon. Then she backs down to one end and charges full speed to the other. An enormous cracking and splintering of ice, but she stops in twenty feet. Again she goes at it. And again. And then again. Old Wäinämoinen is as vicious as a mad bull and as stubborn as a mule. To us it looks hopeless, but her captain, standing on the bridge all fattened up in huge fur coats, slugs her at it again and again and then again. 'Damn the expense!' he seems to say. 'Coal is made to burn; pitch it into her furnaces.'

Then comes the last charge. Down the lagoon she comes, water boiling out from bow and stern, suffocating clouds of smoke pouring from her funnels. She hits the ice ridge a terrific punch — and goes through! On this side is a smooth ice-field across which the Wäinämoinen romps at *increasing* speed with a sound like gigantic scissors ripping cambric cloth. A tremendous report seems to run through the ice to the furtherest horizon and a long slit instantly appears down through which the water squirts up for hundreds of yards.

And so we dined in Helsingfors the night of the twenty-ninth. We had been two days crossing the Gulf of Finland, but, somehow, nobody complained that what last summer used to take two hours in a destroyer, should have taken two days. After all it was better than having to struggle on foot across those icy wastes, after abandoning our baggage to whatever fate overtook the little old Poseidon.

A BUSINESS TOUR OF BALTIC STATES

To Hon. W. Cameron Forbes

HELSINGFORS, FINLAND
February 3, 1920

DEAR GOVERNOR:

I have written you and Conrad once or twice about the five thousand dollars you were good enough to entrust to me in 1916 for relief purposes.

This letter is merely to say that there still remains a balance from this sum, which I am finding abundant opportunity to spend in this part of the world. For example, when in Riga a couple of weeks ago I left thirty pounds with John Gade, the American Commissioner to the Baltic Provinces. Gade had already been so moved by the distress in Riga that he had started a little relief project of his own, carefully supervised and administered and used for special cases. Before the war, Riga was a city of five hundred and fifty thousand people; today it does not count more than two hundred and twenty-five thousand. In 1914, it was a flourishing trading and manufacturing city; today it is a dead city without a ship entering or leaving its harbor, without a factory operating, cut off from the interior of Russia (for which it was the natural outlet) by the fighting against the Bolshevists, and with the railroads which serve it almost completely broken down. In addition it has to suffer from an amateurish and inefficient government set up by the Letts under the principles of 'self-determination.' Under these conditions you may imagine the distress that prevails. Gade's little relief project is primarily for special cases among the older people and the children of families that were formerly very prosperous, but are now starving. The American Red Cross and the A.R.A.'s (Hoover's organization) Children's Relief care for the great mass of the destitute, but do not reach the kind of cases which Gade looks after — old ladies who have had to stand the Russian winter up to January without a stick of wood to warm their rooms; families of professional people slowly starving to death on a meagre ration of gruel; disabled and paralyzed officers turned out of the hospitals without a penny; and other cases of this nature.

Gade started his relief efforts with personal funds and with money contributed by his wife and friends at home. The work is in direct charge of one of Princess Lieven's daughters, who personally investigates each case before any funds are allotted and follows up every case where help is given — if you want to know about the Lievens, I refer you to Peter who met the father and mother in Paris where the Prince had gone for medical treatment for the very serious wound he received while fighting the Bolshevists last spring. A full report on the expenditures made from your thirty pounds donated to this work will reach you in due course of time.

Last week I also gave thirty pounds from your fund to Lieutenant-Colonel Wilson, Chief of the British Military mission in Esthonia, for the care of nurses and doctors who may fall ill while fighting typhus at Narva. This was done after I had made a trip to Narva and personally investigated the appalling conditions in the so-called hospitals at that place. In and about Narva are concentrated the remnants of the

Russian Northwestern Army, commanded by Judenitch, which almost captured Petrograd some months
ago. This force has ceased to be an army and has
become a mere rabble of refugees, without discipline,
organization or morale. Naturally disease has broken
out and today there are thousands of cases of flu,
dysentery, frost-bite, fever and spotted typhus. The
so-called hospitals we visited were requisitioned
factory buildings without hospital equipment, supplies or conveniences of any kind — even beds were
lacking in every hospital we visited but one, and there
they were quite insufficient for the number of patients. Into these buildings hundreds and hundreds
of sick were crowded and lay on the floors in the filthy
rags in which they had campaigned, without care of
any kind in most cases. A handful of doctors and
nurses struggled against these conditions — and it is
for them when they become sick that your funds will
be used. The slackers disappeared long since; those
who have remained at their posts are the devoted and
plucky ones. A large majority have already become
sick and others will follow — to show what they are
up against I may say that two of the five members of
the British Military Mission at Narva have already
come down with spotted typhus (we brought one back
with us in our car from Narva) and of four nurses who
came out from England, one is dead and three convalescing from typhus. Unless private funds are
available, the doctors and nurses who become sick are
likely to fare little better than the poor wretches I
have described above. With funds, provision can be
made for them in private houses. Wilson will report

directly to you on the disposition he makes of your funds.

I have gone at length into these two cases of use of your relief funds to show you typical instances. It was my understanding that you wanted these funds used in cases that fell outside of the regularly organized relief efforts of the American Red Cross, the A.R.A. (which is feeding seventy thousand children in Esthonia alone), or in districts where no relief organizations were operating. There are, of course, always many pathetic cases which fall outside of regular relief efforts, and I have made a special effort to search out such cases. I trust that I have been carrying out your wishes.

A general summary of relief allotments from your fund show that they fall under the following headings:

(1) Polish relief;
(2) Belgian relief;
(3) French relief;
(4) Russian relief.

An accurate account has been kept of most of these expenditures, with supporting vouchers, etc. But in many cases Russian relief has had to be administered under conditions that did not permit of securing vouchers and receipts. In the majority of cases, however, the paper record is complete and will be submitted to you, together with a general report, when I come home. This will supplement the report on Polish and Belgian relief already sent in. French and Russian relief will account for the greater part of the original fund of five thousand dollars.

My private job, which brought me back into this

part of the world, is proving very tedious and long-drawn-out. I am keen to get it over with and be home. But I have contracted to see it through to its conclusion; so must stay here until that has been done. Of course one's experiences in this part of the world are most interesting — the greatest problem of modern times is being fought out here — but I am very homesick.

Sincerely yours

WARWICK GREENE

P.S. In this part of the world, one never knows what will become of a letter after one has posted it. However, Finland has so far made good as an independent country and conditions are immeasurably superior to those in the new 'States' of Esthonia, Latvia and Lithuania which complete the Baltic Front of what was once the Empire of Russia. So I am hoping this letter goes through. But I know that much of my mail has disappeared.

To Mrs. Charles A. Lindley (Edith Greene)

HELSINGFORS, FINLAND
February 20, 1920

DEAR EDITH:

Your letter of December 12th has just reached me — a trifle over two months en route. But in this part of the world one is delighted to get a letter at all. I don't speak of Finland — she has done well under her independence and is now a reasonably well-organized State. Soon she may be entitled to rank as a fourth

215

Scandinavian State. She assumes some moral responsibility about mails and delivers them. Probably she has a secret censorship, but she passes on your letters after having read them. There are delays owing to the ice and to the fact that at this time of year there are only bi-weekly connections with Sweden. Aside from these delays, the Government post functions reasonably well.

But in the little Baltic 'States,' my Lord! In the wild-cat Republics of Esthonia, Latvia and Lithuania you will probably never hear again of a letter you are incautious enough to trust to the mail. Nobody dreams of entrusting a letter to 'Government' post; they are handed, instead, to any old friend who happens to be travelling. And if no friend, to some fellow countryman. And if no fellow countryman, then to some Britisher or Frenchman. So letters wander up and down the land in the hands of members of British, French and American Missions, of Red Cross and Hoover's Relief people, etc. Very haphazard and no responsibility.

As I am much in the Baltic 'States,' do you wonder that my mail connections are a bit sketchy?

As for travel conditions in the Baltic 'States' — ask Mamma to show you a diary I sent her of my last trip. A quite typical trip.

In your letter you describe a few fleabites of troubles at home — a sick and obstinate President, helped down his road to ruin by an over-ambitious wife; a trifle of a coal strike, finally settled; some disgruntled Cabinet officers resigning; a Senate quite properly suspicious of a Peace Treaty which is handsomely seconding the war in ruining the world — and then you say, 'enough of gloom.'

Good Lord! You people at home don't know Gloom! You never met him. Come to Central and Eastern Europe if you don't believe me; what you call gloom there, here would seem sparkling sunshine. From the Rhine to Vladivostok the world is a ruin. The wreck, begun by the war, is fast being completed — and in very generous measure — by the Old Men at Paris. The Tiger gets back to his lair not only with the scalps of both Wilson and Lloyd George, but also with the bones of enough babies to build a pyramid over his grave out-topping that of Cheops — babies murdered by George's policies as inevitably and directly as though he had been a real striped tiger and had killed them with his own claws. Central and Eastern Europe — that incalculable agglomeration of peoples from the Rhine to Behring Straits — will remember Clemenceau — for centuries! Unfortunately the France of a later generation will expiate for these present policies that are framed in blood and starvation. Clemenceau has sown the wind; young France will reap the red or black — Bolshevist or Reactionary — whirlwind out of the vast stretch of territories and peoples he and his generation have wronged. Perhaps it will be both red and black. The old man himself will be gathered to his fathers, full of years and honors. He saved France from one great peril, only to commit her to another which you outsiders are just beginning dimly to see. There was only one Peace possible — a Peace of good will and reconciliation. France spurned that; she faces a future in which both German and Slav are staggering to their feet, hand in hand against her.

And Clemenceau's remedy? A band of border states between the two, his 'barricade of barbed wire' to control Russia and Germany and keep them from joining. Esthonia, Latvia, Lithuania, Poland, Czecho-Slovakia, Rumania, etc., are to be fostered on condition of saving Europe both from the Red peril and German revenge. What a senile dream! As well expect a litter of quarrelling guinea-pigs (to vary the metaphor) to stop a bear and a wolf. While the Russian Bear and the German Wolf are stunned... perhaps! When they recover and combine forces... well! you may hear a few squeals. That will be all.

Think, in your cold common-sense, of a policy that bases its control of giants like Germany and Russia on Balkanizing a strip of Europe from the Black Sea to the Baltic (and with a generation of experience in the Balkan Peninsula behind us!); of an attempt to protect Europe from the danger of a union of the German and the Slav by a rickety fence of squabbling jerk-water republics. And Poland — temperamental, attractive Poland, unstable as water — as the centre post of the fence!

No step could have been better calculated to bring about the feared result. To the German as a natural enemy of the French people, Clemenceau's policy has now added the Slav. By preaching and stimulating hatred and discord from the Rhine to Asia, the Tiger has aroused huge forces of hatred which eventually are going to coalesce against France. England will not escape, nor we (though America is in for only a fraction of the retribution); but in all this part of the world France bears the brunt of the odium for the intolerable sufferings into which the populations have been plunged — the Peace Treaty and the Russian Policy of the Allies are considered to reflect accurately the atmosphere of Paris.

Even the French finally got panicky and packed the old Tiger, loaded with deserved war honors, back to his native Brittany and that old Mongolian or Turanian prehistoric stock from which he is said to have sprung — and you have only to look at his face to see that some, at least, of his forefathers were Kalmucks. There let him growl out his Memoirs, which should be marvellous reading if he writes as he has talked for the past two years. But with the problems of reconstruction before us, let us get Europe forever free from his bloody claws. At last France learned that Tigers are better for war than for peace — perhaps she learned it too late.

Your affectionate brother
WARWICK GREENE

To Mrs. Francis Vinton Greene

COPENHAGEN, DENMARK
Sunday, May 2, 1920

DEAR MAMMA:

Might be dated New York, 1920, this clipping, mightn't it? At least to judge from your letters and what one reads in the papers. Expensive luxuries, wars! And the bills keep on coming in for years and years afterwards. But somehow in the long run they get settled and prices come down again. And, after all, the American bill for the war is very light — fifty thousand dead in battle or from wounds, thirty or forty billions as the direct cost of the war to us and high prices and unrest as the indirect. But oh, so light compared with what European countries have to pay! And for that very light cost we have run off with the plums of the war — for we have whatever cash and prestige it has yielded. Think of the price France, Russia and Germany have paid — not to mention the lighter but still very heavy burdens on England, Italy and the rowdy Balkan States. As for poor Austria, she seems to be the permanent 'mutilée' of the war.

Speaking of high prices and abnormal conditions, let me tell you more about the cost of living and money exchange as they fluctuate about this little Baltic Sea — I have already written you something about this, but let me amplify.

On the western side of the Baltic lie the neutral Scandinavian countries, healthy as possible, their people fat as butter. And Stockholm a close second to New York as the most expensive place in the world. You pay seven to eight dollars a day for a very ordinary room at the Grand Hotel, Stockholm, and six to ten dollars a day additional for their heavy meals. Copenhagen can't quite keep up this pace, but is expensive enough. Danish and Swedish exchanges have fallen as compared with the dollar and the Swiss franc, the latter having climbed to a pinnacle of high exchange where it holds even the dollar in scorn, but nothing as compared with most European currencies.

A BUSINESS TOUR OF BALTIC STATES

So much for the western shores of the Baltic.
Everywhere sleek prosperity and high prices. There's
lots of grousing, but nothing really worth grousing
about. But take a motor boat and run out of Copenhagen not so very many miles to the south. There
you come to lean, crazy, miserable Germany. Little
food, less work, and everybody abysmally unhappy.
The mark, normally a quarter in our money, now
worth between one and two cents in exchange. As a
consequence prices are grotesquely high in Germany
for the inhabitants, but grotesquely cheap for us who
have the privilege of buying marks with dollars. I
remember having a room at the Kaiserhof in Berlin
for $.65 a day and a wonderful dinner at one of the
best restaurants for $1.50.

Now let us run to the northern end of the Baltic,
where we find Finland, really a fourth Scandinavian
country in her cleanliness, her thrift, her capacity for
self-government and her self-sufficiency. For generations she had to grin-and-bear the rule of Russia; but
when Russia went finally mad, Finland shook herself
free and set up her own national housekeeping, of
which so far she has made a go. Well, when I was
there in January the dollar was worth thirty-four
marks (normally the Finnish mark is about twenty
cents) and living for visiting Americans was most
attractively cheap — twenty-five to forty marks for a
room at the best hotel and that hotel just as good as
you would find anywhere. Then, zip! up went the
mark and down the dollar until one dollar bought
only twenty marks. As prices were rising all the time,
it meant that the cost of living for the visiting Ameri-

can doubled in six weeks. Under these circumstances do you wonder that business in Europe has a sick headache most of the time? With such fluctuations how can anybody calculate out a business deal in advance? With prices and exchange looping-the-loop and going into spinning nose-dives like this, how can a poor merchant export timber and import American cotton unless he figures at least two hundred per cent profit no matter how exchange goes! A wonderful happy hunting ground is exchange — for the profiteer!

Then from Finland you cross the little Gulf of Finland and come to Esthonia and so down the east coast of the Baltic Sea. In distance you are only a few miles from well-to-do Scandinavia, but in communications, living conditions, political organization and human happiness you are on another planet. Of the general demoralization and disorganization I have already written you; now let me describe the fever chart of prices and exchange in tiny Esthonia. This fragile, baby republic has, of course, its paper money printing-press running full blast, printing its currency, of which the mark (normally worth about twenty cents) is the unit. The Government controls exchange and says the pound sterling is worth 270 Emk. and the dollar Emk. 70. I said control, but what I really mean is that the Government attempts to control exchange, fixing these artificial levels with fines and imprisonment for anybody trading at higher prices. Of course everybody does trade at higher prices and when I left the pound sterling fetched 585 Esthonian marks.

At this exchange the price of 'home' products such

as houses, rooms, servants, beef, pork, veal, butter, milk and potatoes was fantastically cheap for a foreigner, though very dear for the natives. For example a steak, filet mignon, or Vienersnitzel, would vary from $.12 to $.25 according to the restaurant. And this included potatoes, cooking and service. Then a breakfast of tea, white bread and butter and two boiled eggs — very large and very fresh ones — would come to only fifteen cents of our blessed money. And on my hotel bill I find one item of ten marks for hot roast beef and potatoes. About seven cents in U.S. money! Servants were from seventy-five cents a month to two dollars and a half — at the latter figure you would need a machine gun to keep the mob of applicants from breaking down your door. And good, faithful, hard-working servants, too. In passing I may add that a captain in the Esthonian army receives seven dollars a month (one thousand marks), about one tenth of what you say a kitchen maid gets in New York.

So much for home articles in Esthonia. Imported goods is another story. Miserable apples cost $.18 each. And even the little shrivelled-up native apples are eight marks apiece, for during the winter months it has been practically impossible to obtain fruit in Esthonia. Sugar was $.40 to $.60 a pound and other foreign articles still higher.

And then the dirt, discomfort, grit-in-the-food (they cook everything along with all the dirt it has acquired in transit), and the monotony quite indescribable. But, renting one's own house and keeping one's own servants, one could live extraordinarily cheaply and comfortably in Esthonia, for the basic commodities are so cheap that they overbalance the imported luxuries. For a thousand dollars a year you might have an excellent house (a fine old mansion of the Baltic nobility with lovely gardens, if you liked), plenty of servants and an abundance of simple, good food. Yes! for 140,000 Emk. annually a family of two or three could live magnificently in Esthonia — and it would all come to less than $1000 if one made a good bargain in exchange.

Did you think there were such places left on the globe?

But isn't it preposterous that prices and living conditions should present such contrasts around this little Baltic Sea? How artificial it all is! Lean, swampy Finland and rocky Scandinavia blessed with comfort and prosperity, while the more favored eastern shore, with a vast, rich hinterland stretching to the Black Sea and Asia behind them, are in want and disorder. All due to the character of the people. The frugal, strong, hard-headed Scandinavian makes his granite hills to bloom like a garden, while across the little salt lake called the Baltic the Russian peoples live in filth and misery above a fertile soil.

The prices faithfully register the difference — as always in this world you pay for what you get. For security, stable government, high prosperity, abundant luxury and easy living the cost is high, in Stockholm and Copenhagen as in New York. Yet everybody grumbles at everything, as in New York. But high as the prices are the people have the wherewithal to pay them (which on the whole seems also to be the case in America), whereas amid the ruins of that imperial sky-scraper that was built on sand, Russia, they can't even pay at the ridiculously low prices I have quoted.

On the other hand, the law of compensations also works out to the advantage of the visitor. On this side of the Baltic he can snuggle down to soft beds, fine bathrooms, rich meals; friends, dinner parties and dancing (if only I did!); theatres and operas (in unknown languages, however), newspapers (real ones, not the badly printed emotional little rags of Baltic Russia), and enticing shops. In short, all the pleasant accessories of opulent civilization. Yet your visitor finds it a bit flat (after a few days of thorough enjoyment) as compared with the living drama that goes on 'over there' on the borders of Russia. There, midst all the deterioration and degradation there is an immense flavor and interest to life. Beyond the precarious borders of these tiny new states the Red Experiment is in progress which is trying the nerves of the entire civilized world; within their petty borders the small tradespeople and the peasant proprietors have rudely pushed aside the land-owning aristocracy and the upper city bourgeoisie and taken all the power into their own hands. Underneath them the landless peasants and the city proletariat are probably dreaming reddish dreams. Yet for all their unattractiveness and all their blunders one cannot help admiring the courage with which Esths, Letts and Lithuanians have fought their little Republics into being. In spite of the general mess one feels that a strong new order of things is evolving. But the destruction of the old order is a cruel process to watch going on under one's own eyes. Everywhere culture, good breeding, education, good manners, good taste, intelligence and property rights are being greedily torn down by coarse hands and to the accompaniment of vulgar abuse. The new social order is petty, dreary, uncouth, venal, suspicious and very squabblish; yet one feels, if one has the American bias, that it is all leading somewhere and probably to greater heights than the old Baltic civilization. But it is going to take time — and lots of it!

I have pasted on an Esthonian 5 penni 'shinplaster.' It takes twenty-eight to thirty of them to buy one cent in American money, say three thousand of them to our dollar. Yet they actually buy things in Esthonia. Doesn't it give you some idea of the present poverty of these people? To complete the row I have also pasted on others.

With dear love

Your loving son

WARWICK

To Hon. W. Cameron Forbes

COPENHAGEN, DENMARK
May 19, 1920

DEAR GOVERNOR:

On my return here I find your letter of March 31 — I may explain that I use Copenhagen as my mail base and have mail forwarded to me only when I am sure of my 'line of communication.' Otherwise I am liable never to receive it, though of late conditions have improved in the rather wobbly palisade of little new countries which have been erected, or have erected themselves, about Red Russia.

With regard to your cousin: don't discourage anybody who wants to help out in the wholesale mess Eastern Europe finds itself in after the war and during the pigmy wars which have followed the main one. It is all needed; and private help should be increased now that diplomatically (for very good reasons) we are holding aloof from Europe's troubles.

In general I favor help through the regular organizations, Hoover's A.R.A. Children's Relief or the American Red Cross. It is easy enough to point out instances of mismanagement and extravagance in these organizations, but in the long run they accomplish the big and permanent results, whereas individual relief efforts are apt to fizzle out and often leave unpleasant misunderstandings and heartburnings behind them. Women generally want their own ventures in war relief, and the more gifted they are, the more they balk at the big organizations and the dreary character of the rank and file of these big organizations. But, as you know, second-rate people backed by powerful organization will generally achieve more than the most brilliant individuals working by themselves. Of course there are plenty of exceptions to prove this rule and sometimes the private effort fills a gap for which the big organization is not fitted, but in the long run I believe it best to put one's money on and into the big relief organizations whose weight and momentum are sufficient to carry them through the difficulties that usually finish off the best personal independent relief efforts. The relief problems of Europe (like its economic problems) are too gigantic to be tackled except wholesale. So my advice to friends is to back Hoover's and Davison's organizations if they want their dollars to do any real good — and jump on handy fellows like Eliot Wadsworth when things go wrong in these organizations, as they often do!

A lot of fine and energetic relief people, like Miss Anne Morgan for example, disagree violently with this point of view. They claim that the big organizations are cumbersome and wasteful and that the real good is done by direct and personal work carried on by small devoted groups outside of the 'Relief Trusts.' My answer is that the misery of Europe is too great to wait on scattered efforts at relief, and that if the big organizations are not all they should be, then we should put our efforts into reforming them rather than in competing with them on a tiny scale.

So if I had a sister or cousin with money and stamina, who was willing to put two or three years into European relief work (and I don't know a better occupation for such a girl), I should advise her to finish her regular nursing course (in the mean time giving money to Hoover's Children's Relief or to the Red Cross), sign up with the Red Cross for six months' work in that part of Europe for which she has special sympathy, and then either work on up in the Red Cross or branch off into some independent personal relief effort where she *had learned the local conditions at first hand*. Otherwise she runs the risk of returning from Europe rich in experience and disillusionment, but with little real good accomplished.

A BUSINESS TOUR OF BALTIC STATES

The sordid post-war conditions in the wrecked countries are little dreamt of by high-minded girls at home,
and the opportunities are very great for their fine
little individual relief efforts being exploited to serve
various local intrigues and ambitions — and purses!

Of course a high-bred and enthusiastic girl will
chafe tremendously under the American Red Cross.
She will find herself working under a rather scrubby
lot of Americans, with plenty of jealousy, incompetence and squabbles abroad in the organization, and
the petty-mindedness of her chiefs may drive her into
an explosive revolt unless she has lots of grit and
common-sense. But if she sticks it out and learns to
work with a big organization, she will do far more
good for her Poles (or any other people she may
select) than if she tries to go it on her own from the
very start. With six months' practical experience
behind her she is equipped to push ahead in the Red
Cross (and the Lord knows they need high grade personnel) or to step in and help out some crying local
need overlooked by the big relief organizations or for
which their methods are not adapted.

Of course this is not popular advice to give young
American girls, who usually want the glamour and
freedom of working with a tiny band of enthusiasts
in some personally selected field of war relief, but if
their real object is to fight war misery, they had better
join up with one of the big organizations, just as their
fathers, cousins and brothers had better contribute
their money through Hoover or Davison. At least
this is my opinion, based on four years of batting
about warring Europe in relief, war and diplomatic

jobs. With the big organizations there is discipline and responsibility; they should be under a constant fire of criticism to keep them healthy and active, but they should be supported.

For, since relief work in Europe has to be on a big scale, the same principles apply as in war and big business. Had we sent a hundred thousand volunteers to Europe to fight, their average quality would have been higher than the A.E.F.; their special efficiency perhaps greater and undoubtedly they would have died gallantly and splendidly, to the last man, somewhere between Meaux and Fort Valérien, but they would never have stopped William marching into Paris. Whereas the great machine under Pershing, clumsy as it was in many details, did — with a jolt!

And so now that it is a question of fighting typhus and famine in Europe, instead of the Prussian, it seems to me that a girl had better enlist for the work under Hoover or Davison, just as her brother had to enlist under Pershing and submit to the hard grind under 'Regulars' in place of enrolling in some band of free fighters, for whose dramatic efforts the efficiency of modern war leaves no room. The business of fighting the famine and stopping typhus in Europe is too grim for amateur enterprises which divert money and human talent every scrap of which is needed by the professional organizations.

You see I am really fanatical on the subject! Whatever lingering doubts I may have had were dispelled by watching Colonel Ryan and the American Red Cross wade in and knock the typhus epidemic in Esthonia and among the forlorn remnants of Judenitch's army, on the head. He is efficient and energetic. With the A.R.C. behind him, he cleaned up that situation as quick and slick as one could want — and the conditions among that typhus-stricken, rotting army at Narva were unbelievable. I have seen few worse sights than Narva in January of this year before the A.R.C. got going; or few more encouraging sights than the way the misery and suffering melted away after Ryan got to work.

Sincerely yours
WARWICK GREENE

To Lieutenant-Colonel E. T. Dawley [1]

COPENHAGEN, DENMARK
May 20, 1920

DEAR DAWLEY:

Your letters — one dated October 14, one November 13, and your wedding announcement — have finally all reached me.

First my warmest congratulations on your marriage and my greetings to Mrs. Dawley, whom I am looking forward to meeting and becoming acquainted with when I finally reach home. It was a great disappointment to me to miss the wedding. It is splendid and I envy you heartily.

Now as to my own doings since I last saw you. To put it in a word, I am still wandering about Europe, mostly in these parts and in the Baltic 'Provinces' or 'States' as you best like to call them. Just before I

[1] See letter of July 27, 1919.

left the Army I was asked to undertake a certain matter. I accepted and have been busy on it ever since. However, I am hoping to finish up with it before long and get home — I have not seen those good United States for over four years. Long enough to be away at one stretch, I'm thinking.

Perhaps you may be interested in hearing about some of our common friends in the Baltic. I have just lunched with Gade, who got in from Libau via British destroyer this morning, and we have been chatting over Baltic matters. He has left the Service and is on his way home. He has done a good job.

And since lunch I have been talking to Prince Lieven, who is here waiting for a Lettish visé in order to return to his own country. He has been here for some weeks patiently waiting. Gade tells me he thinks that the visé will now be granted — it was one of the last things he took up with Meirovics before leaving Riga. Pretty rotten way of treating the Prince, 'n'est-ce pas?' when one remembers the stand he took last spring during the Balt coup, as well as the man's part he played in recapturing Riga from the Bolshevists.

Esthonia, as you know, made peace with the Bolshevists, the first of the border states to do so.' Consequently she expects to reap lots of trade advantages — how much she will ultimately get out of it remains to be seen.

Törnisson returned to the Prime Ministership, and lately has also had to take on the portfolio of Industry. He is probably the only man able to clean the grafters out of that bureau and perhaps get a bit of trade started.

Laidoner got out. The Social Democrats were too strong for him. His departure was sugar-coated with a Lieutenant-Generalship. Rink is now very much to the fore and is really the head of the Army.

In Riga they are pegging along. The elections turned out fairly well. The Social Democrats can be outvoted by the other parties combined. Ulmannis is still Prime Minister, but is not expected to last. They are negotiating with the Bolshevists for peace and their Peace Commission has been at Moscow for some weeks. Negotiations are reported to be going very slowly.

Of course the great event is the Polish offensive. Personally I am leary of it. In the first place, I don't think Poland is in any conditon to stand much strain being put on it. And in the second place, the penetration of Polish troops so deeply into genuine Russian territory is apt to turn the war into a national one and rally to the support of the Bolshevists elements which would otherwise oppose them. Had its effect been to crack up the Bolshevist Government at Moscow immediately, it might have finished with it. But it didn't do that. And I am thinking that it may provoke the kind of boomerang its supporters are not looking for.

In short, while I was an 'interventionalist' last summer, I am no longer. It had to be done then or else Russia left to evolve her own salvation. Picking at the scab with Kolchaks, Judenitches, Denikins, Petlouras and Poles only makes the abscess worse.

There were two remedies, to cut it out firmly and sharply with a good surgeon's knife, or to allow rest and good food to cure the patient naturally. Neither was adopted and the picking at the abscess continues.

Sincerely yours

WARWICK GREENE

From Greene's portfolio of miscellaneous writings

BERLIN, *August* 18, 1920

He was a little hobbling man, dressed in remnants of 'Feld-Grau.' His face seemed of cold clay and where his eyes had been, merely two unintelligent holes were left. A dirty pasteboard sign across his shabby breast signified in German that he had been totally blinded in the war. It was mid-August in post-war Berlin. A malevolent sun dragged its way across searing skies. Warm and jaded Berliners were far too torpid to respond to the scores of aged or war-wrecked human beings that begged along the dirty streets.

So lean, indeed, were the pickings on Unter-den-Linden that afternoon, and long the waits between occasional doles...

Yet after dark the glare of pleasure would spring up the length and breadth of that avenue, and restaurant and dance-hall would rock with the spendings of the 'Schiebers' (war profiteers) who had snatched hasty fortunes from their country's need and were more hastily spending them, ever with an anxious eye on the Red Tornado whirling down on them from Russia, that, if it came, would scatter their paper fortunes like dried leaves before the opened doorways of hell. Yes! when the sun had gone under and the heated night darkness had descended on the city, the Schiebers, the raucous stranger within their gates and their trooping harlots would crowd about the pleasures of the table, the bottle and the bed — while the slums of Berlin went to bed with gnawing stomachs, and the waifs of the war, gathered again into their slum homes, would count the occasional one-mark note that had fluttered into their grasp. But be sure of one thing — from every one of those lean hearts from the jammed slums, a prayer to Lenin was rising to the August heavens!

As brazen dusk settled down on Unter-den-Linden, a boy of eight or nine, with bare legs and bare feet and two shredded garments, appeared. The ears of the soldier, already sharpening at the expense of the lost eyes, quickly picked his footsteps out of the multitudinous shuffling of the crowd and something like a smile came over that face of putty.

The youngster trotted up, with bright eyes shining out of his dirty blond face and eager questioning on his lips, which died to disappointment when the tale of the meagre earnings of the day was mumbled.

But presently they are off, wavering down the street, the soldier's arm about the neck of the lad who guides the pair through the traffic. From time to time they stop and stand in begging attitudes, hoping for softening hearts somewhere in that August crowd. But no bits of paper descend, while darkness is beginning to mug up the streets.

At last they give up hope and turn up a side street. Here a passing honest Haus-Frau finds a fifty-pfennig bit (whose purchasing power in 1920 Berlin is merely a speck!) and then waddles on. The shaver props the young soldier up in a doorway, darts into a near-by shop and emerges with a broken bit of bread. They chatter together in subdued friendliness while they munch the shared black crusts. Presently the boy reaches up and arranges the bit of soiled black and white ribbon in the soldier's buttonhole. Perhaps he hears, for the manyeth time, of how the Iron Cross was won in France or Russia. Perhaps he hears only oaths or obscenity against all authority — a foul curse on all kings and capitalists.

They resume the way, boyish strength supporting a bit of lost and battered young manhood. But the affection between the two lights the dreary monotony of the street, for all who have eyes to see or hearts to feel. They disappear, headed towards that grey Berlin, nearly breadless, almost workless, that laps its grimy immensity about this little smear of cheap fashion, this slough of squandering, that festers where aristocratic Berlin once played its part and where bronze Hohenzollerns (oh! many of them), black as iron, look down uncomprehending on ruin. Indeed, they that live by the sword shall perish by the sword; but with them shall go down to the houses of death and mutilation, the Youth of their race.

Back in these endless brick jungles, where the cost of war is counted with each breath that is drawn, the 'junked' youth and the skinny boy will be among their own again — where all hearts are beating time with the drums of Moscow, where all ears are listening for the Red guns that are rumbling forward over the ruins of Poland.

V

NORTHERN ITALY AFTER THE WAR

From a Diary

Ran across Melvin Hall and lunched with him at the Cercle Interallié. Lunch over, Hall departs for England by airplane.

In the evening to the Gare de Lyon to catch the Italian Express, Mrs. Wolcott, her son Lyman Bass and his wife, and little Susan Bass, all at station; also Mrs. Schoelkopp, who accompanies us. Finally the flutter and confusion is over and the train departs, bearing Mrs. Wolcott, Mrs. Schoelkopp, Susan and myself, and leaving Mr. and Mrs. Bass on the platform. Poor Susan, of course, is in tears at leaving her mother.

Saturday, October 2, 1920

Morning finds us swiftly running along the base of Swiss mountains whose upper slopes are drowned in mist and rain. The drenched pastures and orchards are vividly green. Later, the country widens out a bit and we slip past Lausanne and through the wet have a glimpse of Lake Geneva, usually so bright and sunshiny. The region is well known to me, as I was often here in Rockefeller Foundation's days, little suspecting that near Lausanne and Vevey, where I often used to go, was then living a shabby Russian refugee, spending fourteen hours a day in public

237

libraries, known as Vladimir Ulianoff, who today is shaking the world as Lenin. As in those days I met many of the Russian and Polish refugees who thronged Switzerland, I probably heard the name, but it made no impression on me.

By and by we begin to ascend the Rhone Valley, still wrapped in mist. A touch of Italy appears in the architecture; then we plunge into the longest tunnel in the world, the Simplon (over twelve miles long and at one point seven thousand feet underground), and emerge into Italy.

But sunny Italy, no! A cold rain is falling and only the lower flanks of the vast mountains that hem us in are visible. Down we go rattling between the glistening rocks, swinging over great bridges, the atmosphere warming up as we descend, but the rain ever thickening. Mulberry trees and vineyards, Italian villages, Italian faces, the Italian touch; then Lake Maggiore. But today no turquoise sheet of water! The little we see of it under the driving rain squalls is a slate green. How disappointing! Especially for Mrs. Wolcott, who loves Italy with all the strength of her robust soul, and who has brought her little chick, Susan Bass, down to thrill and delight her with glowing Italy bursting into view at the foot of the Alps. But today Italy refuses to glow, and Susan — whose fourteen-years-old mind has been crammed with England and France during the past few weeks, with National Galleries, Louvres and Châteaux of the Loire, and who is mourning her mother left on the platform at Paris — refuses to be thrilled.

By and by the mountains dwindle down to foothills, widen out, and we slide into the plain that lies between the Alps and the Apennines. Then in quick succession: Milan, Brescia, Verona, and Vincenza. Cities to stir the imagination, but all we see are platforms, wet people and famous names on dripping statues.

Finally a rumble over a long causeway; the guard yells 'Venezia,' and out we get. The usual battle over baggage finished, we emerge from the station to find salt water lapping the station's steps and gondolas awaiting. Though Venice is huddled up in night, yet its charm penetrates even our tired understanding, as we slip through its water streets. It is raining no longer and we are in a city of strange, if shabby, beauty that seems to grow right out of the waters of the sea. Its charm is an old story, but each new visitor feels it afresh.

We slide through many water alleys and then emerge into a stately water avenue, the Grand Canal, and down to another building whose stone steps are also lapped by salt water; the Grand Hotel, where we are to stay.

Mrs. Wolcott is fully radiant to be again in her beloved Venice, but Susan is too crammed with travel, new ideas and heavy travel dinners to respond.

Sunday, October 3, 1920

We gondolier to the Piazza and see Saint Mark's and the Ducal Palace, which we are to visit many times during our short stay, and as I mean to write of them again — as well as of what lies within them —

and of the Church of Frari, and expeditions to the Lido, and gondola trips up and down the Grand Canal, and the Church of the Miracoli, and all the other wonders of this light and fantastic city, which has thrilled every visitor for ten centuries — and which Ruskin, Browning, Shelley, Byron, Goethe, Wagner, Pater, Howells, Symonds, Duse, and hosts more of imaginative people have tried to render with words, music and the brush — I shall hurry along now, skip Sunday and take you to:

Saturday, October 9, 1920

— when you see us bundling over to Mestre on the mainland. Mrs. Schoelkopp had departed that morning for Paris, which is disappointing, as she is a very agreeable person and we shall miss her; especially Susan, who has warmed up to her enormously. Mrs. Wolcott and I spend our time in acrimonious battles over Venice, she, steeped in the Byron-Browning traditional place, and I fancying that I represent a newer generation which finds those old worthies have their place, but hankers for a fresh interpretation of Venice. Mrs. Schoelkopp quarrels with nobody's theory of art, and tones down too much intellectual discussion with a real interest in bonnets and gowns, a very soft heart for beggars and people in trouble and a genuine love for children. Susan, who is a kind, sweet little duckling, finds her most sympathetic, while Mrs. Wolcott and myself, with our fights over Teutons, Tintoretto and Titian and our wrangles over Doges and Donatello, must fatigue her greatly.

NORTHERN ITALY AFTER THE WAR

At the station a Spa automobile awaits us with a chinless chauffeur, whose receding forehead contains about five small cells of grey matter, as we later find. Off we whirl across the Venetian Plain, following up the Brenta River, passing old Venetian villas where the declining aristocrats of that sumptuous city spent their summers in the eighteenth century. Mrs. Wolcott loves even the eighteenth century in Italy, but I do not. It was a great century in England and France, but can be quickly skipped in Italy. We stopped for an instant to look at the vast Villa Pisani at Stra, on which the greedy eye of Napoleon happened to light, and which he promptly secured as a palace for his Viceroy of Italy, Eugène Beauharnais. What an eye he had for plunder, that Buccaneer from Corsica!

And so to Castelfranco, where we explored the dim church that contains an enchanting picture by Giorgione. A great age that, when an enthusiastic young artist could paint himself in shining armor as a knight of the Church at the feet of his lady love, disguised as a charming Madonna — and make the picture one of the world's masterpieces!

The sun has come out in full force and Italy puts on her bluest skies as we rush onward across the plain. The great ramp of the Alps marches towards us, valleys and ridges articulating with magnificent light and shadow effects as we draw nearer. Out from the mass stands Mount Grappa, a huge brown bastion of earth and rock boldly protruding forth as though an Alp wished to leave his brothers and find more elbow-room in the plain. No wonder it was a vital point during the war and that there were so many battles for its possession.

In its shadow fought Italians and Englishmen and Frenchmen coming from the south; and from the north, Germans, Austrians, Magyars, Slavs, Yugo-Slavs and Czecho-Slovaks.

Bassano we find with its walls and roofs still nicked by shell and bomb. Also an excellent lunch, really Italian, with Rizzoto, and 'polenta' and fried fishes and the inevitable veal and foaming Verona of the best ruby color, on which Mrs. Wolcott and I dote.

Then to the very foot of Grappa, where we look up at the many military roads and trails that zigzag up and down; and winding lines of jagged trenches and galleries and dug-outs in the rock; and places where the great military cableways ran from crag to crag.

We turn to the left skirting the foot of the mountains to Marostica, where we attack the mountain over a road that was an important military supply artery. Up we go out of the plain in a great swoop, doubling on our path every two minutes on hairpin turns. The windpipe of the automobile has some obstruction so that the Chinless One must pump gasoline by hand, at the same time that he is sounding the horn and steering round breathless curves on the edge of many hundred feet of nothing — occupation for three hands, not for two. When Mrs. Wolcott has confidence, she has it very completely; when she has not, she has none whatever. Confidence in the Chinless One she lost at the first glance at him in Mestre; so she is soon in a great panic as we whirl around the precipice edges, the chauffeur concentrated on pumping gasoline rather than on steering. So presently we stop; Susan is pried out of her seat in front, which I take in order to pump gasoline, leaving the Chinless One both hands and all his small brain to concentrate on steering us around the airy turns.

Now we have climbed the first range, leaving the dust and warmth of the plain behind, and are on the grey stony plateau of Asiago. Heavy battles were fought here. Trenches and wires run across the bleak landscape; the little towns are heaps of powdered brick and stone.

We come to the city of Asiago, in the heart of the plateau, a strategic key position of the fighting. The Asiago that was is flatter than Ypres or Lens, but here there is no waiting for outside help. No. Everybody to the last tot is busy sawing, hammering, hauling and building. Already a good part of the city is rebuilt, luckily for the most part on the traditional architectural lines of the region.

And here I may say that this was our experience throughout these mountains — everywhere the sturdy mountaineers are rebuilding, so that in a year more the towns and villages will show scarcely a trace of bombardment.

From the plateau we climb again. This time to the very clouds. A bony ridge stands behind the Asiago Plateau, for whose possession much human blood was shed. Through the long pass that we climb and then descend, the traces of war are incessant.

An interesting district known as the home of the 'Setti Communi' or Seven Communes of Teutonic blood who inhabited it. Tradition says they are descended from the Cimbri, the remnants of whom took refuge in the mountains after the Roman General Marius had defeated them in the plain below. In any case, here is a Teutonic enclave in the Italian population, and the blend of Gothic and Italian blood, combined with the vigorous life of mountain, has produced a very good-looking race. We are enthusiastic over the handsome people we pass, Susan especially so. Now that we are in the real mountains, with clear air and fresh scenery, she has lost the lethargy of Venice and is full of interest and enjoyment. She loves the mountains and finds these mountaineers, vigorous and comely, very refreshing after so many canvases and statues. Susan is quite right!

Darkness comes on us amid a great mass of mountains, but presently a tremendous radiance of light appears far down the valley. It is Trento, but we cannot account for such an illumination. The chauffeur thinks the city must be on fire, and I am inclined to agree with him. Of course, Mrs. Wolcott scouts the idea, but can't give an explanation. Presently we run into the city and find it a-flutter with the green, red, and white of Italy's gaudy tricolor hung from every window, draped on every façade, and flying from every flagpole; while the streets are ablaze with electric lights, candles and colored lanterns. Trento, it seems, is celebrating its formal annexation to Italy, which takes place tomorrow. No wonder the city seemed on fire!

After hours of running through wild and desolate mountains, scarred everywhere with the marks of war, it rather takes one's breath away to dash out of

244

the dark into this well-built handsome city, a blaze of light and color, entirely undamaged by the war, and the streets thronged with a rejoicing crowd.

Up we drive to the great Trentino Hotel, its façade blazing, a band crashing away before it, and marvellous uniformed creatures in three-cornered hats on guard at the door. Italian Generals and Senators dash up in cars, two to the minute. Three tired and dusty Americans cut very little figure. Rooms! 'Mon Dieu,' says the porter, 'all the rooms have been engaged for three weeks, and the Italian Government has requisitioned every hotel in Trento.'

It is the same story at each hotel; so we return to the Grand Hotel, Trentino. I give fifty lire to the porter with the result that some Socialist Deputy, who has carelessly left the hotel to stroll about the street, is dispossessed, and Mrs. Wolcott and Susan installed in his place. Later on, a small room on the top floor is found for me, and a table-top in the hall for the chauffeur.

For all its external glitter and imposing dimensions, the hotel is wretched. The huge rooms are dirty; the service most indifferent. On my floor there is an enormous bathroom equipped with the most modern plumbing from Switzerland — but nothing works. The bathtub is full of broken crockery; in some of the fixtures the water will run in, but not out; in others it would not run out if it could run in. In my bed the sheets have done duty many times since their last trip to the laundry.

I interrogate the manager, whom I discover to be an Austrian, 'Why are things so bad?' His shrug is eloquent. Translated into words it says: 'Don't you see, you poor deluded fellow countrymen of Herr Wilson and disciple of self-determination, its all *your* fault! *Why* did you give our beautiful clean Austrian city to these dirty Italians?'

The dining-room, as well as the adjoining corridors, are in the throes of preparations for the great banquet tomorrow. However, we get a good dinner. The room is full of uniforms and glitter. One large table is occupied by an Italian General of the Pershing type and his staff, and the other by a general of the Tasker Bliss type. The first, I believe, was the General who captured Trento; the second has been the military governor during the occupation period. The verandas are alive with natty young Italian swells in uniforms.

Bang! Whang! goes the band outside, crashing into the Italian National Anthem. Everybody stands at attention, Generals and waiters, Aides and Americans. At its conclusion the crowd roars a happy, happy roar. The city rocks with music and excitement — only the Austrian manager looks sardonically on like a misanthrope watching the antics of children.

Sunday, October 10, 1920

Last night was only the preliminary, today is the great day of the fête, the celebration of the formal annexation of the Trentino to Italy. This handsome city, cuddled down in its valley in the midst of mighty mountains, that was a nest of concentration for Austrian armies attacking Italy during the war, today gives itself completely over to the joy of becoming Italian. Everybody is in the streets and everybody seems happy. The 'dirty Italians' seem popular with everybody except the Austrian hotel manager. Where the other Austrian sympathizers are I don't know; hidden in the deepest cellars, I suspect, for this holiday mob would like nothing better than a few Austrian victims to top off the festivities with.

Yet they tell us that to the north, at Bozen and other places where German blood is in the ascendancy, the cities are today hung with black. So says the manager, and so also the 'Morning Post' correspondent, whose clipping on the annexation of the Southern Tyrol I enclose.

Yet, be that as it may, Trento seems wholly happy; cannons are banging, soldiers marching, Senators and Socialists embracing, Generals and pacifists hobnobbing. Everywhere there are bands and banners, flags and fireworks, speeches and sputter. We spend a couple of hours enjoying it.

And so we leave rejoicing Trento and roll on the rest of the day through a jumble of mountain country. At times we are in long valleys that are rich and green with pastures; at times on fertile river bottom lands where corn makes a try at mountaineering; at times on the flank of mountains which are copper green with vineyards; at times in brave groves of highland chestnut trees. Everywhere the architecture is a happy blend of Alpine and Italian styles; everywhere are sleek cattle and tanned and healthy peasant faces. No matter how deep you penetrate into the Alps, you find a mountain world that has long since

247

been tamed and humanized. There is nothing really wild as in the Rockies.

War has marched through this mountain land of the Southern Tyrol, but only where it halted has it done much damage. You pass a score of villages where the sole trace of war is an occasional roll of barbed wire; then you come to a village where two or three houses have had their crowns crumpled in by shells; and then to a village where Mars sat down very heavily, indeed, and left only a pile of splintered brick, stone, and tile, with charred beams, to tell of his revels. But always as at Asiago, hammer and trowel are busy.

By link after link of the winding road we lift ourselves to the great Broconne Pass. Up from the vivid green fields and succulent pastures; up from the rusty vineyards; up through splendid forest of oak and on pine and larch; and finally up to the great stony pastures fit only for goats, that end in the stark rocks of the final ridges and peaks.

Tucked away in a fold of the bleak pass is an inn. Here we have lunch in a clean room, with clean coarse linen, and clean cutlery — the first clean knife and fork I have seen in Italy. The outer room is full of pedlars, mountaineers and goatherds, and is very warm and friendly, but another room is made ready for us where we can lunch in state and secretion. Lunch is excellent — wholesome bread, new butter, smoking omelettes from eggs the hen has just hopped off, good cheese, and the best of wines. We are served by the daughter of the house, with hair like new, yellow flax, and looking as if she had just stepped out of Grimms' fairy tales. The son of the house, who helps with our automobile, is a ruddy shepherd lad such as the Bible says David was. Through the window the sky is a turmoil of mountain peaks. How cold those Dolomite pinnacles look, but how exciting to climb!

Susan Bass, surfeited with art and civilization, takes it all in — the clean bare rooms, the appetizing plain food, the atmosphere of good will and hospitality, and the friendly simplicity of the people — and says she wishes to stay a week here; that she loves the mountains and the keen cold air, adores the food and the people, and particularly wants to climb the peaks in the neighborhood.

And but for a very firm grandparental hand laid on those foolish whims, I believe she would still be there. I sympathize with her.

After lunch our host tells of war — how his little property was stormed and taken by Italian and Austrian forces in turn; how all the houses were shelled, the barns burned, the cattle killed, and the movable property looted; how his first two sons were killed quite unnecessarily; how he, born on a strip of soil unluckily colored Austria on the maps, was hustled over to an internment camp in Sardinia; how he came back after the war to his heap of ruins and his lost sons, and painfully rebuilt. 'And who will repay me for all I have lost?' he plaintively asked. Like the rest of these border people, what to him are Italy or Austria, except two rival powers forever fighting for these mountains? How they envy the Swiss, where Germans, Italians and French, having combined into a mountain republic, keep themselves out of European wars. To all intents and purposes the Austrian and Italian Tyrol, the Bavarian Alps, and the Savoie district of France, are parts of Switzerland; and I have seldom met a mountaineer who did not wish that the Swiss Republic might embrace the entire Alps in its protection.

Well, lunch over, and the landlord's tale of the war finished, Susan is vigorously yanked away from the lure of the simple life in the mountains, and off we go, down, down, down, with smoking brakes.

Night overtakes us at a place with the operatic name of Fiera di Primiro. We put up at a large Alpine inn. The town is full of drunks who roister about the streets until early morning. Whether they are of Italian blood and celebrating the town's annexation to Italy, or of Teutonic blood and mourning its loss to the venerable wreck of Austria, or simply drinking bad luck both to Italy and to Austria, does not appear.

Monday, October 11

By the early morning light Fiera is an enchanting place. Enormous mountains shut in most of the sky, but what does appear is deep, blood blue; a gurgling ice-cold river runs through the fragrant pastures; plump and placid cows graze within a few feet of the village streets; and the architecture of the town is a handsome Alpine, yet with a pleasant touch of Italy and Venice brought up from the plains below.

But we have a long delay obtaining benzine, which is a rare and rationed commodity in Italy today. The

NORTHERN ITALY AFTER THE WAR

sole proprietor of the article has not yet recovered
from last night's spree, but abundant lire finally induce
him, though grumbling, to leave his alcoholic bed.

At last we are off. And still in a world of endless
mountains. Soon we hoist ourselves up to another
pass, the Rolle, to Susan's great delight, her spirits
going up in proportion as we mount, and Mrs. Wolcott's going down, as she does not like the cold. In
this pass, the burned inn has not yet been rebuilt; its
blackened ruins look very desolate in the bleak
Alpine pasture. There is no sign of rebuilding.
Probably the entire family were blotted out by the
war.

This pass behind us, we let ourselves down into
more narrow valleys, warm and green. We are now
in the midst of the wonderful Dolomites, and on the
great Dolomite road, built by Austria in 1908, and
now an involuntary present to Italy.

We pass the ruins of the castle of Andraz, perched
on an inaccessible rock. Once it was the lair of a
robber band and was destroyed by some condottiere
soldier of Venice or Milan sent up here to put an end
to its activities. During the late war it apparently
sheltered a very comfortable machine-gun nest, from
which the main road could be peppered for several
miles in each direction.

And now a tremendous climb up and over the
Pordoy Pass, nearly seventy-five hundred feet above
sea level. It puts more roses into Susan's cheeks, and
Mrs. Wolcott dons an enormous motor coat. The
Italian Government should certainly heat these
mountain passes if they wish tourists to come!

251

Barbed wire and trenches criss-cross the pass and run up to the snow-line.

From Pordoy we dipped down into a valley where war has laid a smashing hand on every village. In the valleys every house and church is flat, and to the edge of breathless precipices cling fantastic ruins. What a fantastic war it must have been, shelling from one huge range to the other, with burning villages lighting up the dusk of the very deep valleys! I saw a little of the war in the Vosges in 1918, but after all they are small hills compared to these Dolomite Alps.

In the centre of a valley stands a church on a promontory, whose steeple has been cleanly knocked off by a shell. Otherwise the building is undamaged. A beautiful shot! I remark that the gunner who knocked it off probably won a carton of cigarettes, or made the battery set him up to wine at that evening's mess. Mrs. Wolcott rebukes my levity, especially as the shot obviously had come from some Italian batteries we had passed. She has the orthodox view that only 'Huns' do such things. My stars above!

We skirt the foot of the famous Col di Lana, a mountain which occupied a strategic position and was strongly fortified by the Austrians. So the Italians — who are magnificent engineers and workmen, as you know — slowly burrowed under, loaded the burrows with dynamite and T.N.T. and neatly blew off the top of the mountains with all the Austrians thereon, much as in the Philippines we used to put a sliver from a dynamite stick under a giant anthill and scatter sand and dead ants over the landscape.

As you look at the great crater at the top of the

252

Col di Lana, you feel sure that the mountain is an old volcano, for it seems incredible that tiny man could conjure up such an explosion. In 1917 I saw the tremendous craters on the Messines Ridge (while they were still comparatively fresh and very smelly), and after the Armistice, the prodigious craters at Berry-au-Bac in the Champagne, but they are pock-marks compared with the Col di Lana.

And now up to our third pass this day — the famous Falzarego. And here we have a marvellous panorama, every horizon clouded with the peaks of the fantastic Dolomite Alps. How they flash and burn in the sunlight, these pinnacles of iridescent limestone! All the known colors are there: purples and pinks, blues and greens, dead whites, rosy reds and saffrons, sparkling and gleaming with different bursts of color at every new shift of sun and cloud.

The pass is very interesting. Crowded with trenches and rusting wire. Guns and shells are still lying about. On either side the grey fields run up vast spires of chromatic rock, powdered with the everlasting snow. If you examine these peaks closely, you see that up to their very tip-top they are honey-combed with rock galleries, dug-outs and machine-gun nests and gun positions. To the rear of these peaks, protected from hostile gunfire from the opposite range, are wooden barracks and shacks, weathered to grey, and looking like swallows' nests clinging to the eaves of titanic roofs.

Susan is fascinated and longs, audibly, to climb up and explore, as I do too. Our childish desires are sternly repressed by grandmother, and we descend to the warmth of the valleys, to tea at Cortina, where, beside a blazing fire, Mrs. Wolcott gradually thaws out.

Cortina used to be a great summer resort. Today it seems rather melancholy. During the summer, some of the great hotels are again tentatively open; at the time of our visit they had tightly closed again. It will take some time for the effects of war to pass from these mountains.

And then down a magnificent road — all have been magnificent, but this fairly surpasses itself for the breadth of its way, the hardness and smoothness of its surface, and the splendors of its masonry in bridges, parapets and retaining walls. The Roman traditions of solid building have never left Italy. Today the Italians are still par excellence the stone-masons and road-builders of the world.

Down from the mountains, down to the foothills, and out into the warm and close air of the plain. We pass the night at Vittorio, famous as the scenes of the final Italian victory over the Austrians. The town, however, escaped serious damage. This is a splendidly built place at the very feet of the Alps. We remember it for the affable proprietor, and for the dreariest and most garish of modern cheap Italian hotels.

Tuesday, October 12

We race over the hot plain, pulling up finally at Udine to send a telegram and to look at the charming bit of Venetian architecture at the Piazza. From the hill close by, Attila is said to have watched the burning of the Roman town Aquileia, whose refugees were later to found Venice in a lagoon.

And now we see the Isonzo River, the scene of so much fighting. We are in a region of blazing sunshine and barren hills, where every village and town has been blotted out, as on the Somme or in the Champagne. And so into Gorizia, which shows considerable war damage, but is still inhabitable, and is carrying on business much as usual. You will remember that it was originally in Austrian territory, that it was captured by the Italians in 1916, and lost by them to the Austrians after the disaster at Caporetto in the fall of 1917. I remember being in Switzerland in 1916 when the news of the taking of Gorizia came to Berne. The Austrians were greatly depressed. 'Its capture lies on our heart,' they said.

At first Mrs. Wolcott refuses to believe that the town is Gorizia, as some gushing propagandist, who had addressed the Colony Club in New York, had persuaded these gullible ladies that Gorizia lay in the very peak of the Alps — probably to make it sound more romantic to her audience. So when we come to a Latin town, half-wrecked by the war, squatting in the hot sun on tiny hills beside a slow-flowing river not two hundred feet above sea level, Mrs. Wolcott refuses to believe that it is Gorizia. The gushing propagandist must have been right; the chauffeur and I are certainly wrong!

Susan, brought back again to heat and to dusty civilization, and longing for the cold splendors of the Dolomites, is a bit sick. We enquire for the best hotel. We are directed to a certain one which turns out to be a pension. The landlady, though surprised at transients, soon makes Susan comfortable. I ask her, 'But they told me this was the best hotel in Gorizia.' 'The best hotel *morally*,' she answers; 'the others are bigger and finer, but the goings-on! "Ach lieber Gott, diese immoralische Italienische leute!"' 'Why didn't you follow your "moral" Austrian army away, then!' I answered, but she merely fixes me with a look that lowers the temperature in the room at least ten degrees.

What would become of wars if the women on both sides didn't keep up the hatred?

Susan soon bucks up, and we go to one of the 'immoral' Italian hotels for an excellent lunch.

We leave sweltering Gorizia behind, and climb the famous Carso, a rugged blistering plateau, where more Italian and Austrian blood was poured out than on all the other fronts combined. For the spectacular war in the rocks and the eternal snows of the Alps was comparatively bloodless. But here on the Carso, parched under an eternal sunshine, it was bitter. Inch by inch, yard by yard, in bloody offensives, the Italians slowly pressed forward. The waterless Carso was the key to Trieste; once it had fallen into Italian hands, Trieste was theirs. And so throughout 1916 and 1917 they hammered away slowly, crawling forward — and then overnight came the disaster at Caporetto, and the entire Italian force had to be rushed back to the Piave, almost to Venice, before they held.

Caporetto was a result of Ludendorf turning his attention to Italy; he planned one of his able offensives and despatched some German divisions in order to make sure that it would be a success.

We descend from the Carso, the Monfalcone, and follow the Adriatic south. The sky is burning blue, and the country a blaze of tropical sunshine.

We pass the ruined castle of Duino — a splendid and well-preserved mediæval structure until the guns of this war scattered its stones over the hillside — climb some heights and look down on Trieste, sitting on a long curve of the coast. A wonderfully handsome city in a gorgeous panorama. And a splendidly built city it turns out to be as we ride in. Fine walls, spacious buildings, streets paved with great flagstones, as in Roman times.

But the hotels are crammed. We go from one to another of the best ones in vain. Porters simply laugh insolently in our faces when we enquire for rooms. I wish you had some idea of after-war manners in these parts of Europe!

At last an enormous bribe induces the porter in a wretched fourth-rate hotel to let us in as a great privilege; Mrs. Wolcott and Susan share one dirty room; I have a filthy cubbyhole under the stairs. All the call bells are out of order, and no servant makes any pretence of coming no matter how loudly or how long you call. If you do collar one and bribe him or her to stop long enough to listen to your request, he or she departs with your bribe and never comes back. No wonder we see that sinister name Lenin written up on the walls everywhere we go. You can feel the Bolshevist undercurrent rather strongly in Italy of today, although it seems to be lessening.

As Mrs. Wolcott says, the insolence and indifference of the servants is so monumental that you almost forget to be angry. To add to her trials, a large party of Croats are drinking, playing cards, and quarrelling at the top of their lungs in Croatian in the adjoining room, separated from Mrs. Wolcott and Susan by a very thin pine door. Croats, as you probably know, are merely another set of minor ruffians that we have liberated in Europe and allowed to set up their crazy Government under the banner of 'Self-Determination.'

The final straw is that there is no running water, the city waterworks being turned on only for two hours a day. Why this is so, nobody can explain. But for twenty-two hours a day the city of two thousand people is waterless except for what they have stored up in pitchers and cans.

Wednesday, October 13

Another gorgeous day. I cannot describe to you how regal Trieste looks set in her great amphitheatre of hills, with the violet Adriatic at her feet.

And now we turn homeward. Back by Monfalcone, across the Isonzo, and then the Tagliamento; Latisana, Portugruaro, Oderzo; across the Piave at Ponte di Piave; finally Treviso and Mestre. From Duino to the Piave we follow the line of the Italian retreat after Caporetto in the fall of 1917. A terrible affair — an entire army racing back to save itself from annihilation, with the German and Austrian wolves ever on their flanks, coming down from the mountains to the northward. All the hard-won positions of Gorizia and the Carso, which had taken many months to gain, had to be given up in as many hours. And the entire Front we had seen up in the Alps crumpled up in a few days. An appalling affair; I remember it well in France where we were negotiating with the French over our Aviation program, when everything had to be dropped, as the French Staff was entirely occupied with the hurried transport of British and French troops to Italy to save the day. At the Piave the Italians finally stuck. Ludendorf then pulled his German divisions out of Italy and hurled them on some other front.

Thereafter the Italian Front settled down to quiet until the final victory and rout of the Austrians in 1918.

Mrs. Wolcott thinks I am too hard on the Italians in saying that they and the Austrians were the tail-enders of the war; but, as a matter of fact, neither were to be compared with the English, French or Germans for staying qualities. In spite of their five hundred thousand dead, one never felt that the Italian soldiers had their hearts in this war the way the French or English did. They had a fairly lively hatred against the Austrians, but were quite calm about the Germans. The Socialists were always against the war, and were very powerful in Italy. In many ways it is extraordinary that they stuck as well as they did.

It is a wonderful day and we run very slowly so as to take in the full flavor of the country. Also so that Mrs. Wolcott and I can chat freely between the front and rear seats — I still have to pump gasoline, as the car's windpipe is still clogged.

LETTERS OF WARWICK GREENE

To the north lies the long wall of the Alps, stretching in a solid mass to Munich in Germany. It has ever been the barrier between Italy and the Northern races, and I do not suppose that the fighting of this war is by any means the last it will see.

And so safely back to Mestre and Venice.

My respects to Mrs. Wolcott. What energy and will power to go on such a trip at seventy and some odd years! And enjoy every minute of it. She is a wonder. I admire her greatly, and although we differ totally about war, art, and the management of granddaughters, yet we always have a splendid time together. She adores her little granddaughter, but the pair often remind me of an old bull-dog that has adopted a Persian kitten.

To Mrs. Francis Vinton Greene

BOLOGNA, ITALY
October 17 (*Sunday*), 1920

DEAR MAMMA:

Arrived here this evening, having left Venice this morning in the same Spa car we made the trip to the battlefields in. Came through Padua, where we had another look at the bronze statue of Gattamelata which we saw when we were at Padua about two weeks ago. A wonderful equestrian statue and I never know which I like the best — Gattamelata at Padua or Colleoni at Venice. Both were mercenary soldiers-of-fortune (condottieri) who rose to be commanders-in-chief of the Venetian armies at the period of her greatest military glory. In their careers

260

they were alike — very successful — but one — Erasmo da Narni, surnamed, or rather nicknamed Gattamelata ('the honey-cat') — was a baker's son, the other, Bartolomeo Colleoni, was the fugitive son of a murdered nobleman. Both served Venice faithfully and won great honors and wealth thereby. But the third great mercenary generalissimo of the Venetian Republic, Carmagnola, proved a traitor to her and was executed. Venice was rich and paid her mercenaries well, in money, honors and privileges, but was merciless to those who served her ill. 'Results wanted' with the great merchant princes of that wealthy Republic.

After leaving Padua we passed by the foot of the Euganean Hills and saw the very attractive château which was the property of the Archduke Francis Ferdinand of Austria (whose murder at Sarajevo started the landslide of the Great War) by virtue of his inheritance of the title of the old Dukes of Este of Italy. A charming place on the lower slopes of the Euganean Hills and to my mind much more attractive than the more grandiose Palazzo di Pisani which we had passed at Stra on the Brenta Alps, coming to Padua, and which Napoleon gave to Eugène Beauharnais when he made him Viceroy of Italy.

We had a good Italian lunch at Rosigo, crossed the huge river Po swimming lazily to the sea between its great artificial banks (the level of the water is higher than the surrounding country, as with the lower Mississippi), ran through Ferrara, stopping to gaze at the vast brick castle, with its moats and drawbridges, which once housed the mighty House of Este whose Dukes ruled Ferrara so long and so well, who did so much for art and whose adventures have been the subject of so many legends and romances.

And so to Bologna for the night, where we are staying at the Hotel Brun, whose comfort, service and general efficiency are in refreshing contrast to the other hotels we have so far encountered in Italy. And the cheapness of the place! I have a huge double bedroom with a most modern bathroom attached for $1.20 a day! And Mrs. Wolcott and her granddaughter Susan Bass have two enormous double bedrooms with bath attached for $2.10! With twenty-five lire to one dollar, life is cheap for Americans here, though appallingly dear for Italians.

But the efficiency of the hotel is what surprises us, after the languid attentions of the staff at the Grand Hotel, Venice; the filth, insolence and indifference of all the hotel employees at Trieste; the chaos at Trento, and the general dilapidation of such hotels in the mountains as had not been burned during the war — we could get no advance information about places in the war areas in the Alps. With good appetites and high expectations based on maps and pre-war guide-books, we would arrive at places where we expected to find good hotels — only to gaze on jagged pinnacles of blackened masonry rising against the blue of Alpine skies.

Bologna is in the throes of the 'social unrest' of Italy — if I may use that euphemism! Day before yesterday the mob tried to rescue an agitator who had been arrested, and in the mix-up three soldiers

262

were killed. At their funeral yesterday a revolutionary Socialist refused to lift his hat as the cortège passed — which started a fight in which one man was killed and many were wounded. Furthermore, the 'Nationalists' took advantage of the row to sack and burn a news-stand selling revolutionary reading matter. I have just been down to the corner, looking at the charred remains of stand and papers, which are guarded by twelve soldiers with rifles. The Palazzo Communiale is alive with soldiers and a motor-truck load of them have just gone crashing off to some disturbance in the suburbs.

Sounds dangerous to you, does it! Well, it is absolutely safe to those who mind their own business. Otherwise I should not be here with an old lady and a little girl fourteen years old.

I have just been making mental comparisons between these Italian soldiers standing between the City Castle and the proletariat and the German soldiers whom I saw doing the same thing at the old 'Schloss' in Königsberg, East Prussia, a few weeks ago. And the Germans were behind barbed wire and in full panoply of war — steel helmets, hand grenades, etc. Now from Bologna to Königsberg is a long, long way and the similar conditions show how widespread is this disease of 'social unrest.'

But it is all very tame compared with what we used to see in Baltic Russia in 1919.

Yet one should not underestimate the crisis through which Italy is passing. One reads posters and notices calling on demonstrations in favor of Soviet Russia, and the name Lenin is frequently scrawled on walls —

in all the towns. And even on the base of the statue of Gattamelata we saw 'Socialism' in large letters.

Well, I am off to bed in my huge room, as we shall be up early tomorrow morning to see a bit of this interesting town before taking the road to cross the Apennines on our way to Florence, where we are due tomorrow night.

Good night.

With dear love

Your devoted son

WARWICK GREENE

To Mrs. Francis Vinton Greene

FLORENCE, ITALY
October 19, 1920

DEAR MAMMA:

I wrote you a fairly long letter from Bologna dated Sunday night, October 17. As the envelope was too large to go in the local post-box, I left it with the portiere of the hotel, which was an unwise thing to do, as I have been cheated so much in Italy that I am quite capable of believing the portiere will cut the uncancelled stamp off the envelope and drop the letter in the waste-paper basket. Do let me know if you ever receive it.

Well, Monday morning, October 18, we spent prowling about Bologna. We saw the Piazza Nettuno and the Piazza Vittorio Emanuele II and admired their handsome Romanesque-Gothic-Renaissance buildings. Then we went to see the two leaning towers (Pisa is not the only Italian city that has a leaning tower — leaning was a characteristic of these old Italian towers, though the one at Pisa is the best leaner), and admired one of them, the Asinelli, very much indeed. It is a very impressive, slim, handsome affair.

Then to the Museum to see the chef-d'œuvre of the Bolognese collection — Saint Cecilia by Raphael, of which I enclose a photograph.

Sight-seeing over, we boarded our Spa car and were soon climbing the long valley that leads to the passes on the highest and most direct road across the Apennines to Florence. The highest point our motor reached was thirty-one hundred feet above sea level, and so not to be compared with the mighty passes we went over in the Dolomite Alps when we were between seven and eight thousand feet above sea level and the wind was as keen and cold as though it had been cradled in glaciers.

But while the Apennine scenery is not as sensational or as grand as the Alps — especially where the ravages of war in the High Alps were still to be seen — yet it is lovely beyond description. The long, sweeping, friendly mountains — somewhat like our own Appalachians; the little ripening grain-fields; the chestnut groves; the tiny vineyards; and, as we came down into Tuscany, the olive trees, all made it as sweet a bit of mountain landscape as the world has to offer. And no advertising signs and no blatant, hasty modern houses mar the picture. High, red Tuscan cars drawn by mules in gay and jingling harness clatter up and down the steep roads, and one valley was filled with Italian soldiers on the march, pouring into the villages with great stir and bustle for the night's billeting.

Lunch we had at a little peasant inn — peasant bread, good butter, omelette, cheese, fruit, and sweet wine — all as good as can be. Simple food, but delicious tasting, and it never gives you indigestion — there is no adulteration and no false seasoning. We stuffed ourselves — particularly Mrs. Wolcott and myself, who adore this kind of food.

And so in the early evening into Florence and to the Hotel Italia, where we are staying.

Today — Tuesday, October 19 — Mrs. Wolcott and little Susan Bass have been resting (even an old lady of iron like Mrs. Wolcott occasionally has to admit that she rests), while I have started to see my beloved Florence, which I have loved from far for over twenty years, but which heretofore I had always looked on with the eyes of the spirit and not the more trustworthy ones of the flesh.

But of the detailed delights of my first sights I shall write you later. This morning I took a gallop through the place — the Battistero, the Duomo, Giotto's Campanile, the Piazza della Signoria, Palazzo Vecchio, Uffizi Gallery and the Bargello. A big meal of beauty for one day! Giotto, Brunelleschi, Donatello, da Vinci, Raphael, Botticelli, Cellini, da Bologna and Michael-Angelo — not to mention hosts of others. Tomorrow, and the days after, I start in to digest them slowly; to compare the actual bronze and stone impressions with what one has seen in photographs and casts and read of in books.

In the afternoon we went out to Arthur Acton's

villa on a hill overlooking Florence, for tea. He is a cousin of the Lord Acton (son of the distinguished one) whom I knew as Minister to cold and turbulent Finland. His wife is an American with a ton or two of money. His taste, backed by his wife's money, has enabled him, in thirty years or so, to accumulate a wonderful collection of things beautiful, so that his great villa is a delight to visit and ramble through. It is a villa that had great owners in the past — cardinals and such-like — and lends itself to a hand-chosen collection of Italian art such as Acton has filled it with.

She is good-looking and seems agreeable. After batting about so long in hotels, it was a delight to relax in a gentleman's great house and enjoy a well-served tea — with a charming hostess, quiet serving-men, a friendly Alsatian wolfhound and lovely things to look at — tapestries, pictures, bits of sculpture and handsome brocades.

Nor could I help thinking of the many noblemen's and great gentlemen's houses I saw in Baltic Russia last year — with the pictures stolen, the tapestries ripped down, the windows broken, pigs and chickens squabbling on the parquet floors, and hairy peasants clumping up and down the stairs — or drunken, brawling soldiers in the cast-off uniforms of Russia, Germany, England and America — for that was the Esthonia, Latvia, and Lithuania that lay before my eyes in 1919 — and wonder whether or not the same things are coming to pass in Italy. Probably not — but who can predict these days? Certainly, as we gad about drinking in the great Italy of past days, present

Italy is settling beneath our feet. One sees the sinister name of Lenin scrawled up everywhere — on the pedestals of old statues, on the walls of public buildings — even on the outside of post-offices in little Italian villages. Yet, when I last saw you, that name Lenin was utterly unknown to the world and the holder thereof an obscure Russian political refugee in Switzerland. Today he is more feared throughout the world than ever was the Czar of all the Russias and the former lords of Russia are the penniless refugees in foreign lands. In so short a time has all this come to pass — so who can predict today what will be in four years more? But we can hope that the common-sense — a quality always lacking in Russia — of Italy will save her from the Red Nightmare of Russia.

And so back to dinner at the hotel and this letter to you.

Good night.

With dearest love
Your devoted son
WARWICK

VI

PARIS AND VERSAILLES IN 1920

To Miss Emily Sever

PARIS, *October* 28, 1920

DEAR AUNT EMILY:

Though not in the least war-worn in health, I am a little war-worn in spirit as a result of seeing at close hand too much of the misery which the Peace Treaty has imposed on Europe. The colossal suffering of the war was bad enough, without the additional human pain that the Treaty of Versailles has imposed during the past two years. We went to war for the sake of humanity, and we have allowed our representatives to impose a peace that has raised a monument to itself of old people and babies starved to death on a large scale. The vindictiveness of Clemenceau, added to the insane egotism and autocracy of Wilson, have not been much behind the Kaiser in the woes they have inflicted on the innocent. Fortunately, the fair-mindedness of the English, added to the sense of realities which the Italians possess, is slowly leading to necessary modifications of the Treaty — necessary in the interests of humanity and of the reconstruction of Europe. The more I know of the British, the more do I take off my hat to them — to their common-sense, integrity, and sense of fair play.

I am too far away from America to know how the campaign goes, but, of course, I fervently hope for Republican victory, first because I am a Republican, second because I think Wilson's intolerable vanity and personal autocracy need the severest of lessons, and third because I think it will clear the way for necessary modifications of the Peace Treaty and for some Association of Nations founded on maturer judgments than the present League of Nations and one that will be framed away from the vindictive atmosphere of Paris — unavoidably vindictive after France's sufferings during the war. Even the French have had the good sense to put Clemenceau away; and when the Americans have retired Wilson, the stage will be cleared for some constructive action towards a peaceful world. Lloyd George is no obstacle, having always been the most moderate and humane of the Councillors of the victors gathered at Paris.

As for the candidates, Harding and Cox, they seem to be rivals in commonplaceness; Cox inclining to cheapness and superficiality and Harding to unctuousness. Whichever wins, it seems to me we shall miss the dignity of Taft and the distinction of Roosevelt and Wilson — for much as I dislike Wilson, I must grant him great distinction.

The reaction of the American people against Wilson and too much meddling in European affairs — if it materializes — has been very sound and eventually will prove to have been of enormous benefit to international problems. Wilson's work at Paris was entirely too much of a one-man job to deserve endorsement from a democratic people. Without any consultation he was hurrying them into ventures which would have brought us all sorts of embarrassment and not a few real dangers. The American people were asked to sign, on the dotted line, contracts which had been framed in the dark as far as they were concerned, and from which they should instinctively shy off. It was like asking a hard-headed farmer to sign a document — long, involved and elaborate — concerning his property in the drafting of which he had never been consulted. Naturally he refused.

Your affectionate nephew
WARWICK

To Mrs. Francis Vinton Greene

PARIS, *November* 10, 1920

DEAR MAMMA:

Yesterday, as I had some time off waiting a telegram of instructions from New York, I went out to Versailles, which I had not seen since the signing of the Peace Treaty in June, 1919.

Feeling energetic, I walked the entire distance. After all, no more than did the thousands and thousands of women, poorly clad and poorly shod, who trudged out one historic day in 1789 — and brought back a live but frightened King, his Marie Antoinette, his Dauphin son, together with the grain and bread supplies of the Palace, chanting, 'We're not going to starve, now that we have the Baker, the Baker's wife and the Baker's boy!'

From the Louvre to Louis the Fourteenth's Palace is one of the most interesting walks on earth. First the Gardens of the Tuileries where stood the Palace of Kings that vanished before a mob's Red fury in 1870 (and France today the greatest enemy of the Reds except the United States!); then the Place de la Concorde, where they once chopped up Kings and Aristocrats — and Reds and Radicals, before they got through, just so there would be no favoritism!; then the most sumptuous Avenue in the world, climbing to the Arch that seems to stand at the World's End and to lead to the skies beyond; then the Arc de Triomphe itself, the most triumphant bit of architecture ever built; then the sleek and rich Avenue du Bois de Boulogne; then the glossy and enchanting Bois de Boulogne (with Longchamps and all the rest); then the handsome Seine under Mount Valérien; then the steps up to the Gardens of Saint-Cloud, site of the Palace the Prussians destroyed; then the loveliest of cultivated forests; then a string of obscure but pleasant French villages; then the royal and garrison town of Versailles, whose essential character Republican France has never changed, and which still stands in all the restraint and good taste of its seventeenth and eighteenth century architecture; then the vast Palace and Park which the 'Sun King' built as a fit setting to his glory and which surpasses the settings of all other Grand Monarchs even as he surpassed them all in person.

This walk begins with the vista from the Louvre through the Arch of the Carrousel, the Place de la Concorde and the Avenue of the Elysian Fields, to the giant Arch of Triumph; and ends with the truly imperial vista from the Terrace side of the Palace of Versailles, where the vast stairs seem to have lifted you to the top of the world, and, with the great façade of the Palace ranging behind you, your eye roams over the forest park that stretches to the horizons and gives the illusion of having no end.

To Versailles we came repeatedly in 1917 and 1918, not to see palaces, but to visit the great French aviation dépôts and repair parks at Versailles and Saint-Cyr, very near by. In those days Versailles, in addition to these aviation stations, was a vast army motor-truck reserve dépôt. Thousands of motor vehicles, of every make, were parked along its broad streets, ready to be slung anywhere along the fighting Front where an emergency had arisen. Indeed, Versailles was then a barometer of the Front; if the town was plethoric with motor trucks, you knew that the Front was quiet from Belfort to Arras. But in the Verdun days and during the German offensives in the spring of 1918, these great motor reserves melted away. The sun would go down on street after street crammed with orderly rows of Berliets, Saurers, Renaults, Panhards, de Dions, Whites, Pierce-Arrows, Packards, Fords, etc.; and would rise on bare streets with only oil spots on the macadam to show where the motor hosts had been. Off they had hurried, in the dark, hundreds and hundreds of them, to pick up reserve divisions of soldiers and hurry them to some point of the line that had given way. Affairs were grave when the streets of Versailles were empty of motor vehicles; for this was the last great reserve, called on only in emergency.

Today you would never know a motor truck had parked in its decorous streets.

And the Palace is quiet compared with the bustling day in June, 1919, when the Treaty was to be signed and the World and his Wife were hurrying out there to see it. Lord! what a jam of diplomats, soldiers, and civilians were there, crowded inside the gilded iron gates and fences! And such a strumming of airplanes overhead and booming of guns and playing of fountains when the signatures had been fixed to that wretched Treaty — I was watching it all from the Great Terrace. The world had been made safe for Democracy, the last thing the builder of the great Palace would have wanted. To find a fit setting for their great fête, the rowdy democracies had to borrow the spacious and superb kernel the vanished French autocracy had left behind it!

But not a bad place to sign the downfall of what we hope was the last of the great imperial autocrats, William the Second. Potsdam outlasted Versailles nearly a century and a half, but it would have pleased Louis the Fourteenth's vanity to have known the fall of the last Lord of Potsdam was consummated and celebrated in Louis's own Palace.

Yesterday there were only shabby strings of sightseers wandering through the Palace and its grounds.

I took time to see the Museum, the Royal Apartments, and the other sights of the place. Miles and miles of historical paintings, mostly battles, with some coronations, treaty signings, proclamations, etc. The battle scenes are all much alike, whether of Clovis and Charles Martel, or of Napoleon and the war of 1870. In all, the horses are carefully groomed, the men shaved and their hair brushed and curled, the scenery like a park, and the uniforms spotless and bright. Evidently for centuries artistic tradition has

274

it that battles were fought immediately after Dress Parade. And the warriors fight and die in carefully contorted attitudes; the horses plunge and cavort like sleek circus pets. Of the mud and filth and disarray and haggard agony of actual battle as we know it, there is not a trace. The tournament ideal of fighting persisted in art long after tourneys ceased. Of course, in the leisurely centuries, battles were fought in a more leisurely fashion, but even then they could not have been like these great decorous canvases, which are valuable only for their portraiture and for their record of the arms, dress and accoutrements of the times they represent. And even these are often quite imaginary. The brutal, livid stress of actual warfare is shown in the paintings of the Great War, but none of these have yet intruded into Versailles.

Nevertheless, one finds these endless panels of well-bred battle scenes not uninteresting.

The glittering Hall of Mirrors was quite deserted. There were no sight-seers (it was getting late); the shades of William the First and Bismarck, if present, were invisible (I fancy that since the last Treaty was signed here they find little pleasure in revisiting the scene of their triumph); and Clemenceau, Lloyd George, and Wilson, of course, are scattered to the ends of the earth (Clemenceau is at present in Ceylon).

But, after all, the royal apartments are more interesting, in their regal intimacy, than the pictures or the Hall of Mirrors; and the exterior of the Palace, with its façade at once noble and sumptuous, and the spacious terraces, great stairs, jubilant fountains and lordly park, are the real and enduring glory of Versailles.

I walked to the very end of the Park and then back, climbing the steps just as the Palace was washed in all the colors of the setting November sun and the autumn reds, greens and golds of the forest park were disappearing in a blue mist. I assure you it was splendid beyond words.

November 11, 1920

Today the Unknown Soldier was carried to his grave with all the sorrow, pride and glory of France behind him, just two years after the victory. The procession had little or no remembrance of Russia, Belgium, England, Italy or America; it was not Allies' day, being reserved exclusively for France's homage to her own nameless son, 'un soldat de France, inconnu, mort sur le champ d'honneur.' Preceded by blue soldiers, the standards of the French Army and the heart of Gambetta in a golden catafalque, came a 150 mm. gun, bearing a simple coffin covered with the tricolor; following it on foot, Millerand and all the great dignitaries of France, and her Marshals and Generals, Foch, Pétain, Joffre, Gouraud, Mangin, etc. Marching soldiers closed the procession. Slowly it covered the route from the Panthéon to the Arc de Triomphe, where the nameless poilu is to have the most glorious resting-place it is in the power of France to give him.

A most moving and imaginative ceremony, at once proud and martial, and tender and loving. Few could watch it with dry eyes. 'My greatest and

dearest son, this unknown dead common soldier,'
France seemed to say, 'these poor mouldy bones of
the Average Frenchman who died for his country
are the holiest relics in my possession. President
of the Republic! Marshals! Generals! Senators! walk
humbly and reverently on foot behind them! He
who was the least among you, is today the greatest!'

November 12, 1920

Last night there were tremendous fireworks, torch-
light processions, etc. The Gardens of the Tuileries
were a glare of white magnesium flares, while up the
Seine the towers of Notre-Dame burned with red
fire. Captive sausage balloons floated overhead,
carrying strings of French flags lit up by the rays of
searchlights, of which there were a great congregation
in the Place de la Concorde. The streets were
jammed with people, but there was little boisterous-
ness — not at all like the first Armistice Night, when
Paris was a crazy hullaballoo of joy from one end to
the other, to which the thousands of American doughboys contributed at least their share of noise. Today
khaki has disappeared almost utterly from Paris and
the sense of honor to the dead and the thought of
the heavy sacrifices which had made the victory possible seemed uppermost in people's minds. Consequently, there was no noisy celebration. It was
the day of mourning for the dead, symbolized in
the passing of the coffin containing the Nameless
Soldier.

There was, of course, a lighter side to things yesterday, though not in the least detracting from the underlying solemnity of the occasion. Instead of watching proceedings stiffly from some grandstand (as I saw the Victory Parade in July, 1919), I mixed with the crowd, where you get the real flavor of passing events. I saw the procession first with the crowd from in front of the Chambre de Députés; then ducked round (processions move very slowly) to the Rond Point of the Champs-Elysées and saw it again; then up to the Arc de Triomphe for its finale.

At the Chambre, Millerand got a good reception from the crowd, as did Foch, Gouraud, and Mangin, especially the latter, the fire-eater who broke the German lines on the night of July 17–18, 1918 (incidentally with the help of our First and Second Divisions). In 1917 he was the 'butcher,' and the poilus and mob were everywhere yelling for his blood; after the shambles and failure in Champagne. But in 1919 and 1920 he has been one of the heroes in every parade. 'Vive Mangin!' is yelped out whenever he appears. Gouraud is also very popular; the people remember that his army stood like a rock between Rheims and the Argonne during the last great German offensive, that of July 15, 1918. He lost an arm during the war — and the people appreciate a General who shares his soldiers' risks.

At the Chambre there was also one stout old rough fellow who would bellow nothing but 'Vive la République.' He had probably seen the inauguration of the Third Republic, and leaning on his soldier son, wanted everybody to know that Presidents and

Field Marshals didn't matter very much, but that republicanism did. So he roared for the Republic like a Bull of Bashan all the while the Notables were passing, quite drowning out the other 'Vives.'

At the Rond Point I secured a perch high up on a truck. Presently a plump lady is boosted up beside me, maintaining her equilibrium (in spite of very high heels) by grasping both my hands firmly, just in time to see Unknown Poilu go by. 'Ah, peut-être c'est mon Henri. Pauvre garçon!' she said, sways for a few moments more on the perch, holding on tightly to me, and then flutters down again.

At the Arch, as soon as the heart of Gambetta and the bones of the Unknown Soldier had come to a rest beneath the great arch, the crowd swept police and soldiers aside and surged in — Frenchmen suffer authority as a necessary evil to an orderly life, but they have no respect for it. Appears a pompous but rather frightened Senator, with his goatee and his great ribbon of the Légion d'Honneur across the white shirt-front of his dress suit, and raises his hand with the majesty of high authority to still the crowd. 'Comme il est joli, ce petit bonhomme là!' jeers the crowd and jostles him about with great zest. The Great One loses his temper, and storms and gesticulates, waving his fists and calling on police and soldiers to rescue his dignity. Whereupon a huge market-woman bellows, 'Ha ha! Un Sénateur qui rage, ça me fait énormément plaisir! Mais comme il est méchant, ce beau Monsieur là! Allez vous en! ce pauvre gare sous le drapeau, appartient à nous, lui! mort! inconnu! pas à vous, Monsieur Parlementaire!'

And in presses the mob, sweeping the gibbering Senator aside.

With dear love

Your devoted son
WARWICK GREENE

To Miss Emily Sever

PARIS, *November* 10, 1920

DEAR AUNT EMILY:

Your letter from Newport of October 29 is just in. I presume you will be back again in Boston when this reaches you. I am quite homesick for that pleasant town — should like to feel once more the nip of the East Wind and to see the Back Bay Basin on a raw and bracing winter day.

You would find Venice little changed after fifty years. A little shabbier (stucco will fall off!) ... a bit war-worn ... a surrendered Austrian battleship — huge and slate-colored and in complete naval dishabille — sits at anchor off the Public Gardens ... an occasional brilliant-hued naval seaplane drums its fiery way across from the Lido and swishes about in the waters off the Piazza of Saint Mark's — but that would be all. Also the Accademia delle Belle Arte is still closed to the public, though we got in and saw pictures being restored to their places on the walls as fast as after-the-war laisser-faire permits — nobody works hard, these days, except the Red Demons at Moscow. They seem to monopolize all the energy and enthusiasm that is abroad. Which probably accounts for their successes.

Furthermore, that sinister word Lenin is scrawled

280

upon many a wall and many a statue base. And not only here, but also in Padua, Bologna, Florence, and in all Italian cities.

But the Ducal Palace still rises in its cream-and-buff airiness and is still the most enchanting building in the world. Within, Veronese, Titian and Tintoretto and their brethren glow on walls and ceilings as though tons of airbombs had not crashed down on the city only three years ago. Bacchus, or the Adriatic, comes up ardent from the blue sea, ring in hand, to wed his lovely Ariadne, or Venice, while Theseus' ship sails sturdily away carrying that handsome adventurer home to Attica and the conquest of more trusting ladies. Brilliant Doges hobnob (on their knees, to be sure) with the Great Ones of Heaven, or receive Persian Ambassadors, as unconcernedly as though their gossamer-like Palace had never trembled to the sound of modern guns which erase cities as though they had never existed.

And Saint Mark's is yet there in all its exceeding glory. Even the sand bags have been removed. The Greek horses, which went to Rome for safety during the war, lift their clean bronze legs as jauntily as ever. During their long lives, these young and sprightly horses have roamed on many journeys — to Greece, to Rome, to Bysantium, to Paris — and this last little trip to Rome has not affected their spirits in the least. 'Glad to be back again,' they seem to say, 'but we don't mind travelling in the least, so long as we don't have to go to Vienna! However, we like this gay portico roof best of all the places we have been.'

Within, gold and porphyry and mosaic gleam in their old and sombre splendor, as though a single shell in 1918 might not have kicked it all to many colored bits.

Too beautiful, too dear and too fragile is Venice to have modern warfare trailing about in its neighborhood — modern war whose iron jaws overnight can masticate a city to fragments. Fortunately, there was no military object in bombing the vicinity of Saint Mark's and the Austrians were too civilized to do so out of wantonness; so in this war it luckily escaped. But had the tide of Austrian advance after their victory at Caporetto in the fall of 1917 continued, Venice might have become the scene of a grim tussle for its actual possession. Then one trembles to think what might have happened; for friend and foe alike spare nothing when they are engaged in a life-and-death struggle for a place.

Affectionately

Your nephew

WARWICK GREENE

P.S. And of course there is a new Campanile since you were in Venice fifty years ago. It is sharp and clear and not soft and mellow as yours was, but it looks just as yours did when it was first built.

VII

AMERICA AND POST-WAR THOUGHTS

To Robert Hale, of Portland

62 EAST SEVENTY-SEVENTH STREET
March 10, 1921

DEAR HALE:

Thanks for your letter of March 7th.

Forget the 'Colonel'! I liked it while I had it, but never considered myself more than a camouflaged civilian. Now there is not even the camouflage!

I have just returned to this country after over four years' continuous absence. New York I find superficially changed, but not essentially. Otherwise it seems much the same U.S., a bit noisy and raw, but free from the implacable racial hatreds with which all Continental Europe seems poisoned. We are a bit bumptious, but our fundamental tolerance towards all white races and all decent creeds makes the wheels of life run much more smoothly than in tortured Europe. It is very saddening to see the beauty and tradition of the Old Countries tottering on their bases from the hatred of each neighbor for his neighbor of a different language or a different ritual. We went to war in the interests of fair play and tolerance; and now see our dear associates in the struggle infected with the same disease we condemned in their and our enemies. We took up the challenge of German Militarism and gave our money and our men to

283

defeat it — only to find French Militarism growing up in the soil we thought we had cleared for peace and mutual understanding based on justice and good will. I hope that the voice of our country will soon speak (it will certainly eventually speak) against Gallic inhumanity, as it did against Teutonic inhumanity.

I spent all of the winter of 1919–20 in Finland and the regions of Baltic Russia we knew so well — as a simple civilian, getting a worm's-eye view of what I had formerly seen from the bird's-eye view of an official.

I hope to see you sometime, and to chat over old times again. If you come to New York, be sure to let me know. I expect to be in New York, Boston or Washington during the next few months. The address at the head of this letter will always reach me.

Sincerely and cordially yours

WARWICK GREENE

To Robert Hale, of Portland

62 EAST SEVENTY-SEVENTH STREET
May Twenty-seventh, 1921

DEAR HALE:

Thank you for your fine letter of sympathy to me for the loss of my father. I deeply appreciate what you say in it.

As you say, no foreknowledge of the coming death of a parent robs the final parting of its great shock and sadness to a son. I had looked forward to several years of companionship with my father when I finally got home after so many years of foreign serv-

WARWICK GREENE (SEATED) AND EDWARD BOWDITCH
Shanghai, 1911

ice. Indeed, I had hoped to coax him abroad with me this summer, to spend several months going over the battle-fronts in France and in Poland and Lithuania with the thought of thereby stimulating him to undertake several final military books with which to wind up his life. His own connection with the U.S. Army, his earlier campaigns in Russia, his many books on the history of our Army and his prestige as an American military critic had, it seemed to me, peculiarly qualified him to write an impartial history of the A.E.F., written with the scale of the whole World War in his mind, and assigning to the A.E.F. its just place in the greatest military effort the world has ever put forth. His previous training as a military critic equipped him for the task; and the fact that he was not identified with the A.E.F. would have made him a very impartial critic. To those who took part in the war, the events with which they were personally identified loom up out of their proper perspective. My father did not have this handicap; he was thoroughly saturated with military history and he knew intimately the record of our Army from its Revolutionary days. So I believe he could have written a work of permanent historical value, and it is a bitter disappointment to me that this strange malady should have cut into his life and deprived him of the finish to his career of which he was otherwise capable.

I was grateful, however, for the three months of uninterrupted companionship I had with him at the end. I was fortunate in being able to finish all my engagements abroad and come home in time to have this short time with him free from all cares or any occupation.

My father was a good soldier to the very end. The doctors told him the truth as soon as they discovered it, but he never quailed and carried on his normal life to the last as far as was possible. Up to the last day of his life he got up every day and went into his library to read and write. So he was spared the usual bedridden ending to this disease; the day he finally surrendered and went to bed was the day he died. But if you know what the last stages of cancer are like, you will appreciate what grit this took.

Well, he had a stirring and eventful life, with much achievement both at home and in foreign lands; he served his country with distinction and devotion both in peace and in war; and he was a fine example of that English New England stock which up to the present has been the leading strain in the development of our country. His ancestor, John Greene, came to Rhode Island with Roger Williams, and all of his line, including my father himself, were born in the little State of Rhode Island. I think I have good reason to be proud of the memory and the heritage he has left me.

Let me know whenever you come to New York, as I should like to see you. My permanent address is at the head of this letter.

Again thanking you for your letter, I am

Yours very sincerely

WARWICK GREENE

AMERICA AND POST-WAR THOUGHTS

From Greene's portfolio of miscellaneous writings

Briand's Speech [1]

Angry, aggrieved, baffled, sorrowful, France speaks on the defensive. Gone is the propitious setting of the Paris Peace Conference — the matchless city; the devastated regions close at hand for all to visit; the exulting march past of the legions of the conquerors under many flags, but all commanded by a French Marshal; the great nations of the world flocking to the city by the Seine; the statesmen of France, old and nursed in old hatreds, arranging the 'decor.' Then the glamour of tremendous victory lay on the conference; France, as of right, took the direction of peace-making into her own hands. The wine of success and adulation had gone to her head; she nourished the illusion that in her old and tired veins the sap of youth ran again; her wisdom and her will were to govern the cub nations who had helped her, but must not have too much of the spoils. The old Latin Lion dreamed of brilliant old days, of great hunting under Louis the Fourteenth and Napoleon the Great, and prepared again for the Lion's rôle.

But at Washington another setting, alien skies, and a new spirit. The young barbarians of the West, summoned to help drive out the hated barbarians of the North, are in the saddle; sulky England lends a cold presence to French oratorical fire. Cool and brisk Mr. Hughes presides, quite fireproof to oratory,

[1] Briand's address was delivered at Washington on November 12, 1921. The text is in the Official Report of the Conference on Limitation of Armaments, page 68.

wishing only to get on with the business, to cut the sob stuff and proceed to the meat of the matter, the reorganization of a very sick and bankruptish world. France is indulged like an old Prima Donna. On the diplomatic stage she appears like her own Sarah Bernhardt, an ancient of days, trailing a great glamour of the past yet démodé, greeted by the affectionate tradition of the young audience, to be assured that her voice is as golden as ever, and the old style of acting still the great style. The applause is friendly but not convincing. It is tribute to the achievements of yester-years; it is respect, not interest; it is polite honor to a tradition and homage to a faded star, not the passionate acclaim of present beauty and power. The seats are all sold, but the venerable star knows that new names are being made up for the next billboards.

Perhaps the cruellest blow is the language. For centuries diplomacy could be spelt only in the French idiom. That tradition is now interred with the bones of the old diplomacy. Alone of the delegations assembled at Washington the French do not speak English. The crude West has arisen, stretched its vast limbs, stepped into the halls of Diplomacy, flung open the windows to the fresh air of publicity, plucked down the French signs on the wall. He treats the old Dame with kindly affection, lets her rant her old lines, hands her a lavish bouquet (without much regard to what she has just said), and then proceeds to run diplomacy as though it were a Ford factory, pitching the old properties out into the lumber room. For the old star herself he has a big armchair in the corner, as far as possible out of the rough draughts of modern ways.

So Briand must speak to an audience of which perhaps one in four really understand his words. Every other delegate can speak directly to the American and British public; even the brown delegates from incredibly ancient worlds. Only France is a linguistic as well as diplomatic back number. The faded star knows only a faded language.

And what an audience to face! The cool, collected will power, the disconcerting plainness, the triumphant common-sense of English-speaking peoples. True, the American is still callow in spite of his strength, and can still be gulled with eloquent sophisms which leave the English and Continental ear cold. In his eyes France is still the great romance of his life; he intends to go on loving her — was not the greatest adventure of his youth the crusade to her lovely land to rescue her from the Ogre? — but it is a romance of chivalry, not of passion. Let the adorable old Dame be sheltered and guarded and humored, but let her stay at home. Let her have a few matinées where the seats will be sold to capacity in respect, but clear the stage for new shows!

So the little Briand, with his agitated mane, speaks in passionate futility. Behind him he is trying to erect again Great France, mother of Armies and Empires, of thought and art, of revolution and raging doctrines, La Belle France, the Light of the World. But the performance is purely histrionic.

LETTERS OF WARWICK GREENE

To Hon. W. Cameron Forbes

62 EAST SEVENTY-SEVENTH STREET
NEW YORK CITY
December 27, 1921

DEAR GOVERNOR,

I see by the papers that a Professor Gilmore, of the University of Wisconsin, has been appointed Vice-Governor of the Philippines.

Now that the matter is closed, I want to thank you warmly for your endorsement of myself as a possible candidate for the position and to tell you how much I appreciated your having so high an opinion of whatever abilities I possess. Also to apologize to you if I seemed lukewarm about the opportunity. It was not that I didn't want to go — good Lord! there was nothing I should rather have done, and had things been different I should have gone after the opening you made for me with both hands and feet and one hundred per cent enthusiasm. My inability to present myself seriously as a candidate was one of the keenest disappointments of my life.

Sincerely yours
WARWICK GREENE

To Mrs. Francis Vinton Greene

376 MARLBOROUGH STREET
BOSTON, MASS.
December 31, 1926

DEAR MAMMA:

A day with the lawyers and at Murray & Tregurtha's; a quiet evening at home and New Year coming fast in the gloom and snow...

AMERICA AND POST-WAR THOUGHTS

A year ago — very different.

The day before, from dawn to dusk, we ride the great red savannas, between brilliant mountains, roaring sunshine over everything, and a heat that melts our bones. I am on our prize mule, Tom, with an iron mouth and a mulish heart, who has run away with everybody and tried to scrape them off his back under low branches; D——, our Texan Camp Superintendent, on Margaret, our prize bucker; the rest of the cavalcade on spiritless mules and burros with drooping ears.

At nightfall we reach the M—— Oil Camp, where a four-day drinking bout of Americans, British and Dutch is ending in brawls and stupefaction. While the superior races celebrate in the thatched main camp, Venezuelans and West Indian Negroes ape them in the peon quarters. We eat a squalid supper — the cook being dead to the world — some slatternly Venezuelan girls helping languidly; and then in the common dormitory have to listen for hours while a half portion of Cockney Camp Clerk, just edging into D.T.'s, rants on, defying all the Americans to lick him, and shrieking his opinion of the cowardice, greed and incompetence of the Chief Driller. Been in the British Army, yes! been through the bleeding war, yes! — it was a bloody shyme he had to take orders from that bloody Yankee slacker. And so forth. And so on. And then all over again. With a glaring, red-headed American giant facing him, and Americans tossing on their cots with fever and dysentery, adjuring him to dry up and go back to his bloody limey-land. Long since the pudgy Venezuelan doctor and Venezuelan engineer have fled from this Nordic brawl.

Next morning we are up while the stars still shine. Soon they pale before the dawn; then the mountains come out as great lumps lying all about the world, hard, blue, opaque. The oil-poisoned ground about the camp comes out in its sterile bareness. We fry eggs and boil coffee; then saddle our mules and pack the burros ourselves. Even the great Bolivar himself could not arouse the peons this morning! There are only three of us; the rest of the crowd sleep on. The little Cockney will awake to a raging headache and the knowledge that he has been fired — there is no justice in a hard world!

We push on all day through the forest, exchanging friendly greetings with the leaders of burro trains that come swinging along the trail. Hotter and hotter it grows with each hour, until at noon it seems as though the very trees must burst into flame. Swamps steam and every fly and mosquito in Christendom is out for the holiday. Our animals are red from the bites of gargantuan horseflies. Monkeys mock us from the branches. Parrots have raucous family quarrels in the tree-tops, heard for miles. Ticks fasten themselves to us quicker than we can burn them off with lighted cigarettes.

Towards dusk we meet a gay and tremendous cavalcade. A dozen dancing girls on burros, their bare brown feet thrust through wooden stirrups, gay in red turbans, green and lilac gowns, and gilt earrings and spangles. Follows the orchestra, also on burros, fiddles, trombones and harps banging against the galled flanks of the little brutes. Bringing up the rear is the wicked old duenna, carried along in a bamboo palanquin by peons. 'Where are you going, my pretty maids?' 'A Motatan del Rio. Los Americanos de California han llegado. Chacos muy guapos. No tristes como los Hollandeses. Habra mucha alegria. Vengad con nosotros!' (To Motatan del Rio. The Californians have arrived. Fine lads. Not kill-joys like the Dutch. There will be a fine time. Come ye with us!)

The sun goes down over the western hills; blue night rushes over the scene. The jungle hugs us in; and wakes to its busy night life. A million prowling, creeping, crawling things inhabit it and begin to move and rustle about. Thousands of fireflies light their showy lamps and dance ecstatically. Everything living celebrates the departure of the tyrant sun.

Suddenly the jungle empties us into a glare of electric arc lights. The roar of oil burners, the throbbing of oil boiling in the stills and clouds of steam greet us. All set against the impenetrable black of the forest. Just like our refinery at Fall River except for that forest and the magnificent array of tropical stars overhead — not the pallid stars we know. We have reached the Shell refinery at San Lorenzo, fed by a pipeline running back through the wilderness to a distant oil-field.

On the concrete fence sit an Englishman and a Dutchman, product of West Indian islands where races have mingled since the days of Drake and the Conquistadores. The post between them supports two brandy bottles; they are drinking from a third.

293

'Hey! You! I don't know your name or care. But you have got to drink this bottle of brandy to the bottom before you can get by! I've the bad luck to be in charge of this refinery tonight, but that won't stop me celebrating New Year's Eve! And you can't pass this gate sober!'

A little later the manager, a quiet-faced Englishman, rescues us. In his clean bungalow we are soon stripping the muddy khaki off and bathing ourselves from head to foot in kerosene to kill the clinging hordes of ticks that will leave sores for days. Then soap and showers. Clad in cool silk we have a pleasant dinner beneath an electric fan. Life is supportable again!

To Mrs. Richard W. Hale (Mary Newbold Hale)

30 ALLSTON STREET
BOSTON, MASS.
June 20, 1928

DEAR MOLLY:

I should love to come out to supper this Sunday at seven-thirty. During the day we shall be somewhere beyond Boston Light, absorbing infra-red and ultra-violet rays, ozone and iodine. All to be had for the asking out on the Atlantic, if you row thirty miles for them and dress African style. Not to be had clothed and on the deck of a yacht. I need them to counteract the New England Oil poison.

Supper and evening at Strawberry Hill tops off a perfect day.

Isadora I shall return to you, Sunday, between two covers. Whereas her charm in life was that she had so little covering to body or soul. Nothing to prevent the innate goodness of both shining out at you.

I withstood the suffocating literary style to the end. In spite of it, I am wholly for Isadora. I vote for more ladies like that, and oftener! One to a generation is short rations.

For she was a real ball of human sunshine. Not a molecule of ill-will, meanness, or malice from topknot to toe-nail. All affection, good will, enthusiasm, impishness, courage.

Adored her Greeks — mistook even the modern ones for Hellenes instead of Helots — without in the least understanding them (except she and Alcibiades would have had 'something common between them,' as Lorelei phrases it).

And her innocence! The innocence that came before fig-leaves, which the daughters of Eve lost and the daughters of Lilith kept. The innocence that goes with a story which Rabinoff told me in Russia: Pavlova and Mordkine were disputing with Rabinoff about some technical point of the dance. Finding him obdurate, they suddenly, laughingly, shed every thread of clothing, and danced their interpretation before him, in the bright sunshine, on the green lawn. He told me it was the loveliest and least licentious thing he had ever seen. If Isadora had been there, wouldn't she have raced to peel with them, just as gaily, just as innocently!

I find her kindness to tired American business men not so innocent, but quite commendable. I am sure it added ten years to ———— ————'s life.

To think of that loving heart having its head

295

snaggled off by a flowing scarf caught in the wheel of a fast-driven automobile! I am sure, however, that Saint Peter somehow winked her through the Heavenly Gates, and that Michael and Gabriel were not displeased, however the Recording Angel may have fumed. If not, Allah, the all-compassionate, the all-merciful, has slipped her in among the houris. That merry lass would gladden any Paradise.

On earth, of course, she would never receive the women's vote.

Affectionately
WARWICK GREENE

From Greene's portfolio of drafts and miscellaneous writings

Who is he, this Lenin? Yesterday a nameless, shabby refugee, hiding on the shores of Lake Geneva; today either a John the Baptist, preparing the way for the coming of Communism on earth; or a fresh Attila, an even more terrible 'scourge of God,' loosing the hordes of the slum with promise of rape, blood and plunder, to tear down present-day civilization.

He is nothing mediocre; nor is his movement. Our silly, senseless, frightened propaganda cannot explain him away nor hide the cold, ferocious strength with which he rules Russia, nor minimize the hopes he has aroused in the downtrodden of all lands. You cannot forget this Bolshevism if you have once seen it face to face; nor can you underestimate its moral or immoral force — whichever it is! It is one thing to peer at it through a blurred and distorted medium — our

Press — and quite another to meet it in its stark reality. Then you realize that there is a new dream — nightmare, perhaps — abroad in men's souls; that for this dream there are men — and women! — ready to die as resolutely as the early Christian martyrs.

For I have seen the city rabble slaughtered by the White Guards — squealing like weasels and kissing the soldiers' boots for mercy — and I have witnessed the shooting of Communists and crack Red Guards, who faced the shooting squad unbound, unblindfolded and unflinching, taunting their executioners to the last thousandth of a second, when the murdering bullets crashed through the brains, and bloody mannequins sat down hurriedly in the ditches digged to receive them. In the first case you knew that plunderers and rapers were receiving their dues; in the second, that men were dying for their faith. As you watched those shining eyes and proud faces twinkle into something shapeless, spouting blood and brains, and saw the grotesque, jerking bodies tumble into the earth — why! you realized afresh that the sword can kill the body, but not the soul; that the bullet can extinguish the brain, but not the light and thought that were in the brain — they leap to other brains, faster far than bullets.

What a clash of emotions one had as one watched the scene! On the one hand you felt law and order; on the other, anarchy and ruin. Here all the nobler qualities of our race, all the Powers of Light given us by our Western and Christian civilization; there all the Powers of Darkness, brewed up from squalor, hate, envy and failure. These are the sons and daughters of Belial, you assured yourself, as you watched them form three by three before the firing squad. This is a righteous if bloody deed! Strength to the finger that pulls the trigger against them!

Then you reflected: so might a minor Roman official in Asia Minor have viewed the execution of early Christian martyrs. This ignorant rabble! These filthy fishermen! These verminous Jews! These pathetic peasants! Why! they are preaching sedition against Rome and all her just Gods and her great laws, trying to drag her splendid civilization down to their own degraded level! Let them perish!

And yet — and yet! As your Roman Consul must have said, and as you say today: Why don't they die like the trash they are? Who gave yonder churl permission to leave his black earth and his grubby wife and children and die for an idea? Who planted something in the brain of that pale scribe which made him throw down his master's counting tables and his vulgar, petty life and go out to shake hands with death as proudly as a knight? Who whispered in the ear of this little harlot and caused her to leave her fleshpots and chuck her light soul so valiantly into this bloody ring?

Yes! Go to Russia on an Allied Mission and you will have great sympathy for Pontius Pilate and for the many, many Pontius Pilates there must have been in the first three centuries A.D. They wore kilts and you khaki, but you feel strangely akin.

From these executions you went home to dine in a quivering city that yesterday knew the Red Terror and today the White; and you saw the funeral pro-

298

cessions of respectable old gentlemen and ladies, shot by the Red hordes as they evacuated the city. Then you hated this foul dictatorship of the proletariat, headed by fanatics, yeasty intellectuals and Jews from the dregs of society; you abhorred 'its chariot drawn by terror and plunder,' as Lloyd George says; you had no mercy in your heart for this effort to establish Communism by a 'tour de force' and without regard to economic laws. Blind hands trying to establish the most grotesque experiment the world has ever known! Diseased brains pushing the world back into the Dark Ages!

You went to bed, and the crackle of rifles through the dark and cringing city, telling where the rats of Bolshevism were being hunted down in black alleys and foul cellars exploded in your sleeping mind with strange effects; the dead of this afternoon rose up from their shallow pits and walked in light; and there came into your dreams strange whispers of a new spirit moving on the waters of history, of a vision of a fresh, freer life for man, of an audacious attempt by force of arms and intellect to right intolerable and growing wrongs.

So much for the emotional appeal of those days in Baltic Russia. When in lurid Russia, it is impossible, if you really feel these things at all, not to lend yourself to its lurid, present-day psychology.

Then you came home to saner, cleaner lands, and saner thoughts ensued. For all its iron strength, its ferocious grip of Russia and its terrifying repercussions throughout the world, you knew this Bolshevism for a rule of extremists and, therefore, probably doomed like the Reign of Terror in France. For months, perhaps, more likely for years, it will last; and then Lenin, Trotzky, and Zinovief will follow the way of Marat, Danton, and Robespierre. If they survive, it will be because in practice they will modify their extreme doctrines, for Bolshevism's greatest danger lies in its present source of strength — its fanaticism. This made it strong yesterday, tryannical today, and will make it intolerable tomorrow. It is too extreme for human nature; men, as comfortable, rational animals, refuse to live long on the heights or in the great depths: the warm plains of average, comfortable living are their natural dwelling-places. They weary of Moses; they crucify their Christs; they burn their Savonarolas; they guillotine their Dantons and Robespierres as readily as they leave their Pharaohs and decapitate their kings. Or they passively wait for their Alexanders and Napoleons to perish in their own egotism; their Attilas and their Neros to drink themselves to death. 'Good riddance,' say the people, and go on with the cultivation of their turnips, the marrying of their wives and the eating of their dinners. So the moujik may blink along for years, dazed by these new prophets and terrorists at the Kremlin, and then one day rise in his crude strength and brush Lenin and Trotzky aside.

And yet I am certain that they have sown seeds in Russia, these Communists, whose harvest will be gathered through many coming generations. Extremists, like Lenin and Trotzky, will either go or become conservative in office; but these doctrines have come to trouble the world for a long time.

In theory Communism is centuries ahead of its time, in practice Bolshevism thousands of years behind. Communism means every man working for the common good rather than private gain, and co-operation and not competition the rule of life. So it is probably still some ages ahead of us.

To bring the Communistic State into being the Bolshevists have laid hands on the most savage weapons known to man. In practice it means an unspeakable tyranny, colder than ice, harder than iron and more ruthless than the worst of the Czars. It has brought cold and hunger into every home; dread and suspicion into every heart; hatred and desolation into every community where the red flag has flown. Under its savage rule civilization is cut down at its stalk, and all humor, comfort, kindliness, grace and happiness crushed out of human life. It fans all the fires of hatred and exploits every grievance without bringing a remedy. Following Karl Marx, it preaches the materialistic interpretation of history — and then it strangles all industry and commerce! To defeat the greed of one class, it appeals to the greed of another — and finally leads all classes, high and low, into the desert to starve together. To get rid of the exploiters of society, it behaves like a man who burns down his mansion to rid it of rats.

And yet, if one can see clearly through the mists of prejudice and dread, a tremendous experiment is going on in Russia. As democracy developed through

301

a reign of terror in France, but by peaceful evolution in England and America, so socialism may grow by revolution in Russia, but by evolution in Western countries.

What is one race's meat is another race's poison; Russia, like France, had to purge itself of the old order by terror and bloodshed, but the stubborn common-sense of Englishmen and Americans should work out the process in an orderly fashion, testing out the new ideas little by little in practice with a sense of tolerance and fair play, gaining here, conceding there, always carefully balancing theory and reality. In that case for the next hundred years or so we should have capitalism, individualism and democracy on the one side, and communism and internationalism on the other as the two, great contending forces in our lives, slowly evolving a new social order more in keeping with the widened outlook on life which science gave us in the nineteenth century.

In this light, Russia is merely the unhappy dog on which an experiment is being tried out from which we shall all greatly benefit.

And, after all, why shouldn't it be Russia's turn? On France were visited the birth-pains of democracy in the world; on America the death-pains of human slavery; on Germany and Austria the expiring agonies of the Grand Monarchism. Huge Russia has ample girth for the birth-pains of the first socialistic experiment. Let us hold our breath and watch and learn. We don't want the destructive doctrine of Lenin in our freer and happier lands; but let us take warning and put our own houses in order. As long as we allow the great festering slums of modern cities, so long are we subject to Bolshevist contagion. Eliminate these slums and there is little danger of Bolshevist infection, for it has small attraction to people who live on the land or in small towns.

Bolshevism itself will probably fail, killed by the cold, the hunger and the despair its fanaticism and incompetency have produced, but its communistic doctrines in modified form will probably survive.

Personally I hate and loathe it. Consequently, last summer I believed that the Allies should have taken strong action in Western Russia, when there was an opportunity of crushing Bolshevism if the Old Men at Paris had taken it. As they let that opportunity go by, I became opposed to all further outside meddling in the internal affairs of Russia, believing it very unlikely that thereafter any military adventurers backed by foreign Powers will ever defeat Lenin and Trotzky. Their principal effect is to consolidate the power of the Bolshevists by arousing nationalistic feeling and so bringing to the support of the Bolshevists elements which in a purely civil war would be opposed to them. Russia is too huge for any outside Power to impose its will on her. She is going through her evolution in her own way and the less we meddle, the better it will be for her and for us.

THE END

Tuesday - June 25th 1935 on board the Theodore Roosevelt — my first Lake Trip of the year.

INDEX

INDEX

Champagne, 12
Chapman, Ace, 182
Château-Thierry, 74, 77, 79; Americans at, 79
Chemin des Dames, 69
Civilized man, 73, 74
Clemenceau, Georges, 108, 114, 217, 218, 275; vindictiveness of, 269, 270
Coblenz, 119, 120
Coincy, 74
Col di Lana, 252, 253
Colleoni, Bartolomeo, 260, 261
Communism, 296–303
Compiègne, 8
Condé-en-Brie, 77
Copenhagen, 220
Cortina, 254
Cost of living, 220–24
Courland, 142, 175
Courneuve, munitions explosion at, 35
Cowan, Sir Walter, 113
Cox, James M., 270
Craig, Major, 201
Croats, 258
Crozier, Gen., 37
Crozier, Mrs., 37
Curtiss, Ace, 182

Dana, ancestry, 53 *n.*
Davis, Dwight, xix
Dawley, Colonel E. T., 92, 98, 100, 113; letter to, 231
Degoutte, his army, 79
Dixmude, 12
Dodd, Lt.-Col., 27
Dolomites, 251–53
Donovan, W. J., xix, 4, 29, 30
Dormans, 74, 77
Dorpat (Tartu), 176, 185
Duino, castle of, 257
Dumesnil, Under-Secretary of Aviation, 83
Duncan, Isadora, 294–96
Dunkerque, 8

Eastern Marches of Germany, 128
Egan, Martin, 87, 88
Egans, the, 84
Ehrenbreitstein, 120
Elverdinghem, 8
Emerson, Ellen, 94
Epernay, 74, 77

Esthonia, 95, 116, 154, 169, 177, 198, 216, 232; prices in, 222–24
Esthonians, 93, 174–76, 199

Fairchild, Mrs. Charles, letter to, 48
Fairchild, Sally, letters to, 81, 83
Falzarego, 253
Fère-en-Tardenois, 74, 77
Ferrara, 261
Fiat Company, Turin, 32, 38, 39
Fiera di Primiro, 250
Finland, 93, 95, 116, 163–68, 174, 175, 215; prices in, 221
Finland, Gulf of, 170, 202–10
Fismes, 74, 77
Fitzgerald, Capt., 197, 201, 207
Fitzhugh, Major, 197
Flanders, 8–12
Florence, 266
Foch, Ferdinand, 47, 278; appointed as Supreme Allied Commander on Western Front, 39, 69; his counter-offensive, 70, 71, 74, 77, 78, 81
Fonck, Ace, 83
Forbes, Gerrit, 43
Forbes, Grant, 32, 39
Forbes, W. Cameron, Commissioner and Governor-General of the Philippines, later Ambassador to Japan, 18 *n.*; takes Greene to Philippines, xvi; letters to, 1, 91, 211, 226, 290
Foster, R. C., 4, 30
France, American relief undertakings in, 6
Francis Ferdinand, Archduke, 261
French Army, 10
French General Staff, 28, 31, 34, 40
French Militarism, 284
Front, the, 22, 84, 85
Furnes, 8

Gade, John A., United States Commissioner to the Baltic Provinces of Russia, 181, 182, 184, 187, 211, 212, 232
Gambetta, Léon, 279
Gapnavalok, 116
Gattamelata (Erasmo da Narni), 260, 261
Geneva, Lake, 237
'German Barons' of the Baltic Provinces, 93
German offensive of 1918, 69, 81

306

INDEX

INDEX

INDEX

Paulding, First Lieutenant in Air Service, 30
Pavlova, Anna, Russian dancer, 295
Peace Conference, Delegates to, 111
Peace Treaty, signing of, 100. *See also* Versailles, Treaty of
Perkins, 7
Péronne, 8, 12
Pershing, Gen. John J., xix, 69, 87
Petroleum Heat and Power Co., of Boston, xiv, xxii
Pfeiffers, Captain, 98
Philippines, the, xvi, 1, 2, 20, 36
Phillips, William, Under-Secretary of State, letter to, 4
Piave, 12
Picardy, 12
Pichon, Stephane, 114
Pisani, Villa (Stra), 241, 261
Poland, William, 94
Polish offensive, 233
Poperinghe, 8, 9, 12
Pordoy Pass, 251
Potter, Lt., 76
Potter, Eleanor (Greene), 76; letter to, 85

Quezon, 1

Rabinoff, Max, 160, 166, 167, 170, 171, 295
Red Cross, American, in Eastern Europe, 229, 230
Relief organizations, 227–31
Reninghe, 8
Retz, Forest of, 77, 78
Reval (Tallin), 94, 154, 155, 169–71, 176, 185, 197–202; Paris to, trip, 117–54; to Riga, railroad journey, 161–71
Rheims, 117
Riga, xx, 93, 147, 171, 181–84, 211, 233; Reval to, railroad journey, 161–71
Rink, 233
Rockefeller, John D., Jr., 30
Rockefeller Foundation, xix, 4, 7, 26, 82
Rolle, the, 251
Rome, 33, 38
Roosevelt, Quentin, 60–62
Roosevelt, Theodore, 61, 62
Rosen, Baron Ernest, 198, 199
Rouen, 8, 9

Rucquoy, Gen., 9
Rumsey, Mary, 183
Russia, 115, 133; roads in, 133, 142; conditions in, 225, 226; her evolution (Bolshevism), 296–303. *See also* Baltic Provinces
Ryan, Col., 230

Sahlitz, Minister of Defense, Lithuania, 97
St. Omer, 8
Sanger, Virginia, 41
Schaulen (Shavli), 141
Schoelkopp, Mrs., 237, 240
Segeja, 116
Sergy, 74
Séringes, 74
Servia, 83
'Setti Communi,' 243
Sever, Anne Dana, 53 *n.*
Sever, Emily, 53 *n.*; letters to, 269, 280
Smith, Gen., in charge of Civil Administration for American Army of Occupation in Germany, 91
Soissons, 75–77
Solbert, Col., Military Attaché at Copenhagen, 100
Somme, battle of the, 8, 12
Steenstraate, 10
Steever, Captain in the Air Service, 30
Stettinius, Mr., 87
Stockholm, 220
Straight, Dorothy, 87, 88, 183
Straight, Willard, 85–88
Sweden, 160

Tannenberg, 132, 137
Topping, H. D., 4
Törnisson, Prime Minister of Esthonia, 232
Torretta, Marquis della, 114
Trento, 244–47
Trèves, 118
Trieste, 256–58
Trotzky, Léon, 300, 303
Turin, 32, 33, 38, 39
Turkey, 82, 83
Tyrol, Southern, 248

Udine, 254
Ulmanis, Prime Minister of Lithuania, 97, 233

309

INDEX